PCs Made Easy
The Official HP & Compaq Guide

PCs Made Easy
THE OFFICIAL HP & COMPAQ GUIDE

Nancy Stevenson

PRENTICE
HALL
PTR

Prentice Hall PTR
Upper Saddle River, NJ 07458
www.phptr.com

A Catalog record for this book can be obtained from the Library of Congress

Editorial/Production Supervision: *Nicholas Radhuber*
Acquisitions Editor: *Jill Harry*
Cover Design Director: *Jerry Votta*
Cover Design: *Talar Boorujy*
Manufacturing Manager: *Alexis R. Heydt-Long*
Manufacturing Buyer: *Maura Zaldivar*
Marketing Manager: *Dan DePasquale*
Editorial Assistant: *Noreen Regina*
Series Design: *Gail Cocker-Bogusz*
Publisher, Hewlett-Packard Books: *Patricia Pekary*

Prentice Hall books are widely used by corporations and government agencies for training, marketing, and resale.

Prentice Hall offers discounts on this book when ordered in quantity for bulk purchases or special sales. For more information, please contact:
U.S. Corporate and Government Sales
1-800-382-3419
corpsales@pearsontechgroup.com

For sales outside of the U.S., please contact:
International Sales
1-317-581-3793

Product and company names mentioned herein are the trademarks or registered trademarks of their respective owners.

Printed in the United States of America

First Printing.

ISBN 0-13-141149-7

Pearson Education LTD.
Pearson Education Australia PTY, Limited
Pearson Education Singapore, Pte. Ltd.
Pearson Education North Asia Ltd.
Pearson Education Canada, Ltd.
Pearson Educación de Mexico, S.A. de C.V.
Pearson Education—Japan
Pearson Education Malaysia, Pte. Ltd.

To Earl, my partner, my friend.

Contents

Part 5

Preface

The world of computing today is a pretty magical one, filled with high-powered but easy to use hardware and software. Computers have broken out of offices and into homes in a big way, making possible all kinds of creative, fun, and productive activities, from designing multimedia greeting cards to managing your family's money.

All Compaq Presarios and HP Pavilions come packed with the hardware and software any computer user needs, and most of it is pretty easy to use. But with so many features, a newer user just might need a guiding hand to get the most out of his or her computing experience. That's what this book is about: how to take full advantage of the tools your Presario or Pavilion has put at your fingertips.

Pavilion or Presario?

Whether you purchase an HP Pavilion or a Compaq Presario, you have made a wise choice. Both computers provide the tools for powerful computing and a wealth of pre-loaded software to explore.

HP Pavilions are a favorite of families with their fun and creative software such as the new HP ImageZone digital imaging software. Pavilions offer ease of setup with features such as the Easy Internet Signup Wizard and ease of use with a powerful help system and advanced keyboard features.

Compaq Presarios are often the computing choice for the home professional or home businessperson. Software such as Quicken for managing financial tasks and the Netscape Navigator browser for researching online make a Presario a formidable computing tool.

In general, this book offers information that applies to both computers equally. However, I've provided two chapters that delve more deeply into model-specific software. Chapter 11 covers multimedia software offered to Presario users, while Chapter 12 covers powerful digital imaging offerings for Pavilion users.

How Is This Book Unique?

This book is like no other book on how to use a computer because it's written specifically for Compaq Presario and HP Pavilion users. You'll learn how to use HP's help system, as well as the software that comes preloaded on every Presario and Pavilion. You'll also get to know the basics of the Windows XP operating system which comes loaded on your computer, and learn how to get connected to the Internet.

Part 1 tells you how to get started setting up—connecting all the cables, turning the computer on, and getting an idea of what's on your computer.

Part 2 explores Windows™ XP, the operating system from Microsoft® that makes your computer run. You'll learn how to get around the Windows desktop, manage the computer files you'll create as you work on your computer every day, and customize Windows and use Windows Accessories.

Part 3 is where you'll learn to use the software that comes with your Presario or Pavilion to write documents, create spreadsheets to calculate numbers, manage finances, and design presentations. You'll also learn to play games, and use multimedia software to create slideshows and play music.

Part 4 shows you how to get online, finding an Internet Service Provider to get an account if you don't already have one, and taking care of online security settings. Using a browser you'll search for what you need online, and set up your home page. Finally, you will begin to e-mail all your friends, download file attachments, and organize your inbox.

Part 5 is where I cover some of the basics of upgrading your hardware, such as adding memory or replacing a disk drive. You shouldn't need to do this to your new computer for a long time, but when you do, refer to this section of the book.

Special Help

Along the way, I've included special elements to help you out:

 tip **Tips give you advice or tricks for getting things done faster and easier.**

 caution **Cautions warn you about potential problems you might encounter as you go through a process or make changes to your computer.**

 note **Notes are little pieces of insight about a term or process or background information you may be interested in knowing.**

Projects are step-by-step procedures to accomplish something fun and useful with your Presario or Pavilion. When you finish a project, you'll have produced a document or set up something on your computer you can use right away.

part

Getting Started

chapter

1

The Box Is Open...Now What?

In this Chapter

✔ Understanding the parts of a computer

✔ Getting your computer, monitor, keyboard, speakers, and mouse hooked up

✔ Learning how surge protectors help keep your computer safe

✔ Getting help

When you get home with your new Compaq Presario or Hewlett-Packard (HP) Pavilion, you have a few things to do (although very few) to get up and running. You can get going so fast because HP has included tons of software you can start using right away, and because of something called plug and play.

Plug and play is a set of specifications that Microsoft and Intel came up with that automatically sets up your computer to work with peripherals. Do terms like peripherals make your head spin? Well, relax. You can consider this chapter your Personal Computer (PC) primer. You'll learn all about peripherals, plug and play, and what you need to get your new computer going right out of the box.

PCs 101: The Parts of Your Computer

When you unpack your computer you'll find several items, including hardware, software, and documentation to help you set up and use your computer. You'll find:

- *Central Processing Unit (CPU)*—This is the computer tower that holds the computer hard drive, which is where all the software and systems for the computer are stored.
- *Keyboard*—Hardware that attaches to your computer, such as a monitor, keyboard, or printer, is called a *peripheral*. A keyboard is an input device that allows you to enter text and move around software programs.
- *Mouse*—The mouse is a device that allows you to select and manipulate items in a software program.
- *Power cord*—The power cord connects the CPU to your power source.
- *Speakers*—Two speakers are provided to allow you to hear system sounds and audio files.
- *Modem/telephone cable*—In order to connect to the Internet or send faxes, you'll need to run this phone cord from your phone jack to your computer.

The Brains: The CPU

The computer tower that you'll find in your box is the brains of your computer. It's where software is installed and all the commands you give your computer through the keyboard or mouse are processed. The CPU is where you turn the computer on and off and where you insert floppy disks, CDs, and Digital Video Disks (DVDs) to run or make copies of computer files.

When you take the CPU out of the box and remove the packaging, find a good spot for it, either on your desk, some other computing surface, or on the floor by your desk. Keep in mind that a power source must be nearby. Unwrap the power cord, and plug the end without prongs into the back of your CPU (usually near the top of the tower).

Getting Stuff In: Keyboard and Mouse

Your keyboard and mouse are used to input data and to select and modify things in your operating system and in various software programs. Each has a cable coming out of it with a color-coded plug on the end. Hooking the keyboard and mouse up to your CPU is as simple as plugging the appropriate colored prong into the corresponding colored hole on the back of the CPU.

Seeing What You're Doing

You won't be able to do much on your computer if you don't have a monitor connected. You may have purchased a monitor as part of your computer package, or you may be using a monitor from another manufacturer. It's easy to connect any monitor to your Pavilion or Presario.

tip **A Presario or Pavilion will work with just about any monitor, printer, mouse, and so on. However, HP consumer products are designed to work better together, so an HP monitor with an HP Pavilion or Compaq Presario CPU will be the most troublefree hardware combination for you.**

The monitor that comes with your computer is color-coded to plug into a corresponding slot on your CPU. If you have a different monitor, don't worry. A little picture of a monitor is on the back of your computer so that you can easily spot the right place to plug it in. You must also connect your monitor to a power source using the power cord that comes with it.

Some monitors come with built-in speakers and sound controls. Most come with brightness and image controls. Check your manufacturer's documentation if you want to make any adjustments to your monitor, but most should work just fine out of the box.

Connecting to a Phone Line

If you're planning to connect to the Internet or to send faxes using a standard phone connection, you'll need to plug the phone cord that comes with your computer into your phone jack. To be sure the jack is working properly, plug a standard phone into it first. If you get a dial tone, the jack is working. Plug one end of the phone cord into the wall jack and the other into the line connector on the back of your computer. The line connector will either be labeled with the word "Line," or a jack symbol, or will be color-coded as red.

tip **If you are using a modem that offers a telephone line switch to access multiple phone lines, make sure the switch is set to 1.**

Starting and Turning Off Your Computer

Now that you've connected your mouse, keyboard, and monitor, go ahead and plug your computer into a power outlet. I recommend that you use a surge protector. Plug your computer into the surge protector and the surge protector into the wall. This protects your computer from damage in the event of a power surge. Now, you're ready to turn your computer on.

Turning Your Computer On

All Compaq Presarios and HP Pavilions have a power button on the front of the CPU, although the exact location may differ somewhat. To start your computer, simply press the power button. It will take a few moments for the computer to start up.

The first time you use the computer you will be welcomed by a Windows XP startup wizard, which will check to make sure the sound on your computer is working and that you are set up for the correct language, country, Internet connectivity, and time zone. When this wizard runs, you can even give your computer a name (which is helpful if you intend to have a few computers on a home network and need to refer to them in your network setup). When this routine is done, you'll click Finish, and Windows XP loads. This can take another few moments, during which time you'll hear your hard drive whirring. When Windows has loaded, you'll see the Windows desktop shown in Figure 1.1.

FIGURE 1.1   The Windows desktop is command central for your computer.

Breathing Life into Hardware: Windows XP

Windows XP is a kind of software program called an operating system. There are different kinds of operating systems, for example, the one that runs Macintosh computers and one called UNIX. Operating systems provide the tools for managing your computer systems and running other software. You can't really do anything with your computer without an operating system.

When you start your computer, after the computer loads all its system files (called booting up), which takes a few minutes, the Windows desktop shown in Figure 1.1 appears. This desktop holds shortcuts to software that is installed on your computer. HP has installed many software programs to get you going right out of the box, so you'll see several shortcuts the first time you turn your computer on. You can install other software programs, which you'll learn how to do in Chapter 6 of this book.

Besides the desktop, you'll use the commands on the Windows Start menu (see Figure 1.2) to get things done on your computer. You'll learn more about this menu and what the choices on it do in Chapter 4.

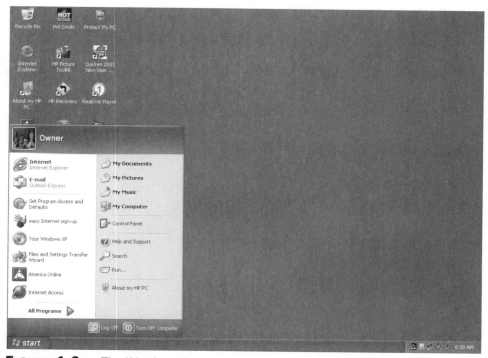

FIGURE 1.2   The Windows Start menu is the gateway to all the programs on your computer and features of Windows.

Get to Know Your Mouse and Keyboard

Your keyboard is what is called an input device. That means you use it to enter text into documents you create using a software program such as Corel WordPerfect. Your computer keyboard is a sophisticated device, with several special function keys along the top. You'll read more about how these work in Chapter 3.

Your mouse is used to move around in documents and to select objects to move, copy, delete, or modify. Together your keyboard and mouse are the set of tools that you use to interact with your computer and documents.

Your mouse has three controls: the left button, right button, and scroll wheel button. The mouse also has a small roller ball on the bottom. When you place the mouse on a flat surface, you can move it around, rolling that ball and moving a corresponding icon called a *cursor* around your computer screen.

The left mouse button is used to select objects and to double-click on certain objects to initiate an action, such as opening up a dialog box to make formatting selections. The right mouse button is used to open shortcut menus. These menus have commands that initiate functions related to whatever you clicked on. When you use the right mouse button, it's called right-clicking, and, when you use the left mouse button, it's referred to simply as clicking.

The scroll wheel button in the middle of the mouse is used to scroll through a document, much as you drag a scrollbar in software programs to move a page or more at a time.

Adjust the Speaker Volume

The speakers that come with your computer play sounds, including system sounds (sounds that occur when an event happens on your computer, such as closing a program), voice, and music.

You can control the volume of your speakers in a few ways:

- You can click the small icon of a speaker on your Windows taskbar, and a small volume control box opens up. Adjust the slider bar there up or down to raise or lower the volume, or click the Mute checkbox to temporarily stop sounds altogether.
- You can go to the Sounds and Audio Devices Properties dialog box from the Control Panel (Click Start, Control Panel, Sounds, Speech and Audio Devices) and adjust the Speaker Volume settings (see Figure 1.3).

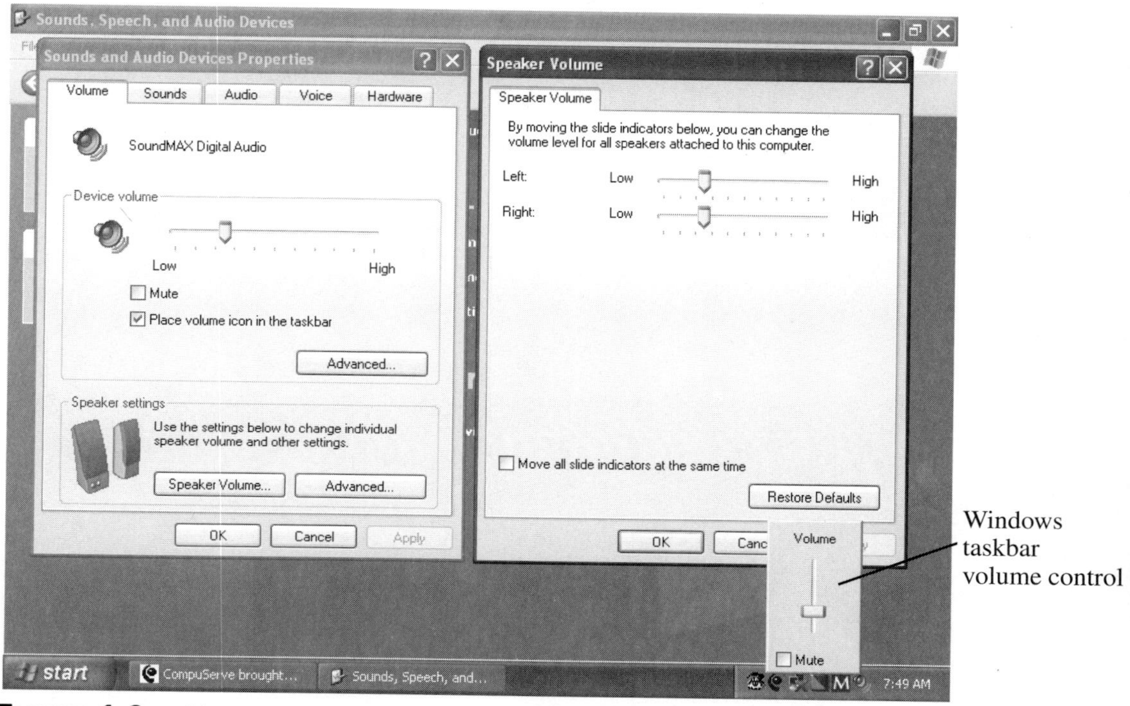

FIGURE 1.3 You can control the left and right speakers with individual slide indicators in the Speaker Volume dialog box.

Finally, you can control the volume of specific devices, such as your music playback, with individual volume control settings from the same Control Panel dialog box (see Figure 1.4).

PCs Made Easy

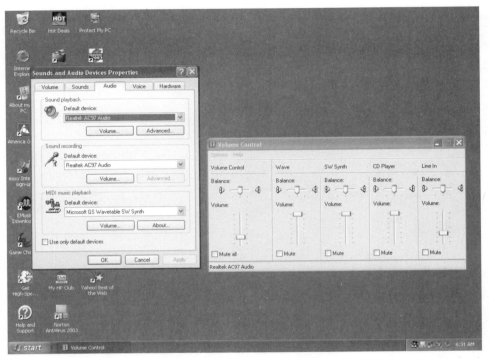

FIGURE 1.4   You can use these controls to make fine adjustments to individual playback devices.

Getting Help

As you begin to use your computer, there may be times when you'd like a little help. Well, you'll be glad to hear that Windows XP provides a lot of help in its Help and Support Center, shown in Figure 1.5.

note   The last chapter in this book, Troubleshooting, walks you through a problem-solving scenario using the Help and Support Center feature. Go there to appreciate the many ways you can find help using this invaluable tool.

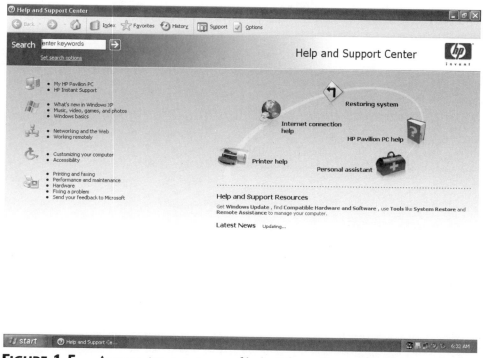

FIGURE 1.5   Access a treasure trove of help information and more from this center.

Help and Support Center

When you first start up your Pavilion, you might want to visit the My Hewlett Packard Computer or My Presario PC section of the Help and Support Center. These provide information about the computer itself, as well as links to features such as a Windows Glossary of computer terminology and an overview of Windows keyboard shortcuts (combinations of keystrokes you can use to perform actions on your computer rather than using a menu or tool button).

✔ **Follow these steps to reach this and other topics:**

1. Select Start, Help and Support. The Help and Support Center shown in Figure 1.6 appears.

2. Click the My HP Pavilion PC or My Presario PC link. The help feature for that category appears.

3. Click an item in the list on the left (see Figure 1.6). That topic opens in the pane on the right. If necessary, you can use the scrollbar in that pane to view more of the information.

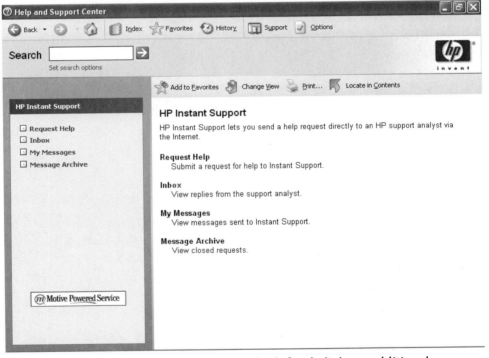

FIGURE 1.6 Each text item in blue on the left side links to additional information.

There are several other features of the Help system you can try:

- *Index*—Click the Index button to view a list of all Help topics (as shown in Figure 1.7). Type a word in the text box at the top of this list to locate an associated topic. As you type, the index narrows down to terms that match that text in the list.

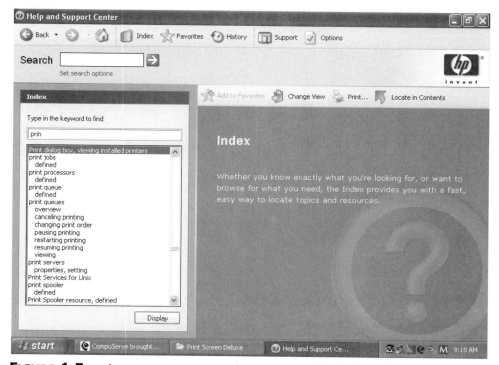

FIGURE 1.7   As you type a topic, a feature called QuickPick narrows down to words in the index that match.

- *Print*—Click the Print button to print the currently displayed topic.
- *Fixing a Problem*—This is a troubleshooting feature that walks you through possible fixes for the problem you're experiencing and sometimes runs tests of hardware settings.
- *Send Your Feedback to Microsoft*—Use this link to email Microsoft technical support about Windows-related problems.

- *Latest News*—This link appears when you are connected to the Internet. It offers links to online help resources.
- *Help and Support Resources*—If you are connected to the Internet, this link appears offering updates to the Windows XP software and tools, such as System Restore (a process that returns your computer to previous settings) and Remote Assistance to help with problems you haven't been able to solve in other ways.
- *Search*—Enter a topic or phrase in the Search box and click the arrow to find related help.
- *Support*—Click the Support button to see options for support, including asking a friend to help you by using the Internet, going to a Windows Web site and viewing information people have posted in a topic forum (an online bulletin board), or using HP Instant Support (more about that shortly).

note **The feature called Remote Assistance is explored in Chapter 20. Essentially, it is a way for somebody else to take charge of your computer remotely using the Internet. If you have a computer-savvy friend, this feature allows him or her to get onto your computer and fix a problem or make a setting for you using the Internet.**

HP Instant Support

For Pavilion owners, one item in the Help and Support Center that's worth exploring is HP Instant Support. This feature allows you to access a live HP tech support person to help walk you through a procedure or to solve a problem. You communicate using instant messages you exchange across the Internet.

When you click HP Instant Support from the Help and Support Center, you'll see five possible actions, as shown in Figure 1.8.

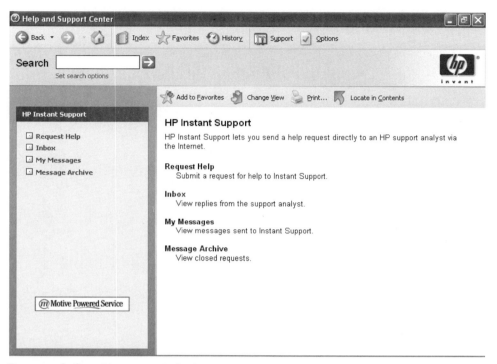

FIGURE 1.8 You can ask for help and track the various messages and responses here.

With the five items in the Instant Support area, you can do the following:

- Initiate a session with a tech support person by clicking Request Help.
- Open an inbox to see if you've received a response by clicking Inbox.
- View messages waiting to be sent in the outbox.
- Review the messages you've sent to Instant Support by clicking Sent Messages.
- View an archive of all messages and responses in the Message Archive.

When you request help, you'll soon be alerted that a response has been sent by a support person. Click your Inbox and then double-click the message to read it. If you want to respond, click Reply, enter your message, and then click Send. The discussion can go on for as many messages as it takes to get the help you need.

If you should leave Instant Support, for example, to try a procedure and reboot your computer, and then need to get back in touch, just open your last message and add new comments. The tech support person who picks up your message will have information on your case available for review when you get in touch again.

When It's Time to Stop

When you've had enough fun playing around with your new computer, you'll need to know how to turn the computer off. There are a couple of options here: placing the computer in a lower energy Standby mode or turning it off entirely.

Put Your Computer on Standby

If you intend to be away from your computer for a while, say to go to lunch, you have the option of putting the computer in Standby mode. Standby uses a lower energy setting, but, unlike when you turn your computer off, Standby keeps everything on your computer as you left it. Programs and documents stay open so that you can get right back to work when you return. You reactivate your computer by simply clicking your mouse button or striking a key on your keyboard.

✔ **To put your computer in Standby mode, follow these steps:**

1. Click Start, Turn Off Computer. The dialog box shown in Figure 1.9 appears.

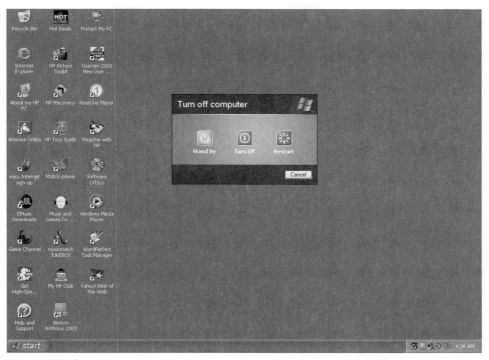

FIGURE 1.9   This is also the dialog box used to restart or turn off your computer.

2. Click the Stand By button. Your computer screen goes black.

3. To reactivate your computer, click your mouse button. A Windows screen appears.

4. Click Owner to log back into your computer.

Turning It Off

Turning your computer off shuts down all programs that are running. It's usually best for you to shut down programs yourself before turning the computer off so that you don't run the risk of losing any data.

You'll learn more about your choices when shutting down your computer in Chapter 3, but I don't want you to have to leave it on until you get there. Briefly, here's how you can turn your computer off:

1. Select Start, Turn Off Computer.

2. At the dialog box shown in Figure 1.9, click on Turn Off.

    That's it!

tip **If you crash, that is, if your computer freezes and won't accept mouse or keyboard commands anymore, you can try two things. Press Ctrl+Alt+Delete twice in succession. If nothing happens when you press Ctrl+Alt+Delete, you can turn your computer off by pressing and holding in the power button. You'll have to press the button again after it's shut down to start it up.**

Chapter Summary

In this chapter, you opened up the box and unpacked your Presario or Pavilion. You connected various peripherals and a phone line. You learned what the Windows XP operating system is and how you use it to control your computer settings.

You modified the speaker volume and learned to put your computer into Standby mode and to turn it off. Finally, you explored the Help and Support Center and learned how to initiate a live help session for your Pavilion with HP Instant Support.

chapter

2

Setting Up Your Printer

In this Chapter

✔ Registering your computer

✔ Connecting a printer

✔ Setting your default printer

When you have finished connecting everything out of the box as you did in Chapter 1, your next step is to register your computer as soon as possible. After that's done, you can hook up to a printer so that you can generate hard copies of documents, newsletters, emails, electronic tickets for airline reservations, and so forth.

Registering Your Computer and Windows XP

Registering your computer is a very important step. After you're registered, HP can notify you of updates for your computer. Also, if you need to contact HP for support, the customer care person uses your registration information to assist you. HP can tell you about special offers if you're registered, and you can receive free newsletters with product information and tips.

note **HP respects your privacy. By registering with them, you do not run any risk that they will share your information with anybody else. They will share your information with HP partners to enable them to make special offers to you only if you give them permission. When you first use your computer, and periodically until you complete registration, a message appears asking you to register. You can register online if your modem is hooked up to a phone line and if you have an Internet account (if you don't, visit Part IV of this book to learn how to get one) by proceeding with the online registration when prompted or going to register.hp.com.**

note **Your computer comes with a one-year warranty, but, when you register, you might also consider extending that warranty. You can pay to upgrade your warranty by calling 888-999-4747 or by visiting www.hp.com/go/hpsupportpack. An extended warranty protects your investment by covering you for three years and by providing toll-free technical support.**

Connecting a Printer

Guess what? The paperless office is a myth and so is the paperless home. Almost everybody needs a printer to go with their computer so that they can print out documents and emails and hand them on to others, stuff them in files, or tack them on a bulletin board.

Printers today come in various types, from expensive color Laser-Jets that print many copies a minute with very high quality, to less expensive black and white Deskjet or inkjet models. Some all-in-one machines even provide fax, scanner, copier, and printer capabilities in a single machine.

Whatever kind of printer you own, and whether it came with your computer or was purchased separately, connecting it to your computer is done in the same way. However, first, you have to have a printer.

Which Is the Right Printer for You?

You may have a printer on hand, or you may have bought one with your computer. However, if you haven't yet purchased a printer, here's some quick advice for how to pick the one that's right for you.

- **Price** is always a consideration. Printers range in price from less than $100 to more than $2,000.

- **Print quality** is important. If you need to print high-quality output, especially graphics, photos, and business documents, you want higher quality. On the high end are impact and laserjet technologies that produce smoother edges to text characters and crisp detail in graphics; on the lower end is dot matrix technology, which produces images and text made up of discernible dots of ink making output appear jagged. One of the great determining factors of image quality is the dots per inch (dpi) setting. The higher the dpi the better the quality. A typical dpi might be 1200 x 600 for higher quality or 600 x 300 for a lower quality resolution.

- **Speed** relates to how many pages a printer produces in a minute. Some printers describe this as characters per second (cps) and others as number of pages produced a minute. If you print a lot, speed can count.

- Do you want **color or black and white?** Color is fun and, for a family computing environment, is usually useful for graphics, greeting cards, posters, and so on. However, color printers of any quality usually cost more, and you usually have to replace two ink cartridges, one color and one black and white.

- Consider **paper size.** Some printers (usually the pricier ones) can accommodate larger paper sizes, such as 13 x 19-inch poster stock. If you'll be printing odd-sized documents, make sure your printer can handle that or that it provides multiple paper trays for different sizes of paper.

The bottom line is that you have to decide how much you'll use your printer so that you buy one that is high enough quality to take the wear and tear. Then, consider the quality you want in the output and how much you can afford.

 caution   **Be sure your printer is Windows XP compatible before buying.**

Connecting and Installing the Print Driver

Your CPU has a plug in the back with two rows of holes in a plastic casing. A little picture of a printer is displayed above this connection. To connect a printer, you have to use a parallel cable that comes with your printer. If you can't locate it, you can buy a parallel cable at any computer supply or office superstore. By default, Windows assumes new printers will be installed on your parallel port.

note   **Printers can also connect to computers using a serial cable. Because parallel cabling is more standardized (pretty much any printer can connect to any computer using this cable) and because the parallel transmits data at faster rates, most printers today do not use serial cabling.**

After you've connected the cable to both the CPU and printer, place the disk that came with your printer into your CD drive. An installation window such as the one shown in Figure 2.1 appears.

Follow the directions in the installation program. During this process, you will probably be asked to confirm where to install the driver (in most cases, just accept the suggested location), and you may be

FIGURE 2.1   This HP OfficeJet installation routine offers a tour of the product to help you get acquainted with it.

asked if you want this printer to be set as the default. The default printer is the one that applications print to automatically, unless you make another setting. (If the installation doesn't make this setting for you, you can do it yourself. See Designating a Default Printer later in this chapter). You may also be asked to print a test page to make sure the connection is set up correctly.

Updating Printer Drivers

If you happen to have a slightly older printer, the drivers that come on the printer CD may not be compatible with Windows XP. In that case, you may get a message that says that the driver is not compatible, and you may have difficulty getting your printer to work. If you get such a message, you should go to the printer manufacturer's Web site (such

PCs Made Easy

as Compaq's, shown in Figure 2.2) and download an updated driver from there.

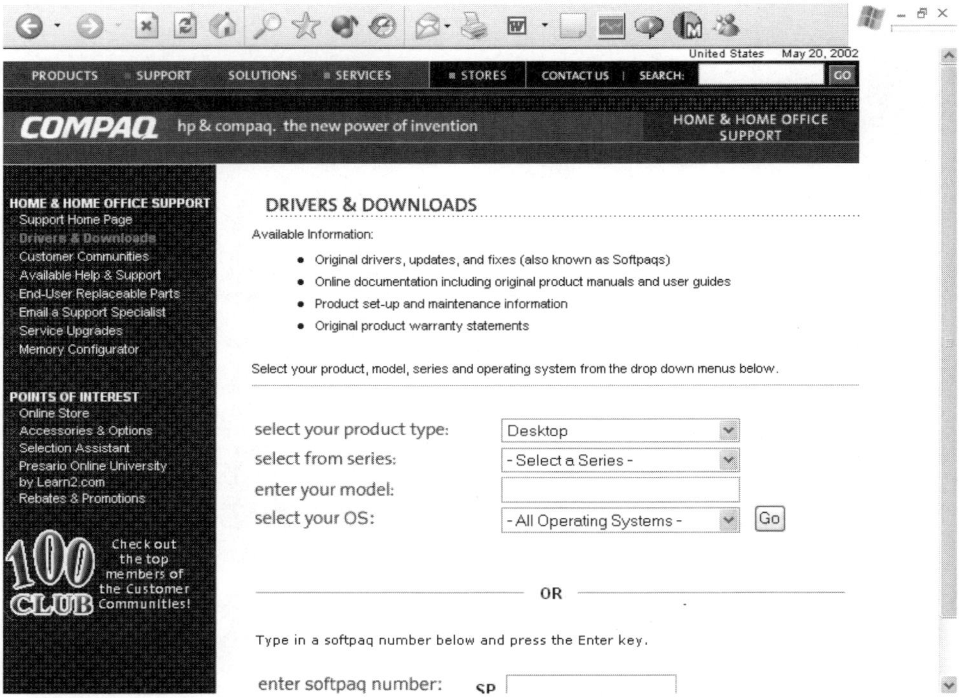

FIGURE 2.2   Look for an area for drivers and downloads on your printer manufacturer's Web site.

You can also download many hardware drivers from Microsoft's Web site, which includes a chart indicating that a product has been tested for Windows XP compatibility (see Figure 2.3).

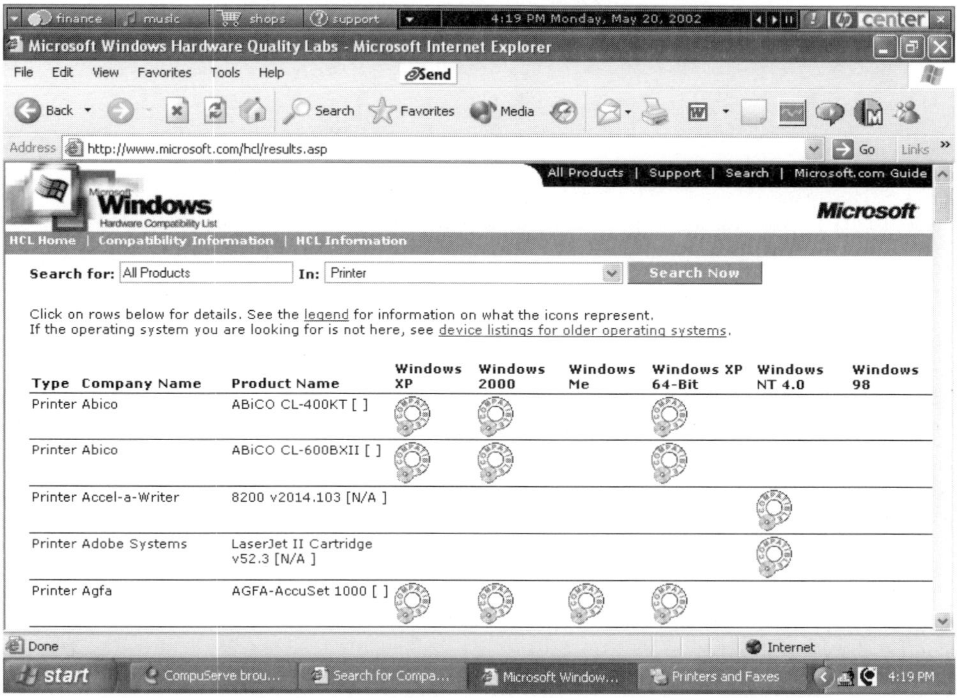

FIGURE 2.3   Microsoft works with hardware manufacturers to update their drivers for Windows XP compatibility and shows you which have been updated.

Designating a Default Printer

You may find that, over time, you will install a couple of printers to work with your computer or set up your computers so that they can access more than one computer through a network. You may also sometimes print to a fax printer.

Your Windows applications all use the printer you have set up as the default printer to print. If you just click a Print button or don't make any changes, that document is headed for the default printer. If you want to print to another printer, you can make that setting in a program's print dialog box.

This default usually saves time because you don't have to make any special setting to print to the printer that you use most of the time. However, if you do want to change the default, here's how it's done:

1. Select Start, Control Panel, Printers.

2. Click View Installed Printers or Fax Printers. The window shown in Figure 2.4 appears.

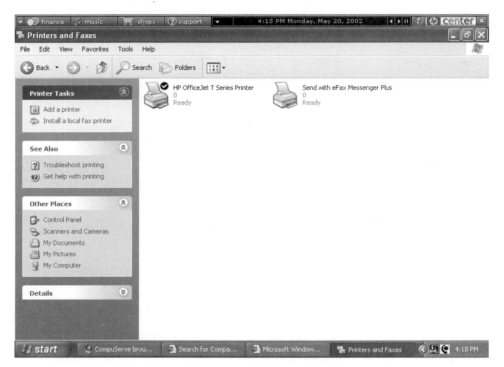

FIGURE 2.4   *The default printer is indicated by a white checkmark in a black circle.*

3. Click the printer you want to set as the default and select File, Set As Default Printer. (Note that this option will only be listed on the menu if you have selected a printer that is not currently the default..)

4. Click the Close button to close the window.

Chapter Summary

In this chapter, you learned about registering your computer so that you could get updates and support from HP. Then, you explored what's involved in connecting a printer to your computer, installing printer drivers, and setting the default printer. You also got advice about buying the printer that's right for you.

chapter

3

Turn on Your Computer: You're All Set to Go!

In this Chapter

✔ Turning your computer on

✔ Getting help

✔ Seeing what you can do with your keyboard

✔ Turning your computer off

With your HP Pavilion or Compaq Presario home PC, after the plugs are plugged in and the power is switched on, you're good to go. However, because so much comes with your computer, it's worth taking a few minutes to explore before you get to work.

There's a wealth of preinstalled software, such as the Microsoft Works software suite, which includes a word processor, spreadsheet program, and more. You'll discover utilities such as Norton antivirus software, which helps to keep your computer in shape. Then, there are programs designed to help you find your way around and to provide help getting started, such as the Windows Help and Support Center. The list just goes on and on. Maybe its time to just take a look.

Don't forget the keyboard that comes with your computer. It offers you far more than an alphabet soup of keys. With it, you can get instant access to your email, Internet shopping, and CD/DVD controls.

A Bounty of Computer Productivity

Starting up your HP Pavilion or Compaq Presario is like opening a treasure box filled with some very cool things. There are programs you can use to play music, write documents, calculate, and play games. You'll find media samples from music to video that you can get creative with. There are Web browsers and email programs and multimedia players.

Turning Your Computer On the First Time

When you first turn on your computer, the Windows XP desktop appears. Windows XP is what drives all the programs on your computer, and the desktop is Windows' home base. Icons on the desktop (see Figure 3.1) represent shortcuts to often-used programs (and you can add more, which you'll learn about in the next chapter). There's a little Recycle Bin, which is where deleted files go. There's also a Start menu, which you can use to access computer controls, software programs, and documents you create.

FIGURE 3.1   The Windows XP desktop can use any picture you like as its background, bringing cheer to your computing day.

note The first time you use your new Pavilion you are likely to be greeted by a little fellow who walks through a door on the desktop and greets you. This professorial-looking chap is Victor, the HP Tour Guide, and he provides an interesting introductory tour of all your HP Pavilion has to offer. You can also invite the Tour Guide to visit at any time by clicking the HP Tour Guide icon on the Windows desktop, or by selecting Start, All Programs, HP Tools, HP Tour Guide.

Finding the Support You Need

For help with your computer, you should visit the Help and Support Center by clicking the Help and Support icon on the desktop or selecting Start, Help and Support. The Help and Support Center appears. From this area, you can find a Windows Glossary, Windows keyboard shortcuts, and information about customizing your computer.

If you own a Pavilion, the Help and Support Center will be customized to display HP-specific support options. Figure 3.2 shows Pavilion's help screen.

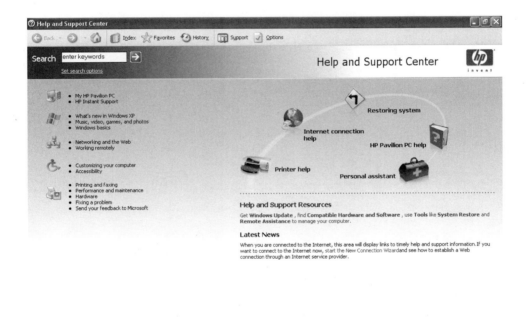

FIGURE 3.2   *Pavilion owners get additional help options.*

Although the HP Help and Support Center is based on the Microsoft help center offered on the Compaq Presario, it also contains specific information about your HP Pavilion and a wealth of tools such as interactive tutorials. By using Instant Support with your Internet connection, you can send requests for help using email and keep an archive of help answers you receive.

✔ Here's how to use Help:

1. Click a topic in the Help and Support main window; you'll be taken to a window offering different items related to that topic.

2. Click one of the subtopics that's displayed; you'll be taken to more and more specific tasks. In Figure 3.3, for example, you'll see the third level of detail when you look for information on printing.

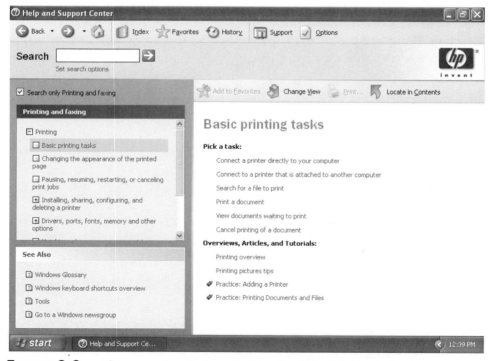

FIGURE 3.3   If you want an index of all topics, just click the Index button on any Help and Support window.

3. When you reach the task you want help with, click it; the system displays step-by-step directions for that task.

4. Click the X in the upper right-hand corner of the Help and Support window to close it when you're done. You return to the Windows desktop.

> *tip* **Do you want to build your own help manual for features you use most often? If you like, you can save help topics you've found useful in your Favorites folder for future reference. Just click the Favorites button on the Help and Support Center toolbar with the page you want displayed.**

Get a Friend to Help

Want help from a flesh-and-blood person? Try Remote Assistance (Start, All Programs, Remote Assistance). You can use this feature to send an invitation using the Internet and Windows Messenger asking for help. When your friend receives the message you can begin to hold an online conversation. He or she can even view your computer screen to help diagnose your problem and to take control of your computer remotely to make fixes from a distance. Learn more about this feature in Chapter 20.

Get Going Fast with Pre-installed Software

Software tells your computer how to perform certain sets of activities, such as drawing or entering text. Different kinds of software enable you to perform different types of activities. Software is also referred to as a program or an application.

In Part III of this book, you'll learn the basics of using some of the software that comes preloaded on your HP Pavilion and Compaq Presario. For now, let me introduce you to the kinds of software you'll find when you first turn on your computer.

✔ **Take a moment to look at what's available on your computer:**

1. Click the Start menu on the Windows desktop.

2. Click All Programs. A list of available programs pops up.

By scanning this list, you'll see that HP and Compaq computers come packed with software. Move your mouse around this list, and you'll see that some of these items contain submenus that list even more programs.

To give you an overview of the types of programs that are available, I've broken them into categories for you. Your computer has the following:

- *Productivity software*—I call this productivity software because it's the kind of software you use to write and design documents, keep track of your finances, and manage data, in other words, to get work done. In this category of software your Pavilion or Presario has included Microsoft Works, an integrated suite of applications that includes a word processor, calendar, database, and spreadsheet program (see Figure 3.4). Another productivity application included is a program to manage your finances: Quicken from Intuit.

FIGURE 3.4   Works is a great suite of products if you like to be led through the process of creating a new document.

- *Internet software and connections*—If you have an Internet account, you'll be glad to see that HP has already placed files for major Internet service providers on your computer that are ready to install. Included may be America Online (AOL), MSN Explorer, Earthlink, or CompuServe (the selection may vary depending on whether you own a Pavilion or Presario). If you don't have an Internet account and you own a Pavilion or Presario, you can use the Easy Internet Sign Up item on the Programs menu, which helps you sign up for an account and get connected (you'll learn more about this in Chapter 13). An email program from Microsoft called Outlook Express also comes loaded on your computer. Use it to retrieve, manage, and send out email and attached files. Finally, the popular Web browser,

Internet Explorer, is all set up to help you find what you need online as soon as you connect.

- *Games*—Windows XP itself includes 11 games, from Hearts to Pinball, and even some Internet games that match you with an online player to play the game in real time through *Zone.com*.
- *Multimedia*—Multimedia can encompass sound and music programs, video and digital imaging, and even animation.

What multimedia programs do you have available? It will depend on your model and when you bought your computer, but typically, here's what comes on your computer:

- HP Image Zone for digital imaging on HP Pavilions
- Multi-Channel Sound Manager
- MusicMatch
- EMusic Downloads
- ArcSoft ShowBiz DVD and Video Editor
- Intervideo WinDVD Player
- RealOne Player
- ArcSoft PhotoImpression
- ArcSoft Funhouse
- RecordNow

If you own a Compaq Presario, you might have these programs:
- Multi-channel Sound Manager
- InterVideo WinDVD
- RealOne Player
- RecordNow
- EMusic Downloads

In addition both computers will include Windows media software such as Windows Media Player. Many of these can be accessed through the Accessories folder on the Start, All Programs menu.

Some of these programs are media players (a player is a computer equivalent of the equipment you'd use to play a CD or a video in your own home). Other programs help you organize multimedia into libraries or to download music or photos from the Internet. Still others allow you to edit or create multimedia files, such as the HP Image Zone (see Figure 3.5) for working with digital images.

tip **Note that several of these programs are trial or limited versions of the full programs. Typically, you can use them for about 30 days before you'll be asked to purchase the software. It's great to be able to play with these programs so that you can find the ones you like best before installing the full versions.**

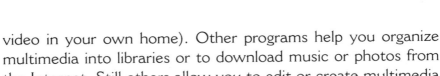

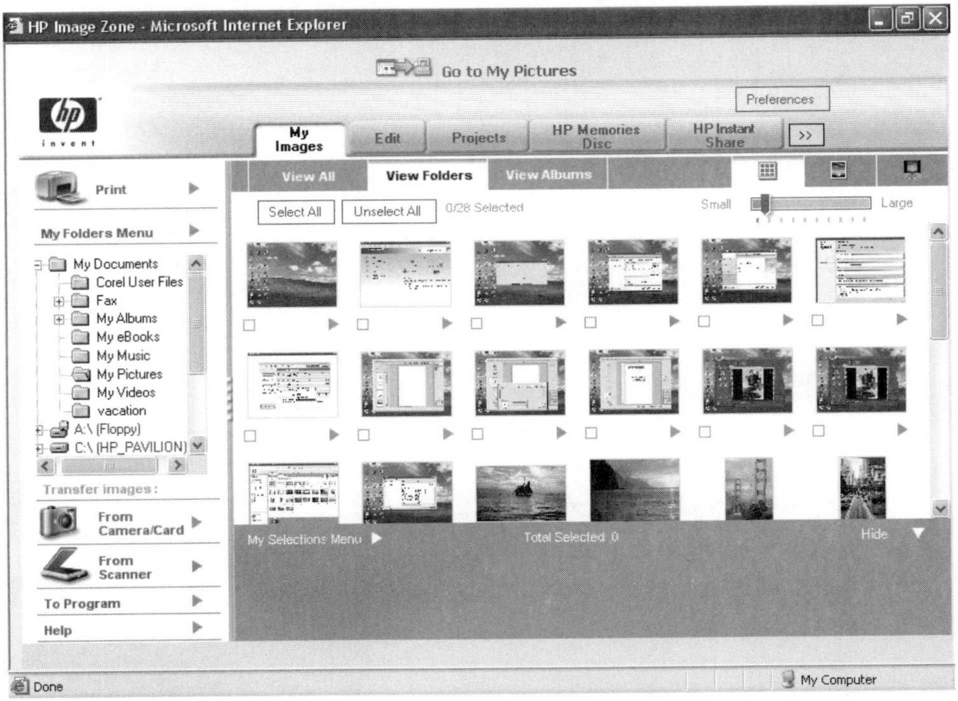

FIGURE 3.5   HP ImageZone allows Pavilion users to work with digital images with ease.

- *Educational*—Many people today are buying home computers as a great tool for kids to do research and complete homework or other educational projects. You and your children will certainly get a lot out of the one year's subscription to Encarta Online Deluxe that comes with Presarios or Britannica that comes with the HP Pavilion. Encarta and Britannica are online encyclopedias, but they're much more. There's a dictionary, atlas, and thesaurus.

- *Utilities*—Utilities are the handymen of the computing world. They root out computer viruses, make backup copies of files, protect your information, and restore your computer if you have a serious problem. Some utilities that come with your HP Pavilion are Norton Antivirus for protection from computer viruses, and Windows Application Recovery and System Recovery to help you if you have a serious problem with your software or hardware.

Getting to Know Your Pavilion Keyboard

Your keyboard is no longer just the thing you tap on to enter text and commands into your computer. It's a fully functional command central for your computer, offering shortcut keys that let you instantly access shopping, your email, and more, as shown in Figures 3.6.

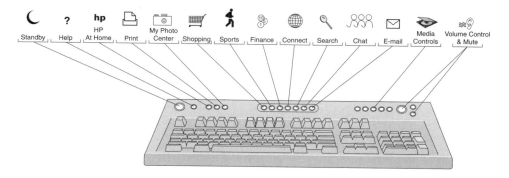

FIGURE 3.6   The Pavilion keyboard offers one-touch access to a wealth of features.

Here's what the special keys on your Pavilion keyboard will do:

- You'll find one-button access to HP, your printer, and Imaging Software on the left side of your keyboard. Using these, you can instantly log on to the My HP Club Web site, go to the Print dialog box to print the currently displayed document, or open the HP Image Zone program to edit or print photos or create photo slide shows.

- The middle section of the keyboard offers keys to instantly access the Internet: Shopping, Sports, Finance, Connect, Search, Chat, E-mail. Note that, if you are not connected to the Internet and press any of these keys, your HP Pavilion is smart enough to use your default connection to the Internet to log you on.

- The question mark button to the left of the keyboard is the thing to hit if you want to go directly to the Help and Support Center.

- CD Player controls are on the right side at the top of your keyboard. You can press the button with a musical note on it to open the MusicMatch Jukebox program (see Figure 3.7) where you can create libraries of CDs or access favorite radio stations (note that you must be connected to the Internet to play radio stations). Then, use the keyboard controls to play, pause, stop, rewind, or fast forward music. You can also use the buttons with up and down arrow keys to adjust your computer's volume or press the Mute button (a button with a little speaker image on it) to temporarily turn off your computer's sound.

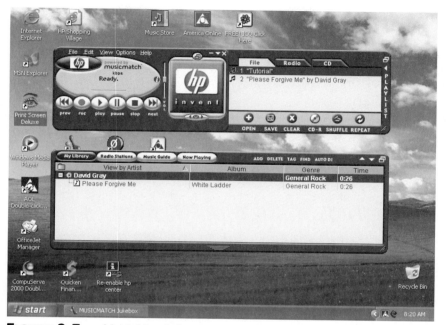

FIGURE 3.7   MusicMatch lets you assemble libraries of music from CDs and the Internet.

- Want to put your computer to sleep? Reach for the snooze button. The Standby button on your keyboard, with the image of a half moon, puts your computer into Standby mode. In this mode, the screen turns black, and the computer uses a lower level of power. However, you will continue to receive any computer faxes or email messages. You can click your mouse to wake the computer up again. When you resume, whatever programs or documents were open will be available, just as they were when you hit the Standby button.

Your Presario shortcut buttons will do the following:

- The Internet button connects you to the Web and a home page you can customize to get your weather, news, sports, or information on the world of finances.

- The button with a question mark on it opens the Help and Support Center where you can get information about your computer, Windows XP, and PC-related peripherals such as printers.
- The Search button takes you online to a search engine site where you can find news and information on the Internet.
- The E-mail button opens your e-mail application.
- The button with a big O on it launches a Web site with special offers, online chat, and discussion groups.
- The Entertainment button takes you online to a site with links to music downloads, streaming video, Webcasts, the latest entertainment news, and reviews.
- The My Presario button connects you to the My Presario Club Web site. This site contains discounts, promotional offers, and how-to discussions for your computer.

tip **You can reconfigure any of the Internet buttons to take you to any Web site or open any program you like. Click Start, Control Panel, Printers and Other Hardware, Keyboard. Use the Keyboard Properties window to change the function of buttons, but remember that the little symbols printed there may no longer make sense to others if you change their functions.**

Turning Your Computer Off

Now that you've mastered turning on your computer and have seen an overview of what comes with your HP Pavilion or Compaq Presario, it's time to learn how to turn the computer off. There are three simple choices to make here:

- *Stand by*—You can put your computer in Standby mode, which uses less power and turns your screen dark, as if the computer were off. Standby keeps everything that you had on your computer screen just the way it was at the point when you went into Standby mode; when you come out of Standby mode (which you can do by clicking your mouse or a key on your keyboard), any programs, documents, or dialog boxes you had open will still be open.

- *Restart*—You will sometimes be instructed to restart your computer, either because you have changed a setting or installed new software and the system needs to start again to implement the changes, or because a problem has occurred and the computer needs to reinitialize itself to solve it. When you choose Restart, your computer turns itself off and then on again.

- *Turn off*—Sayonara. Turn Off means just that. Your computer turns itself off completely, and you'll have to press the Power button on your computer to start up again.

Note that, with the Restart and Turn Off mode, if you have programs running, Windows may ask you to close them, or it may close them itself. To use any of these three modes, follow these steps:

1. Click Start, Turn Off Computer. The Turn Off Computer window shown in Figure 3.8 appears.

2. Click any of the three buttons or, if you change your mind, click Cancel.

That's it, until you're ready to turn your computer on and start computing again.

FIGURE 3.8   Your three options are laid out clearly here: Turn Off will actually turn your computer power off.

Chapter Summary

In this chapter, you got a tour of your HP Pavilion or Compaq Presario and Windows XP. You explored some help features. You learned about some of the special features on your Pavilion or Presario keyboard. Then you discovered the few options available for turning off your computer.

part

2

Getting to Know Windows XP

4

Getting Around Windows XP

In this Chapter

✓ Learning your way around the Windows desktop and Start menu

✓ Creating shortcuts

✓ Navigating around Windows and opening programs and folders

✓ Changing the appearance of things

All the wonderful software and tools that are packed into your computer are like the parts of a car. They are wonderful to have, but, without an engine, they simply won't go. Windows XP is the engine for your computer. Windows is an operating system: It provides the functionality that enables you to use all that software and to give commands to your computer.

I n this chapter you'll climb into Windows, take a look at its dashboard, and kick its tires, that is, you'll explore the Windows desktop and the commands on the Windows Start menu. Then, you'll take a look at where the files and folders that make up your computer programs and documents are kept and take a spin around your computer drives. You'll see a few ways to organize windows of information on your computer screen and explore how to open and close software programs and folders.

Just as you like to look at different colors and upholstery fabrics when you buy a new car, you'll also enjoy looking at the different options Windows offers for changing colors and images that greet you on the Windows desktop.

Discovering the Desktop

In Chapter 3, you got your first look at Windows XP when you turned on your computer for the first time. After the few moments it takes your computer to start up (also called *booting*), you'll see the Windows XP *desktop*. The desktop serves the purpose of keeping the things you need to work on close at hand, just like your desktop at home. However, instead of books and pens and paper clips, what's on your Windows desktop is software, computer files, and menus of commands (see Figure 4.1).

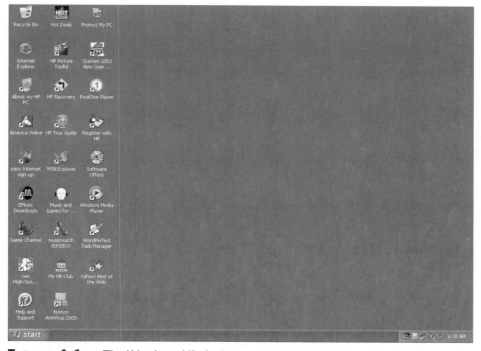

FIGURE 4.1 The Windows XP desktop contains icons that represent shortcuts to software programs, as well as the Start menu.

The icons you see on your desktop are *shortcuts* that you can double-click to open various software programs installed on your computer. HP has placed icons there for many of the most commonly used programs, but you can add or delete these shortcuts if you want (which you'll learn how to do later in this chapter). In addition to shortcuts, you'll notice a bright green button in the lower left hand corner of the desktop. This is the Start menu button.

Exploring the Start Menu

Menus are common elements of any Windows software. A *menu* holds lists of commands that you can click to do something, such as opening a program, going to a control panel where you can make changes to your computer settings, or launching an Internet connection.

The Windows Start menu is located on the *taskbar* that runs along the bottom of the Windows desktop. The Start menu is one of the largest menus you'll find, with a main panel and branches that display a menu of all the programs on your computer, and even some additional submenus (see Figure 4.2).

FIGURE 4.2   Working with this large menu can take a little practice, but you'll get the hang of it.

✔ **Take a moment to follow a branch of this menu to see how it works:**

1. Click the Start button. The Start menu main panel displays (see Figure 4.3).

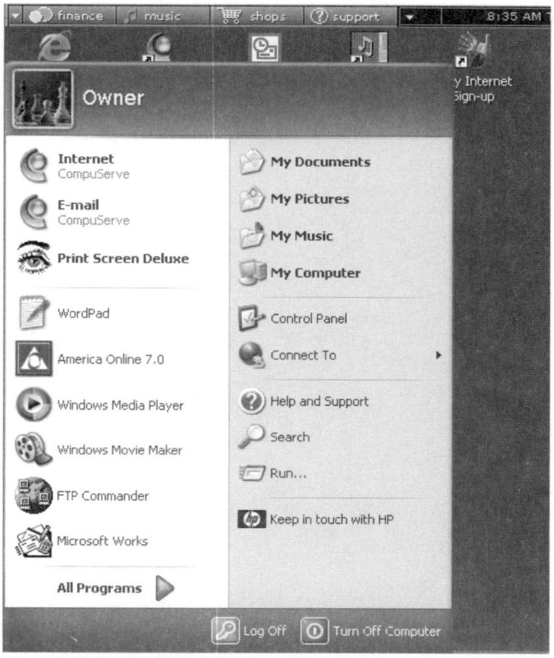

FIGURE 4.3   This panel offers quick access to programs and documents you use all the time.

2.   Click All Programs. The Programs menu appears.

3.   Without moving your mouse up or down, slide the mouse or your trackball to the right so that your mouse is resting within the Programs menu. (Be sure to move only to the right. If you move your mouse up or down even slightly in the main Start panel, you may close the All Programs selection and highlight a different item. You may need to practice this motion a few times before it becomes comfortable).

4.   Move your mouse around the Programs menu; note that some of the programs have a black arrow to their right (see Figure 4.4); this arrow indicates a submenu is available. The submenu appears when your mouse moves over that program name.

FIGURE 4.4   Programs without a black arrow launch immediately when you click them; those with a black arrow offer a submenu of choices.

5. Click the item named Accessories. When the submenu appears, move your mouse to the right (again avoiding moving it up or down within the Programs menu) and drag your mouse to the Calculator option.

6. The Start menu disappears, and the Calculator program is launched.

7. Click the X in the red box in the upper right corner to close the program (this is the close button).

You can use the Start menu to open the folders where your documents or pictures are stored (the My Documents and My Pictures options on the Start menu main panel) or to open any software application stored on your computer. You can also use the Start menu to connect to the Internet and to access computer settings, as you'll learn as you proceed through this book.

Adding and Deleting Shortcuts

The shortcuts on your desktop are placed there for your convenience. However, the people who did that don't really know what programs you use most often in your work, so you might want to modify what's on your desktop at some point.

You can use the Start menu to place other shortcuts on your desktop. For example, if there's a program you use all the time, such as WordPad, you can get to it more quickly through a shortcut than you can by selecting Start, All Programs, Accessories, WordPad.

Project: **Add Shortcuts to Your Desktop**

To personalize your desktop, you should take a poll of those who'll be using your computer and find out what programs they'll use most often. You may have to compromise and leave some off the desktop because you don't want it to get too cluttered. You can then create shortcuts and organize them on the screen, perhaps with those used by each family member in their own corner of the desktop so they can be found easily.

✔ **Follow these steps to add a shortcut to a program:**

1. From the Start menu, click All Programs.

2. Right-click the software you want a shortcut for; a menu appears.

3. Click Create Shortcut. A copy of the item appears at the end of the Programs list (for example WordPad [2]).

4. Click the copy and drag it onto your desktop.

To delete a shortcut from the desktop, follow these steps:

1. Right-click the shortcut. A menu appears.

2. Click Delete. A verifying message appears.

3. Click Delete Shortcut to complete the operation.

tip **You can also create a desktop shortcut to documents you use frequently. Select Start, My Documents and then locate the document and follow the procedure to add a shortcut.**

Opening and Closing Software

In a Windows XP computer, such as the Compaq Presario or HP Pavilion, opening and closing software is done in the same way, no matter who created the software, because those functions are part of Windows.

When you open a program, it appears in a window (hence the name, Windows). You can have more than one program open at a time and can easily switch among the windows.

You have a couple of choices for starting software. You can do one of the following:

- Double-click a shortcut icon on the Windows desktop.
- Use the Start menu, click All Programs, and then click the software (or in some cases, click the software from a submenu, as you did to turn on the Calculator in the last section).
- Locate a document you created in that software on your computer (saved by default in the My Documents folder) and double-click it. When you do, Windows opens the originating software along with the document automatically.

✔ **Try using a shortcut now to open a program:**

1. Double-click the icon that says Windows Media Player. The program opens (see Figure 4.5).

FIGURE 4.5 The Windows Media Player appears in its own window, floating on the desktop.

2. Click the title bar at the top of the window (in the blue bar that contains the words Windows Media Player) and drag the window around your desktop.

3. Click the Maximize button (the middle button in the group of three in the upper right-hand corner). The window enlarges.

4. Click the Minimize button. The program is reduced to a button on the taskbar (the taskbar runs along the bottom of the desktop).

5. Click the Windows Media Player item on the taskbar, and the program opens again.

6. Click the Restore Down button (it's the same button that you clicked on to maximize the program, but, now that the program is maximized, it offers the option to restore it down to its smaller size).

Now that you have a program window open and have played around with moving it, enlarging it, and reducing its size, it's time to learn how to close a program. There are a few options for how to do this as well. (You'll learn that there are usually several ways to do things in Windows programs.)

To close a program, you can do one of the following:

- Click the Close button in the upper right-hand corner.
- Click File, Exit.

Do one of these actions now to close the Windows Media Player program. Note that, if you had opened a file to work on and had not saved the changes you made, at this point, you'd be asked if you wanted to save the file before closing the application.

Doing Windows

Today people do something called multitasking. That means you've got several different things going at once, such as watching TV, memorizing a poem, and feeding the cat. In computer terms, multitasking means that you have more than one program or function of your computer open at the same time. As mentioned in the Opening and Closing Software section earlier in this chapter, you can have several programs open at the same time on your computer and can easily switch between them.

Changing Windows

Try a little multitasking now by opening a couple of programs and moving among them on your desktop.

1. Select Start, All Programs, Accessories, WordPad. The WordPad window opens. If WordPad opens maximized (that is, if it fills your screen), click the Restore Down button.

2. Select Start, All Programs, Accessories, Paint. The Paint program appears. Again, if it opens maximized, click the Restore Down button. The two programs are now both on your desktop, as shown in Figure 4.6.

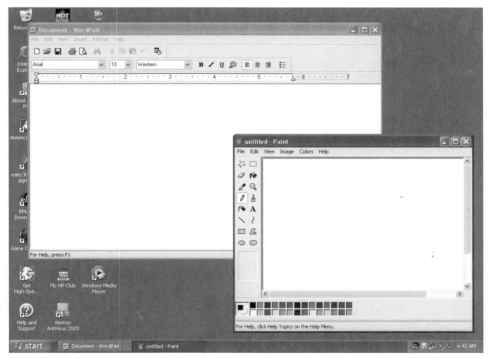

FIGURE 4.6   You can open as many windows as you like on your desktop, but remember that too many open windows can slow your computer down.

You can work in either window by clicking anywhere within it. The *active window*, that is, the window where any actions you take will take effect, will have a darkened title bar across the top. Only one window can be active at any time.

✔ **To switch between the windows, you can perform one of these actions:**

- Press Alt+Tab on your keyboard to toggle between the current active window and the last active window.
- Press Alt+Tab and keep holding the keys down; a box with all open programs appears. Press Tab to move to the one you want. When you release the Alt+Tab keys, that program will become active.
- Click any program name on the taskbar at the bottom of the desktop. If it is open, it will minimize; if it is minimized, its window will open.

Try these various methods now to switch between WordPad and Paint. Also try using the Minimize and Maximize buttons on each window to display or hide the program.

In addition to minimizing and maximizing windows, note that you can resize a window.

✔ **Follow these steps to resize a window manually:**

1. Place your mouse over any window corner until the cursor becomes a two-way arrow.

2. Click and drag to enlarge or reduce the window size.

3. When you release your mouse, the window is resized.

Arranging Windows

You can use the procedures for minimizing, maximizing, and resizing windows outlined in the previous section to help you view and work with several items on your desktop at once. However, Windows has provided a more automated method of arranging windows on your screen that can make organizing your desktop even easier.

You can even use a few different styles of arranging windows on the screen. Figure 4.7 shows windows arranged in what's called a cascading pattern. Figure 4.8 shows those same windows tiled on your screen.

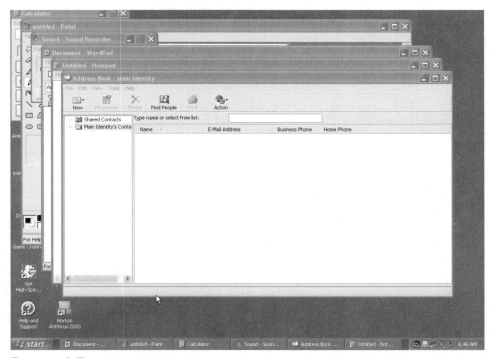

FIGURE 4.7   Cascaded windows arrange themselves like a deck of cards fanned out across your desktop.

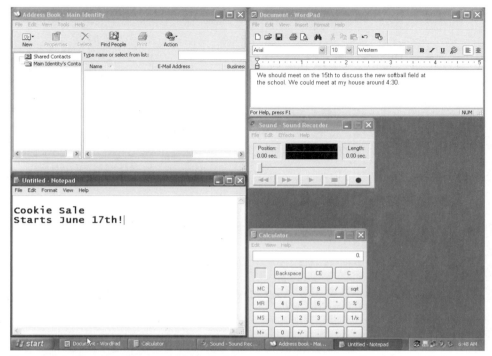

FIGURE 4.8   Windows can be tiled horizontally or vertically on your desktop.

✔ **To arrange windows on your desktop, follow these steps:**

1. With two or more program windows open, right-click (click the button on the right side of your mouse) on an area of the taskbar outside of the Start button or any minimized programs. A pop-up menu displays.

2. Click a selection from this pop-up menu: Cascade Windows, Tile Windows Horizontally, or Tile Windows Vertically. When you release your mouse button, the windows are arranged for you.

3. To undo a cascade effect, right-click the taskbar area again and choose Undo Cascade from the same pop-up menu.

Taking a Look at My Computer

Now its time to look at the contents of your computer a little more closely. Your Compaq Presario or HP Pavilion, like every other computer, stores computer programs and computer files, ready for you to open them up and get to work. The shortcuts on your desktop are just that: shortcuts to launch these programs. However, you can use the My Computer folder when you want to see the various items on your computer and to interact with other media, such as CDs and floppy disks.

Taking a Drive

There's a lot of stuff on your computer that lives on something called your *hard drive*. The hard drive is an actual metal disk inside your computer where bits and bytes of information about your programs, and the files that you create with those programs, are stored. In addition to a hard drive, you also have a floppy drive; a CD drive; and, on most Presario and Pavilion models, a Rewriteable CD (CD-RW) drive.

What's a Floppy?

Floppies are not floppy at all, but they once were. Back in the Dark Ages of computing (say 15 years ago), the disks that you could insert into your computer drive to make copies of your data were either 8-inch or 5-inch plastic film disks that you could literally bend in half, hence the name, floppy. After a while, 3.5-inch disks encased in hard plastic became the preferred storage media because of their size and durability. Though these smaller disks are not floppy at all, the industry continues to use the term "floppy" for this removable storage medium.

The folder on your hard drive called My Computer is where you can access the contents of the various drives on your computer so that you can see what's on them and move and copy items among them.

PCs Made Easy

For example, you might have a file you took off another computer that you want to copy from a floppy disk to a folder on your computer.

To view the My Computer folder, click Start, My Computer. The window shown in Figure 4.9 appears. If you've ever used the Internet, you'll recognize the browserlike interface of this window with buttons to move forward or backward to previously displayed windows, as well as a Search button and other tools for maneuvering around folders.

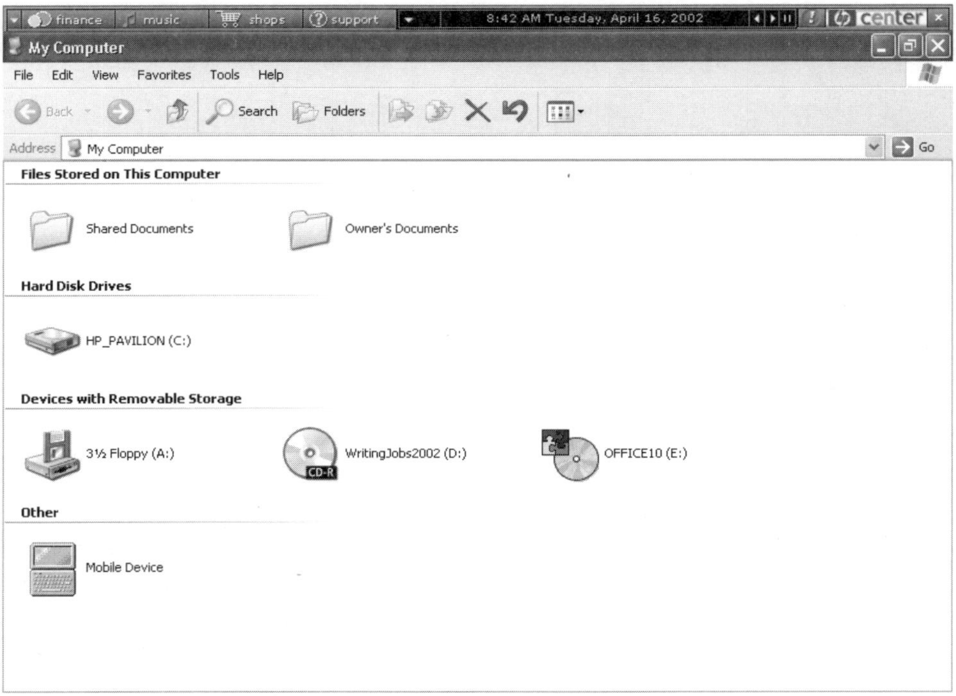

FIGURE 4.9 Your hard drive, documents stored on your hard drive, removable media, and even remote devices can be accessed through your My Computer folder.

The items listed in the Files Stored on This Computer area represent files stored on your hard drive in the Shared Documents and Owner's Documents folders (folders included with Windows for you to store documents in).

tip **You can easily create new folders, rename folders, move folders, or add files to folders. See Chapter 5 for more about file and folder management.**

The Presario (C:) or HP Pavilion (C:) item is your hard disk drive. Although a computer can have several drive letters representing different sections of your hard drive or media drives, C: is typically used for the main hard disk drive.

Devices in the Removable Storage area include floppy, CD, DVD, and CD-RW drives. If a disk is in any of these drives, the name of the disk appears here, rather than the drive name.

You may have an Other section in your My Computer folder if you have installed a remote computing device, such as a handheld computer.

Opening and Closing Folders

Double-click the (C:) item in the My Computer folder to see all that your hard drive contains (see Figure 4.10). You can use the scrollbar on the side of this window to move up and down to view the list of files here. You'll notice that this window contains more folders, designated by little golden folder icons to their left (folders can be nested inside of other folders on your computer), as well as icons representing some individual files.

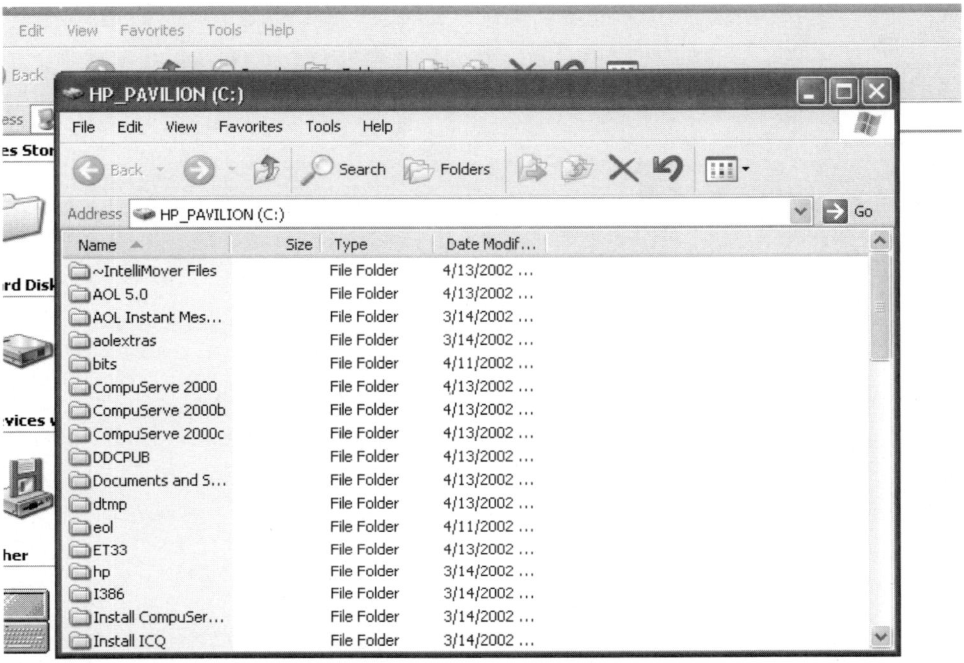

FIGURE 4.10 The My Computer folder contains everything that's stored on your computer hard disk drive—and that's a lot!

You can open a folder and see its contents by double-clicking on it or by clicking on it once and then choosing File, Open. If you double-click a file rather than a folder, a few things could happen. You could launch an application, run an installation program, or open a document in an application.

For now, after you've taken a look at the folders and files (best not to touch any of them at this point), go ahead and click Close to close the C: drive window and then click Close on the My Computer window to close it. You'll see much more of both of these folders in Chapter 5.

Changing the Appearance of Things

When you are on the Windows desktop you'll notice that various colors are used for different elements, such as the taskbar, title bars on windows, and so on. There is also an image behind the desktop, probably a background put there by Hewlett-Packard like the one shown in Figure 4.11.

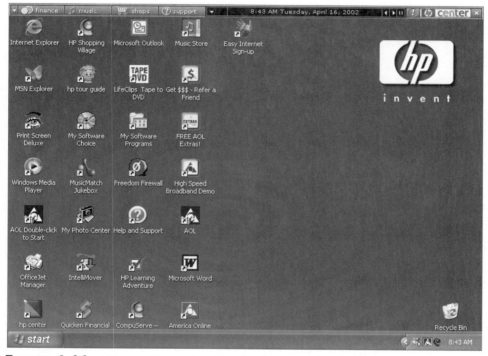

FIGURE 4.11 HP provides a nice blue background, but you'll be surprised at what you can do to change that, if you like.

If you'd like to make your Windows desktop reflect your personality, you'll be glad to hear that you can change colors, the background, and more.

Putting Up Wallpaper

The background image on your desktop is sometimes referred to as wallpaper. Just like wallpaper in a room, the wallpaper on your desktop provides a pleasing background to your computing activities.

However, no two computer users are alike, so you'll be glad to hear that Windows XP provides dozens of backgrounds to choose from. You can even use a picture of your own (your kids, dog, garden, or whatever).

As with all the aspects of your desktop's appearance, the background is set from the Control Panel, which is operations central for modifying Windows settings.

Project: **Personalizing Your Computer Background**

Pick out a photo you'd like to include as your desktop background and scan or upload it into your computer (follow directions included with your scanner or digital camera).

✔ **To change the background on your computer, follow these steps:**

1. Select Start, Control Panel. The Control Panel shown in Figure 4.12 opens.

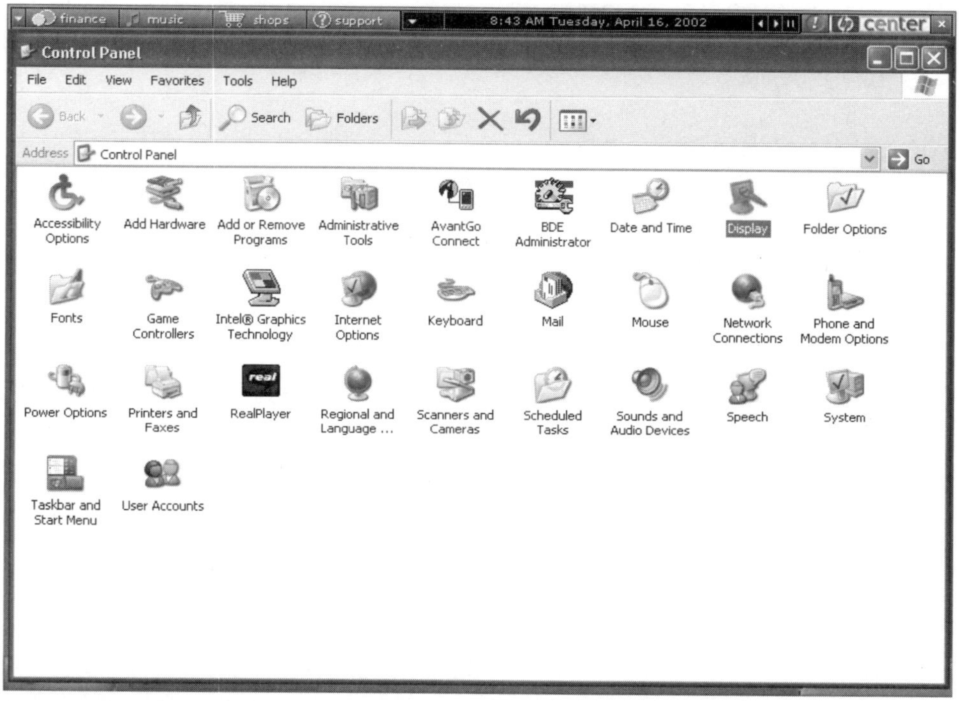

FIGURE 4.12 The Control Panel offers access to all Windows settings in one place.

2. Double-click the Display icon. The Display dialog box (a form used to enter information and make settings in Windows programs) appears.

3. Click the Desktop tab. The Desktop sheet appears, as shown in Figure 4.13.

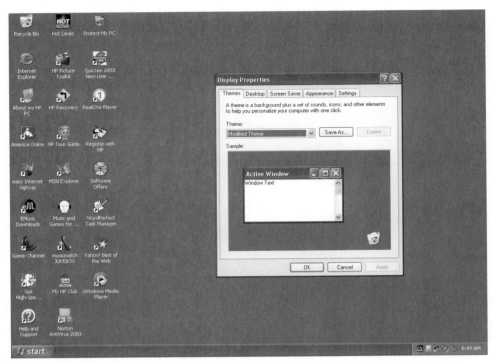

FIGURE 4.13 The Display dialog box contains five tabs; click a tab to modify different settings.

4. To use any image file as your background, when you are on the Desktop tab of the Display dialog box (see Step 3), click the Browse button, then locate the file you want to use, and click OK twice to apply it.

5. At this point, you can click Apply to apply the new background, but not close the Display dialog box, or you can click OK to apply the background and close the dialog box.

note If you want to use a provided background, you can click on any item in the Background list in Step 4, using the scrollbar to the right of the list to move up and down if you need to. The new background is previewed for you.

Getting Just the Right Color Scheme

Computing with a Compaq Presario or HP Pavilion is a colorful experience, in more ways than one. You can pick the colors that most complement your style, changing the colors used on various elements of the Windows desktop and for folders, files, and certain elements in software programs, such as the title bar and dialog boxes.

There are two possibilities for changing the color scheme. One is to choose from a short list of color schemes on the Appearance tab of the Display dialog box. The other is to apply a Theme from the Theme tab in the same dialog box. Themes apply not only a background and color scheme, but also variations on font styles and even sounds that play when certain computing events occur.

✔ **Follow these steps to apply a built-in theme to your computer:**

1. Click Start, Control Panel.

2. Double-click the Display icon.

3. Click the Themes tab to display it, if it's not already displayed.

4. Click the arrow to the right of the Theme list to display it.

5. Click a theme that interests you.

6. Click Apply to apply the theme without closing the dialog box (one advantage to this method is that, if you don't like the theme, you can simply choose another or click Cancel).

7. When you find a theme you like, click OK to close the dialog box.

Note that if you apply a different desktop background, it will replace any background included in the theme, although other settings of the theme will remain intact.

Chapter Summary

You've explored many areas of your computer and Windows in this chapter, including the Windows desktop and Start menu, which allow you to access programs and folders. You learned how to create short-cuts to programs, how to open and close software, and how to open folders on your computer. You used tools in Windows to modify how windows are arranged on your screen and to change the appearance of the elements you look at in Windows and other programs.

File Management Basics

In this Chapter

✔ Creating file folders

✔ Saving files to folders

✔ Moving, copying, and deleting files and folders

✔ Backing up files

✔ Searching for files

Anybody who has ever organized a home filing system or worked in an office knows that there's a place for everything and that it's important that you get all your documents in the right place or you'll be in chaos. The same is true of computer files. You have to know where to find the work you've done and how to avoid confusing multiple versions of the same document. Organizing your computer files involves two key steps: naming and storing files in a logical way.

uckily, Windows already supplies a structure for filing computer documents, and it's essentially a variation on that old metal filing cabinet you're so familiar with. In this chapter, you'll open your virtual filing cabinet and see what's inside; you'll also learn about the importance of backing up computer files on a regular basis.

The Virtual Filing Cabinet

Computer files come in all types and sizes, from files containing photo images to the file where you saved your school play program or taxes. After you've been using your computer for a while, you'll find that you have more files than you know what to do with. If you start out with a good filing system for your documents, you'll avoid a lot of pain down the road.

The filing system that Windows uses is one with folders. Just like the folders you use in a regular filing cabinet, you place related files in Windows folders. In addition, just as you place a manila folder inside a hanging folder, you can place folders within folders in Windows. You can even make copies of files and place them in other folders or move files between folders with ease.

tip **Your home PC comes with several folders already created for you for common types of documents, such as My Music, My Pictures, and My eBooks. All of these are located within the My Documents folder. You can delete these folders, move them around, or rename them as you like.**

How Files and Folders Are Organized

The location for top-level folders on your Presario or Pavilion is the My Computer area. You can add folders at this level or go into one of the existing folders, such as My Pictures, and add subfolders. For example, in the My Pictures folder, you might find it convenient to have My

Family and My Trip folders. You can also create new folders within My Computer.

Take a moment to look at the folder structure shown in Figure 5.1 (you get here by selecting Start, My Computer, Presario (C:) or HP Pavilion (C:), Program Files). The little manila colored folders are shown in a list.

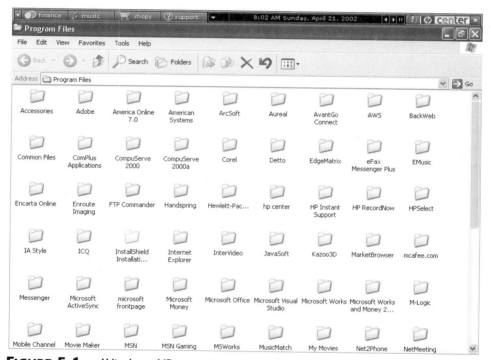

FIGURE 5.1 Windows XP contains many folders to organize the programs on your computer.

Creating Files and Folders

You create a file by saving a document in the software program where you generated the file contents. For example, you might create a letter in the word processor portion of Works and then save it to any folder you like. You can create folders either at the time that you save a file or by creating a new folder using the file menu in Windows Explorer (see

Figure 5.2), which is the feature that displays contents of your computer drives (select Start, My Computer or My Documents, for example, to explore document folders).

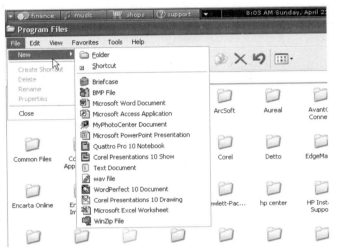

FIGURE 5.2   The File menu allows you to create a new folder wherever you are in Windows Explorer.

Project: **Create Your Projects Folder**

As you work on various projects throughout this book, you and your family may want a place to store them.

✔ **Follow these steps to create a new Family Projects folder in the My Documents folder:**

1. From the Windows desktop, select Start, My Documents. The My Documents folder appears.

2. Select File, New, Folder. A new folder appears at the bottom of the list. Note that the name of the folder is currently New Folder; this name is highlighted and ready for you to edit.

3. Type the folder name Family Projects. When you click anywhere outside of the folder, the new name is saved.

tip **To edit a folder name, just right-click the folder and select Rename from the shortcut menu that appears. Then type the new name. Click outside the folder and the new name is saved.**

Saving a File

Saving a file works the same way in most Windows programs. You use the File, Save command from within any software program and then use the Save dialog box (shown in Figure 5.3) to select a location to save your file. You can save a file into a folder on your hard drive, onto a floppy disk, or onto a writeable CD or DVD.

Create new folder

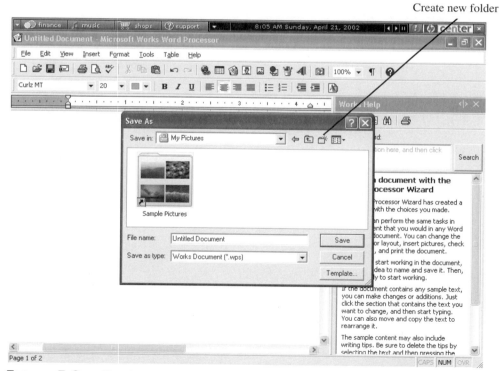

FIGURE 5.3   The Save dialog box contains a button for creating a new folder as you save a document.

✔ **Try saving a file now, creating a new folder as you do by using the Works word processor.**

1. Select Start, All Programs, Microsoft Works.

2. Click Cover Letters and then Start this Task.

3. Click Finish to end the letter wizard and create the letter from a template (you'll learn more about this in Chapter 9).

4. Click to the left of the placeholder text, "Your Name Here," and drag to the right to select it.

5. Type your own name.

6. Select File, Save. The Save As dialog box appears.

7. Click the arrow to the right of the Look in box and select My Documents.

8. Type the file name, "My Letter," in the File Name box.

9. Click Save.

You've just saved a new file to the My Documents folder. If you close Works (click the X button in the top right corner), select Start, My Documents. You should now see a file named My Letter.

Moving, Copying, and Deleting Files and Folders

Not happy with where you saved your file? Want to move or make a copy of the file, or perhaps you don't need the file anymore? Time to learn how to move, copy, and delete files and folders on your computer.

Moving Files and Folders

Although you may have originally saved a file in one folder, you may decide at some point that the file should be moved. For example, you might save a letter in a folder called Writing in Progress while you're drafting it, but then move it to a folder named Personal Correspondence after the letter has been printed and sent.

✔ **You can move a file or folder by cutting and pasting it; you do this by following these steps:**

1. Locate the file by clicking Start, My Computer or My Documents (or another folder listed on the Start menu such as My Music, depending on the location of the file).

2. After you locate the file or folder, click it to select it.

3. Select Edit, Cut. (If you cut a folder, you also cut all the files and folders within it).

4. Go to the location where you want to move the file or folder. (You can click the Up arrow on the toolbar or click the arrow next to the Address box and choose a location of a folder).

5. When you have the folder open where you want to place the file or folder, select Edit, Paste.

Copying Files

You might want to make a copy of a file to store it in two places. For example, you might have a copy of important family contact information in your family finances folder and your babysitter folder. One option is to open the file and save it with a different name in another location on your hard drive. However, you can also use Windows Explorer to copy files and folders.

Copying a file or folder is simple. You can use a method very similar to cutting and pasting a file to move it. However, with copying you would choose Edit, Copy to copy the original file and Edit, Paste to paste it into the folder where you want the copy placed.

You can also use a shortcut menu if you want to copy a file or folder to a floppy disk, the Windows desktop, the My Documents folder, or a writeable CD or DVD.

✔ **Follow these steps to copy the My Letter file to a floppy disk:**

1. Insert a floppy disk into your floppy drive.

2. Select Start, My Documents.

3. Right-click the file name and select Send to, 3 1/2 Floppy (A:)(see Figure 5.4). The file is copied to the disk.

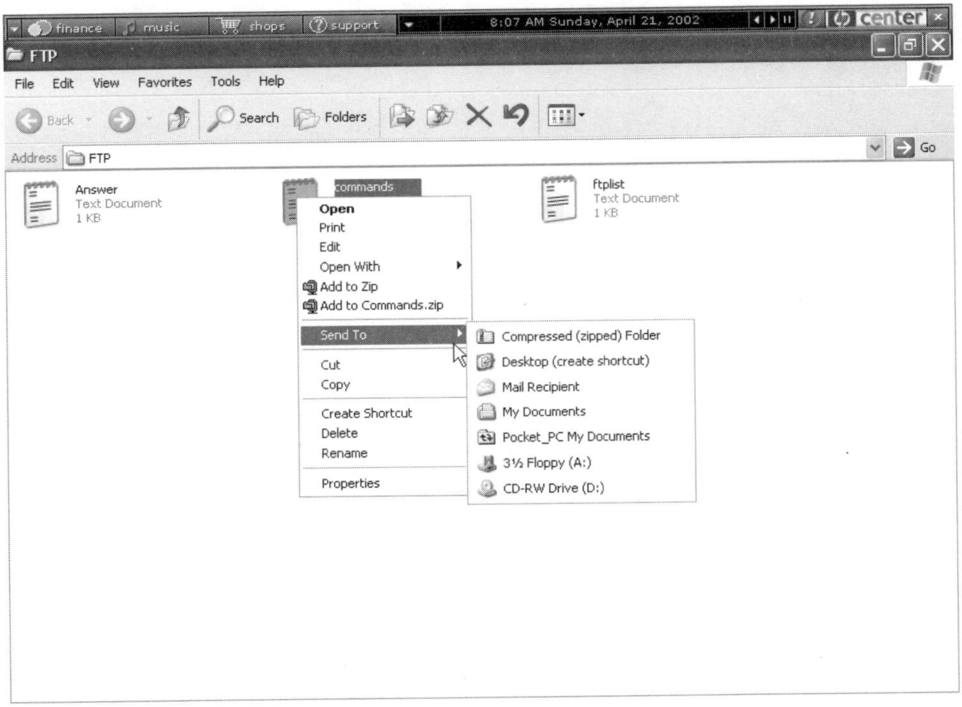

FIGURE 5.4 This shortcut menu offer commands you'll use often when managing files and folders.

4. Click the arrow to the right of the Address box in the My Documents window and then click on 3 1/2 Floppy (A:). The file should now be listed with the contents of your floppy disk.

 caution   Be sure to insert a floppy disk that has enough room to store the file or folder you want to copy to it. If you don't, Windows will display a message that there is not enough space on the disk to perform this action.

tip You can also right-click the file and select the Copy command from the shortcut menu that appears.

Deleting Files

Deleting files is an important part of file management. Because your computer memory gets filled up by all the files you save on your hard drive, it's a good idea to go through and delete files and folders you no longer need on a regular basis. If you like, you can archive old files on floppy disks or writeable CDs or DVDs before you delete them from your hard drive.

✔ **Follow these steps to delete a file or folder:**

1. Locate the file or folder with Windows Explorer (Start, All Programs, Accessories, Windows Explorer).

2. Right-click the item and select Delete from the shortcut menu.

   That's it!

caution   If you delete a folder, you delete all its contents as well. Make sure there isn't a file tucked away in a subfolder somewhere that you need before deleting.

note When you delete something, it is put in the Recycle Bin. This is a folder that keeps deleted files for a time in case you change your mind. To permanently delete a file, right-click the Recycle Bin on your desktop and select Empty Recycle Bin.

Backing Up Your Files

One of the most important rules of file management is to back up your document files. Backing up means saving a copy of your files on some media, such as a floppy disk, writeable CD or DVD, or even on the Internet or a company network.

Why? Because all computer hard drives die eventually. If your computer is new, it should take many, many years, but it will happen. Even before that time comes, you will probably experience *crashes*, instances where the power to your computer suddenly cuts off, or two computer programs encounter a conflict that freezes your computer and causes it to shut down. When a crash happens, you can lose data from your hard drive or the file you were working on when the crash occurred. Having a backup file, even one that might be a version or so older, can save you a great deal of stress if you lose a file.

note **Most Windows software has an autorecover feature that saves copies of the document you are currently working on when you crash and that helps you recover it after you start your computer again. Open the program you were working in after recovering from a crash to see if such an option is offered.**

Backup up should be done daily (or even more frequently if you spend the day creating lengthy documents). You can back up each document you create or change when you're done working with it, or you can back up your entire set of documents at the end of your work day. If your Pavilion has a writeable CD/DVD drive, you can store a great many documents on a single CD/DVD by copying your My Documents folder to it.

note **You can follow the steps provided in the earlier section, Copying Files, to copy files from your hard drive to a CD/DVD or floppy to back up any new or recently changed documents.**

Finding What You Need

No matter how meticulous you are about setting up and using a logical filing system, there will be times when you will simply forget where you stored a file. Windows provides a powerful search tool to locate a file by a variety of criteria, such as a word that might be contained in the file name or in the file itself, the date it was last modified, or the size of the file (if you're looking for a very large file containing graphics, this last choice might narrow down the search).

✔ **Follow these steps to search for a file:**

1. Select Start, Search. The Search dialog box shown in Figure 5.5 appears.

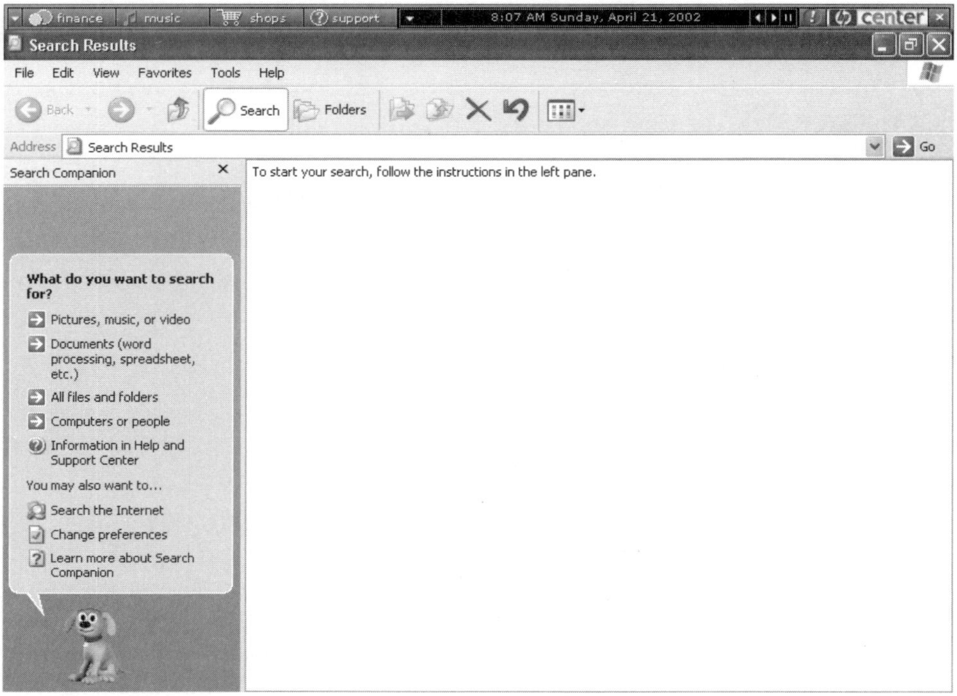

PCs Made Easy

FIGURE 5.5   The little animated dog in this dialog box is your Search Companion.

2. Click the type of item you want to search for in the left pane of this box.

3. Select or enter criteria for your search, such as the date the file was last modified or a word used in the body of the document. If you want additional criteria, click the Use Advanced Search Items link at the bottom of this list.

4. Click Search. The items that match your criteria will be displayed on the right side of the dialog box.

tip   After a search runs, some options will be offered in the left pane of this dialog box. Scroll down to review them. If the search wasn't successful, for example, an option is offered here to refine your search.

Chapter Summary

In this chapter, you learned about the importance of good file management, from storing files in logically named folders to backing up files and folders on a regular basis. You discovered how to search for a file you've saved on your computer and practiced moving, copying, and deleting files.

File management can make the difference between a well-organized computing experience and a frustrating one. Taking the time now to organize your computer will save you time and aggravation down the road.

6

Customizing Your Computing Experience

In this Chapter

✔ Installing software on your computer

✔ Removing software

✔ Adding hardware

✔ Modifying the computer display

The Compaq Presario and HP Pavilion come ready for action out of the box. However, there may be times when you'll want to add software or hardware or remove software you no longer need. In addition to setting up the software and hardware that match your computing needs, you might also want to take advantage of a wealth of graphics and colors that you can use to customize your Windows display.

T his chapter walks you through what you have to do to get what's on your computer set up just the way you like.

Installing Software

Everybody needs different things out of a computer. Some use it for emailing and word processing, while others spend every computing minute playing the latest Lara Croft game or editing home videos. As you use your computer, you'll discover additional software programs that you'd like to use. Luckily, installing software is a simple process.

What to Know Before You Install

There are a few things to keep in mind before you install software. First is computer memory. Your hard drive probably has a tremendous capacity compared to computers of only a few years ago, but everything has its limits. Your hard drive can get filled up with graphics and multimedia files, as well as the software you install. You have to be sure there's enough memory for the program you want to install. During most software installation routines, there will be a message concerning how much memory you need to install the software and how much is available on your hard drive. If those numbers are very close, consider deleting an unwanted program or two so that you're not at your memory limit.

Second, occasionally, programs aren't compatible with your operating system. You may encounter situations where they aren't compatible with Windows XP, especially when you're loading hardware drivers (programs used to run hardware such as printers). Check when you purchase software that you get a version that's compatible with Windows XP, or check with the software manufacturer's Web site to see if it provides an update to the software that you can download to make it compatible with XP.

Running the Installation

Software typically includes its own installation routine. With many programs, as soon as you put a software CD in your computer drive, it opens an installation window and you can simply follow instructions to install the software. Installation usually involves the following steps:

- Designating where to install the software. (Typically, most software is installed in the Windows Programs folder.)
- Indicating whether the installation should be the typical installation, which installs the most often-used features, or a custom installation where you choose what to install.
- Entering information such as your name or phone or fax number. In some cases, such as with faxing software, this information is required to operate the software; in others, it is used to register the software with the manufacturer.
- Choosing whether you want to register the software online now or later. Registering software ensures that you'll get technical support from the manufacturer.
- Restarting your computer to complete the installation.

Project: Install a Game on Your Computer

You can buy a game at most computer stores or office superstores. Pick a game that will appeal to everybody in your family. Some are quite inexpensive. When you find one you like, you can use the Windows Add or Remove Programs feature to walk you through the installation process.

✔ **To access the Add or Remove feature, follow these steps:**

1. Select Start, Control Panel.

2. Click Add or Remove Programs. The Add or Remove Programs dialog box shown in Figure 6.1 appears.

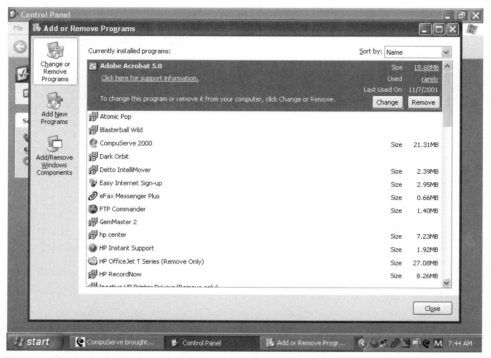

FIGURE 6.1   You can see all the programs you have installed and the amount of memory they are using in the Currently Installed Programs list.

3. Click Add New Programs.

4. Place the software disk or CD into the appropriate drive on your Presario or Pavilion.

5. Click the CD or Floppy button. The Install Program dialog box opens.

6. Click Next.

7. The Run Installation Program dialog box shown in Figure 6.2 appears, confirming the location and name of the setup file. If it's not correct, click Browse to locate the program you want to install.

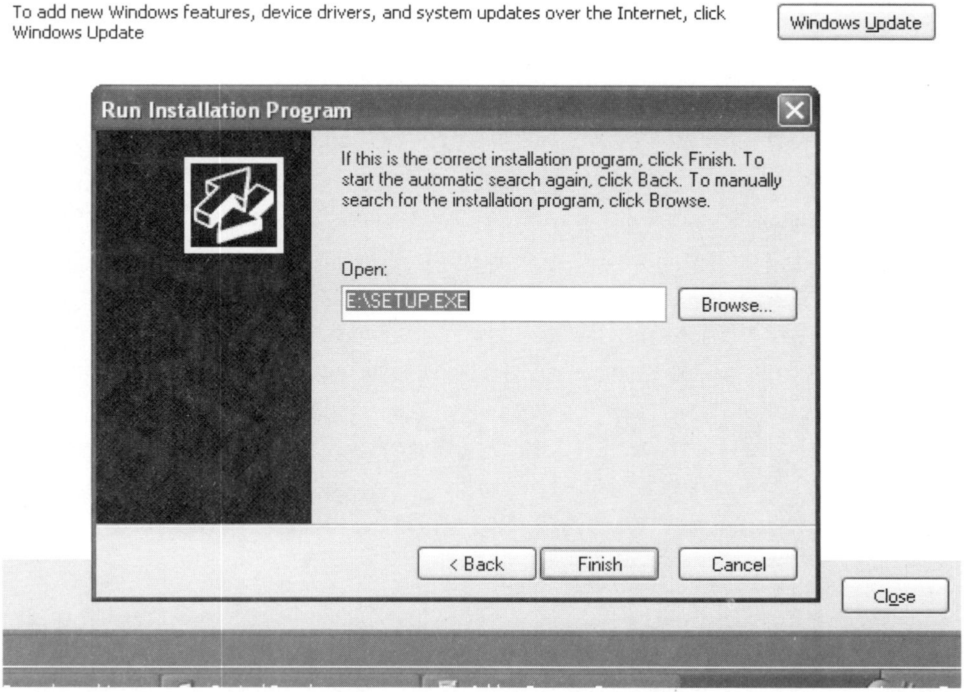

To add new Windows features, device drivers, and system updates over the Internet, click Windows Update

Windows Update

Run Installation Program

If this is the correct installation program, click Finish. To start the automatic search again, click Back. To manually search for the installation program, click Browse.

Open:

E:\SETUP.EXE

Browse...

< Back   Finish   Cancel

Close

FIGURE 6.2 If you have a CD inserted, Windows automatically identifies any executable installation file on it.

8. When the correct file is listed, click Finish. The installation program runs.

You will still have to make choices and enter information as requested by the individual program, but onscreen directions should walk you through that process.

tip **If you're not very familiar with the software you're installing, it's best to select the Typical Installation option. Custom installation requires that you make some more advanced choices.**

Time for a Change: Uninstalling Software

There's no need to leave software you'll never use cluttering up your computer. An overfull hard drive can actually slow down your computer's performance. Periodically, you should archive computer files you don't need and remove any software that isn't useful to you.

Uninstalling software can be tricky business. That's because software programs interact and share certain files. If you delete a folder containing one program's files, you could cause some problems with other programs. In fact, uninstalling programs used to be one of the main problems people encountered using their computers.

Many software products now include their own uninstall procedure, but the easiest way to remove programs is simply to use the Microsoft Windows Remove Programs feature. This step-by-step process notifies you when certain files should be kept.

✔ Follow these steps to remove a program:

1. Select Start, Control Panel. The Add or Remove Programs section of the dialog box should be displayed; if it's not, click that icon to display it.

2. Click the program you want to remove. A Change/Remove button becomes available.

3. Click Change/Remove. A Confirm Uninstall dialog box appears.

4. Click Yes to remove the program or No to stop the process.

With some programs that are made up of several pieces of software, such as Microsoft Works suite or an operating system like Windows XP, when you click the Change/Remove button, you get the option to change the program, allowing you to remove only some elements.

Adding Hardware

Most computers aren't used on their own. They are connected to hardware devices, such as printers, scanners, cable modems, or fax machines, to produce printed output, load files into the computer, or communicate with others.

Most of these devices require a driver, that is, a software program that allows Windows to interact with and send commands to the device. Devices come with a disk that includes their driver. Place that disk in the appropriate drive and follow the steps displayed to install the driver and set up the hardware.

Occasionally, you might not have access to that disk. If that's the case, you can usually download the latest drivers from the manufacturer's site (see Figure 6.3).

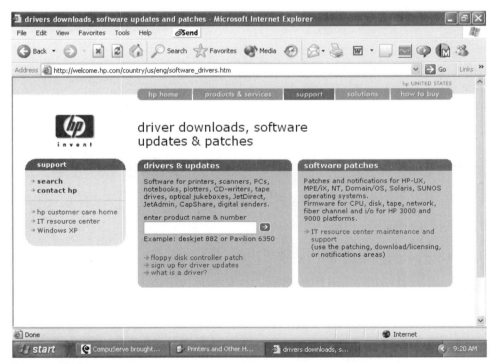

FIGURE 6.3 HP's download center offers the latest drivers for printers, monitors, and more.

What Is Plug and Play?

Plug and Play is a set of specifications developed by Microsoft and Intel for how your computer automates the set-up process when a new piece of hardware is detected. This involves a plug and play expansion card, which all recent Compaq Presarios and HP Pavilions have.

The best procedure when you attach a piece of hardware to your computer is to insert the manufacturer's CD into your drive and then follow the installation instructions that appear. If no installation program opens when you insert the CD, you can select Start, My Computer; locate the CD drive; and click the drive, which should begin the installation.

tip **If an installation window still doesn't appear, look at the CD contents; there should be a file with an .exe extension and possibly named Setup. Double-clicking that file runs the installation routine.**

Using the Add Hardware Wizard

The Add Hardware Wizard is provided by Windows to set up your hardware to work with Windows. It asks little of you, just that you provide a disk with a driver on it or designate the location of a driver on your computer (for example, if you downloaded the driver from the Internet).

✔ **Follow these steps to set up new hardware with the Add Hardware Wizard:**

1. If you have a disk for your hardware device, place it in your floppy or CD drive.

2. Plug the device into your computer. The New Hardware Wizard should appear (see Figure 6.4). If it doesn't, select Start, Control

Panel, Printers and Other Hardware, and click the Add Hardware link.

FIGURE 6.4   You can also use the Add Hardware Wizard if you're having problems with already installed hardware.

3. The wizard searches for new hardware you have attached to the computer. It then displays a dialog box asking you to confirm the location of the hardware driver. (Most times the wizard figures out that the driver is on the disk you've inserted, but, if it's somewhere on your hard drive, you may have to enter the path to get to it.)

4. Click Next and the wizard completes the setup.

Modifying Your Display

Because you'll probably spend a lot of time staring at your computer screen, you might as well enjoy the view. Windows allows you to modify the colors used on Windows elements, such as the desktop, dialog boxes, menu bars, and so on. Also, Windows offers themes, which are sets of sounds, backgrounds, colors, and special icons you can apply as a set. Finally, you can change the desktop background image, designate a screen saver to appear when your computer has remained inactive for a few minutes, and set the screen resolution and color quality levels.

Choosing Color, Background, and Themes

With Windows XP, Microsoft has changed the way you make the most of your computer display settings. In previous versions of Windows, several sets of color schemes and themes were included. Now you have a limited choice, and you have to buy a product called Windows XP Plus to get additional display choices. In some ways, that makes sense, both because all those graphics preinstalled on your system took up a chunk of memory and because today people have access to a great many scanned or downloaded graphics of their own that they can use as desktop backgrounds.

note **Note that if you apply a background, it replaces the background used in the current theme. If you apply a theme, it overrides your background and color scheme setting. If you change color schemes, that changes the theme color setting.**

Project: **Personalize Your Computer with Themes, Backgrounds, and Colors**

Your computer should be a reflection of you, so sit down and brainstorm with your family to pick out colors and images that reflect your personalities. You can even use personal photos that you've scanned into your computer for a background.

✔ **Here's how you go about applying your choice of color scheme, background, or theme:**

1. Select Start, Control Panel.

2. Click the Change the Computer's Theme link. The Display Properties dialog box shown in Figure 6.5 appears.

FIGURE 6.5 If you haven't changed anything since buying your computer, you should have the Windows XP theme set here.

3. Click the arrow at the end of the Theme box and select another theme in the list by clicking it. Windows Classic is the only installed

optional theme if you don't have Windows XP Plus installed, so click it.

4. Click Apply. The new theme background and colors appear on your computer.

5. Click the Desktop tab, shown in Figure 6.6; the background selected matches the one in the Windows Classic theme.

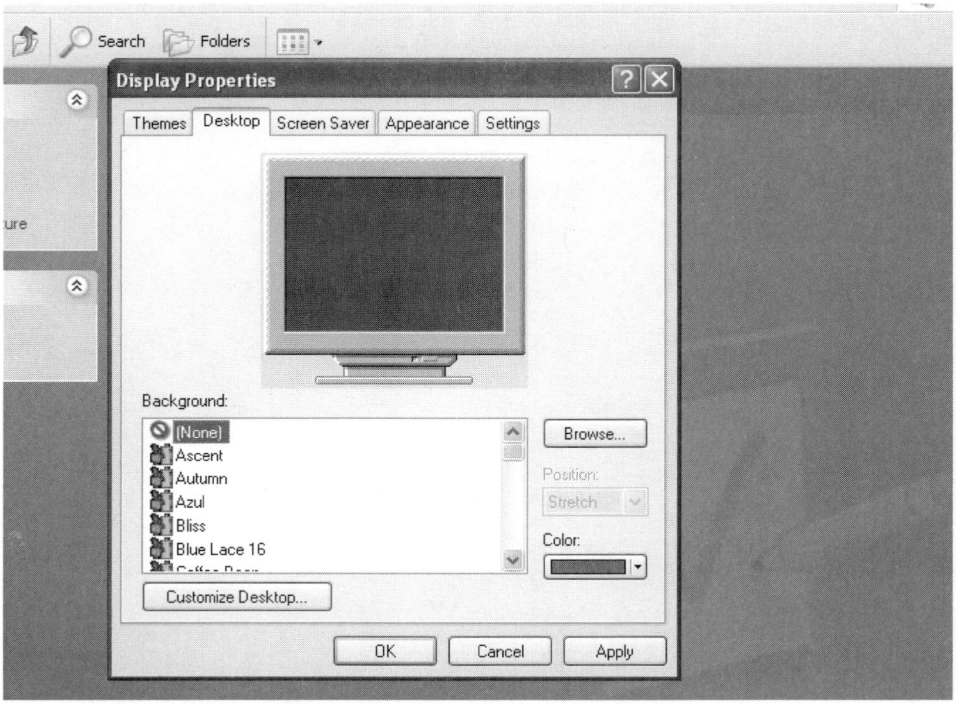

FIGURE 6.6   Microsoft has left you with quite a few background choices.

6. Click a background in the list. A preview of the graphic image displays.

7. Use the up and down arrow on your keyboard to move through the different backgrounds. When you find one you like, click Apply.

8. Click the Appearance tab.

9. Click the arrow on the Color Scheme box and then click a color scheme option. It is previewed for you. When you find one you're happy with, click Apply.

tip **If you want to use an image of your own for your desktop background, on the Desktop tab of the Display dialog box click Browse, locate the file in the Browse dialog box, and then click Open. It is added to your list of desktop backgrounds. Click it and then click Apply to use it.**

Modifying Display Settings

Certain settings in Windows XP will have an impact on the way things look on your monitor. Screen resolution deals with how fine an image you get, that is, how many dpi (dots per inch) are used to form those images on your screen. The lower the resolution, the grainier the picture.

caution **A higher resolution also causes all items to be smaller, which can make onscreen text difficult for some to read.**

Color quality controls how many bits of color information are used in each display dot. Windows XP allows 16-bit color and 24-bit color, with 24 bit being the higher color quality.

caution **Be aware that higher resolution and color quality can cause occasional problems with some software. If you experience problems because programs that display graphics keep crashing, consider lowering these settings a bit.**

tip **If you're using software that requires 256 colors (an older color setting), you can right-click the program name on the Start menu, click Properties, and, on the Compatibility tab, check the Run in 256 Colors option. When you close that program, the computer goes back to your regular color setting.**

✔ **To modify the color quality settings, follow these steps:**

1. Select Start, Control Panel.

2. Click on the Appearance and Themes link.

3. Click on the Change Screen Resolution option. The Display dialog box with the Settings tab displayed appears (see Figure 6.7).

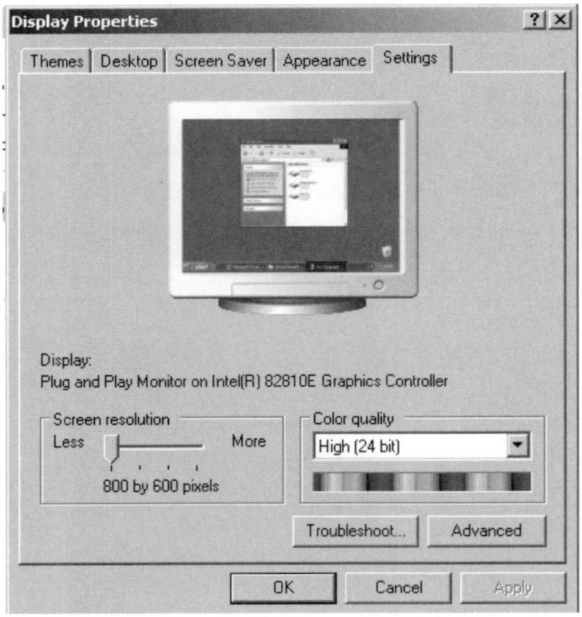

FIGURE 6.7   The little monitor previews how changed settings will affect your display.

4. Click the slider bar under Screen Resolution and drag it to the right or left to change the resolution. Note the changes in image size in the preview as you do.

5. Click the arrow next to the Color Quality box and select another color setting. When you do, the preview bar shows the effect. With the lower setting, the colors are a bit less crisp.

6. When you have the settings you want, click OK. If you decide to save the default settings, click Cancel to close the dialog box without saving changes.

Choosing a Screen Saver

A screen saver is a utility program that automatically displays a random series of graphic images after your computer has remained idle for a period of time. Back in the early days of computing, screen savers were a necessity because having the same image on screen for long periods of time could actually etch an image onto your monitor display. That's no longer the case with more recent monitors. People just set screen savers to display because they produce intriguing graphic images. Also, having a screen saver come on when you're away from your computer keeps passersby from seeing what you're working on.

tip **There are many screen savers available for free download from the Internet, or you can purchase screen saver software that represents your interests, such as mountain climbing, sailing, or gardening.**

✔ **To set a Windows screen saver on your computer, follow these steps:**

1. From the Display Properties dialog box click on the Screen Saver tab to display the settings shown in Figure 6.8.

FIGURE 6.8 *Microsoft provides several predesigned screen savers for you.*

2. Click the arrow on the Screen Saver box and click a name on the list. The preview shows you what the screen saver will look like.

3. If you'd like a full screen preview of the screen saver, click the Preview button. Click your left mouse button when you want to return to the dialog box.

4. Click the spinner arrows in the Wait setting to specify when the screen saver comes on, for example, after 10 minutes of inactivity.

5. Click OK to apply the new settings and close the dialog box.

tip **If you want to prevent other people from seeing what's on your computer, you can check the On Resume, Password Protect checkbox in the Screen Saver settings. Then, only a password you select will turn off the screen saver and return to a normal view.**

Chapter Summary

In this chapter, you learned how to install new software and uninstall software you don't need anymore. You reviewed the process involved in installing new hardware, such as a fax machine or printer, and used the Add New Hardware wizard to set the hardware up with Windows. Finally, you made changes to your Windows XP display, including the theme, desktop background, color scheme, image settings, and screen saver.

chapter

7

Exploring Windows XP Accessories

In this Chapter

✓ Changing settings to accommodate disabilities

✓ Transferring files from your old computer to your Presario or Pavilion

✓ Faxing from your computer

✓ Saving contacts in Windows Address Book

✓ Using multimedia players and playing Windows games

Although every Compaq Presario and HP Pavilion home PC model comes packed with software (you'll learn all about those goodies in the next chapter), you should know that Windows XP itself offers several great programs you might want to take advantage of. Some of these are small utility programs that help you keep your system in shape, others are miniapplications for playing or editing multimedia files, and still others are applications to help you organize your life.

Though there's not enough space here to take you through every accessory option in Windows XP, I've picked a few gems that you might want to check into as you learn your way around your new computing environment.

Set Yourself Up for Productivity

People come in all shapes and sizes: some with less-than-perfect hearing or vision and others who find typing or using a mouse to be a challenge. Therefore, shouldn't you be able to interact with your computer in the way that's most comfortable for you? You should. That's where Windows' Accessibility features come in. They help you to set up your computer in a way that provides optimum visual, sound, and input options.

Meet Accessibility Wizard

Wizards are what Windows uses to make your computing life easy. Accessibility Wizard helps you make all the right choices about how you'll interact with your computer. By walking you through a few step-by-step windows, this wizard helps you set up the text size that's best for you, the input mode that makes sense if you have difficulty using a keyboard or mouse, and other features that assist the vision and hearing challenged.

✔ **To run the wizard, follow these steps:**

1. Open the Start menu from the Windows XP desktop and then click All Programs, Accessories, Accessibility, Accessibility Wizard. The Welcome screen appears.

2. Click Next to move to the Text Size portion of the wizard, shown in Figure 7.1.

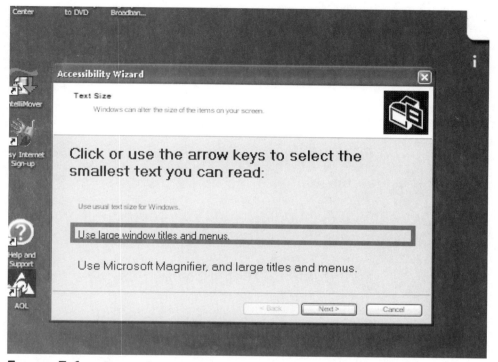

FIGURE 7.1   Pretend you're getting an eye test and pick out the line of text that's easiest to read from this window.

3. Click the size of text that you can read easily and then click Next. The Display Settings dialog box shown in Figure 7.2 appears.

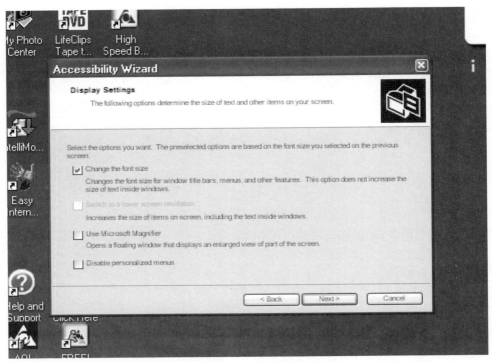

FIGURE 7.2   These display settings include features to help those with vision challenges.

4.   If you selected an increased font size in the previous window, the Change the Font Size option is already checked here. If you didn't make a previous choice and want a larger font size, click that option now.

5.   To enlarge the display on your computer, click one or both of the next two options, Switch to a Lower Screen Resolution, or Use Microsoft Magnifier. A lower screen resolution makes items on your screen larger. (Microsoft Magnifier is a magnification program that you'll explore in more detail shortly.)

tip Note that lowered screen resolution enlarges items, but it also makes for a less crisp screen image because of fewer dpi on your screen, so the tradeoff in readability may not be acceptable to some.

6. You can click to disable personalized menus. This setting helps by keeping choices on menus in a consistent order, so you can depend on the location of each menu choice if you must make those choices without being able to read them easily.

7. Click Next to proceed. The Set Wizard Options dialog box appears.

8. Make choices here depending on whether you have vision, hearing, or input challenges. Based on what you select here, the rest of the wizard windows offer different options.

9. When you've made your selections in this window, click Next to proceed. You are then presented with various options, such as SoundSentry shown in Figure 7.3.

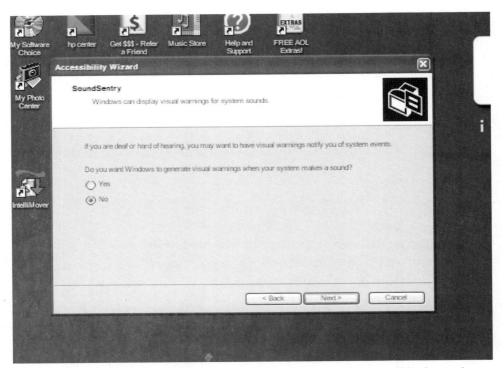

FIGURE 7.3   SoundSentry can generate visual signals whenever Windows plays an event sound; other sound options include ShowSounds, which provides captions for speech or sounds.

10. Work through each wizard window by making appropriate choices and clicking Next. When the wizard has run through all options, click Finish to save all your settings.

Expand Your Vision with Magnifier

Magnifier is a program that allows you to expand the images on your screen. If you've ever used a magnifying glass, you'll know the pros and cons of this feature. It can make elements on screen huge, but you can only see a small area at any one time.

Microsoft recommends that, if you have a serious visual disability, you consider obtaining a full magnification utility program. However if you have only a slight visual impairment and want to zoom in on things occasionally, this utility can be of help.

✔ **To use Magnifier, follow these steps:**

1. Open the Start menu from the Windows desktop and then click All Programs, Accessories, Accessibility, Magnifier. Your window is split in two with a smaller portion at the top showing a magnified view of your screen and the lower area showing the regular view. You'll also see a message about the limited usefulness of this program, with a link to an area of Microsoft's Web site that suggests more robust magnification utility programs.

2. Click OK to proceed. The Magnifier Settings dialog box shown in Figure 7.4 appears.

FIGURE 7.4   The enlarged mouse cursor in the upper window echoes the movements of your regular cursor in the lower window.

3. To see more of the magnified portion of your screen, place your mouse cursor over the bottom edge of the top window until it becomes a two-way arrow and drag down to enlarge it.

4. Move your cursor around the screen to see various portions of it enlarged.

5. If you want Magnifier to stop following your mouse cursor, deselect that option in the dialog box.

6. If you like, you can select a higher or lower magnification setting from the Magnification level drop-down list.

 tip **You can also use the arrow or Page Up/Page Down keys on your keyboard to increase or decrease the magnification setting.**

7. When you're done using Magnifier, click Exit.

Note that Magnifier can be turned on from within any application to read documents or to view images that you might be having trouble seeing clearly.

Bring Your Old Computer with You

The Files and Settings Transfer Wizard is new to Windows XP and can save you time and frustration if you are moving from another computer to your Compaq Presario or HP Pavilion. The Files and Settings Transfer Wizard allows you to copy various files and settings from one computer to another. For example, you can download all the contacts from any address books and transfer settings for hardware or other features from another computer to your Presario or Pavilion.

The easiest way to run this wizard is to have a connection between your old and new computer. You can connect with a serial cable that plugs into the back of your computers or use a network connection. This gets a little technical, but the savings in time because you don't have to reenter information or redo settings can be worth it.

Do It the Old-Fashioned Way

You can also use the wizard without connecting your computers by copying the wizard to a disk (or having your Windows XP disk handy) and then using the wizard on your old computer to perform the process of transferring files and settings to a blank disk. Insert that disk into the new computer and transfer the contents to your new computer. The wizard transfers settings you've made as well as files.

You can use three types of cables for a direct connection, but you're likely to have to buy one, because this type of cable doesn't come with your new computer. You can buy either a LapLink, or null modem serial cable, or a serial file transfer cable from your local computer store, or you can order one online through vendors such as CompUSA or an office supply superstore such as Staples. Each computer must also have a serial port with 25 or 9 pins. Any Compaq Presario or HP Pavilion has such a port, as will most newer computers, but some older computers may not. If you've got the right ports, when you plug a serial cable into each computer, Windows automatically detects the connection and runs the wizard.

If you have a home network set up, you can transfer files and settings between two PCs. Setting up a network involves installing additional hardware in each computer and connecting them with cables or a wireless hookup. Home networks allow you to access the same printers, fax machines, and Internet connections from more than one computer and to easily share files among the computers.

Start the wizard by selecting Start, All Programs, Accessories, System Tools, File and Settings Transfer Wizard. Depending on how you have been able to connect your two computers, follow the instructions to affect the transfer. If you don't have a direct connection, you may be asked to have your Windows XP CD available, or to copy the wizard onto a blank disk.

Connect with Others

Windows XP offers a nice little faxing program that allows you to fax documents saved as computer files. (If you have a scanner, this feature becomes even more convenient because you can scan any document, even a handwritten one, into a computer file and then fax it). In addition, there's an Address Book program that helps you keep all your email and phone addresses straight.

Fax It!

Here's good news. You may be able to throw away that clunky old fax machine forever. That's because Windows XP's little faxing program enables you to send and receive faxes from your computer. The program allows you to create cover sheets and then fax any file to which you have access.

caution **Don't throw away your fax machine if you don't have a scanner. Computer fax programs can only fax documents that exist as computer files. If you can't scan documents into a computer file format, you'll need that little machine to feed hard copy documents into the phone lines.**

Before you can use the faxing program, you have to set it up.

✔ **Follow these simple steps to configure your faxing program:**

1. Select Start, All Programs, Accessories, Communications, Fax, Fax Console. Assuming you've never used the program, the Fax Configuration Wizard shown in Figure 7.5 appears.

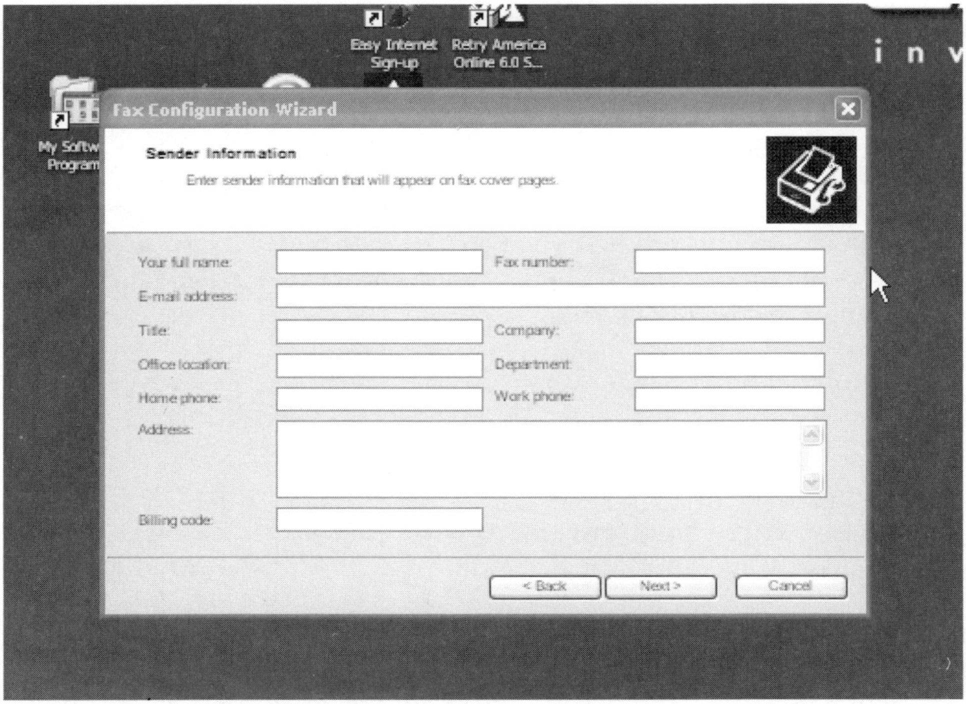

FIGURE 7.5   Some of the information you enter here automatically appears on fax cover sheets.

2. Complete any fields you want included on fax cover sheets; this allows the Fax program to automate the creation of cover sheets. Click Next.

3. At the second (and last) wizard window, click Finish. The Fax Console then appears.

4. Click Tools, Sender Information. All the information you entered in the configuration wizard should be included there. Edit the information if you like, and click OK when you're done.

5. To create a cover page, click Tools, Personal Cover Pages.

6. Click New to create a new cover page. The dialog box shown in Figure 7.6 is displayed.

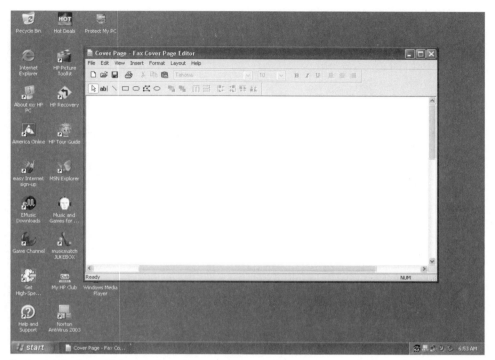

FIGURE 7.6 This simple editing program allows you to add text and drawing shapes to your cover sheets.

7. Click Text and drag on the page to create a text box.

8. Type any heading you want to use for your fax cover sheet, such as the addressee's contact information, your name, your company, phone number, fax number, and possibly the date and subject of the fax.

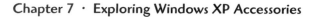 *tip* **Instead of creating a text box, use the Insert menu as a shortcut to insert sender and recipient fields with placeholders for your specific information. After creating these fields, you can move them around the page as you like and format text within them.**

9. If you want, you can use the drawing tools to draw rectangles, circles, and so on. There are also tools to align text and objects on the page.

10. Click File, Save to save the sheet. By default, Windows places the sheet in the Fax folder of the My Documents folder.

Project: **Send a Fax to a Friend**

Create an invitation to an upcoming event, such as a school play or party, and then fax it to a friend. If you don't know your friend's fax number, you'll have to call him or her to get it. Another possibility is to fax an invitation to the next holiday party from your office to your home fax.

To send a fax, you proceed as if you were going to print the document, but designate Fax as your printer.

✔ **Follow these steps to fax a document:**

1. Open the document in the application where it was created, such as Word or Works.

2. Select File, Print. The Print dialog box appears.

3. Select Fax from the Name drop-down list at the top of the dialog box.

4. Click Print. The Fax Wizard appears.

5. Click Next to begin the wizard. The Recipient Information dialog box shown in Figure 7.7 is displayed.

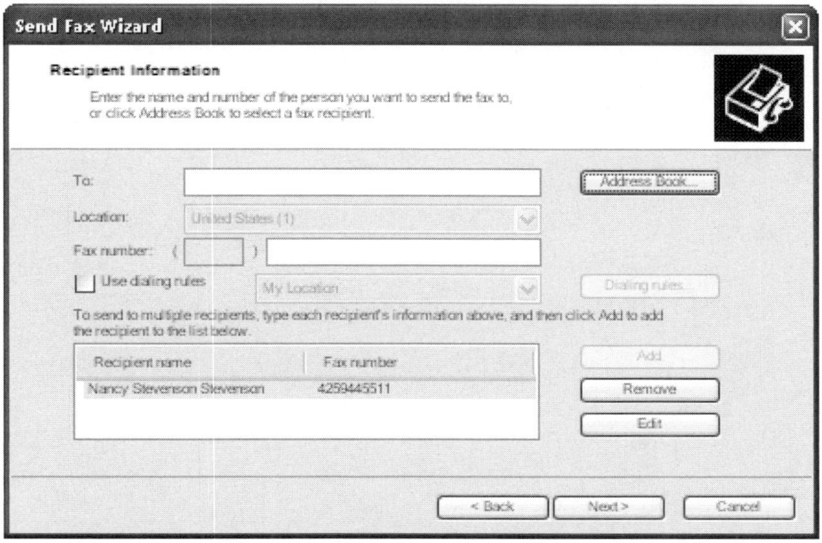

FIGURE 7.7   If you have contacts in an Outlook address book or the Windows Address Book, you can address your fax using the Address Book button in this dialog box.

6. Enter the recipient's name. If you want, you can click the Address Book icon and select a recipient from your stored contact information.

7. Click Use Dialog Rules. This makes the various fields for location and fax number available and tells Windows to use information about your location, phone, and modem settings to send the fax.

8. Enter a fax number. If the default location of the United States is acceptable, just leave that setting alone. If not, you can choose another location from that drop-down list.

9. Repeat steps 6 and 8 for any other recipients.

10. Click Next. The Preparing the Cover Page dialog box appears.

11. Select a cover page from the Cover page template drop-down list. If you created a personal cover page, it will be listed there.

12. Enter a subject in the Subject text box.

13. If you want, you can click Sender Information and fill in any information required by fields in your cover page. Note that, if you chose the recipient from the Address list, any information about them stored in your address book is already available to Windows Fax.

14. Click Next. The Schedule dialog box appears.

15. You can save a few pennies by selecting a time when discount long-distance rates apply in this dialog box. Click When discount rates apply, or click Specific time… to set a time to send the fax.

16. If you are sending multiple faxes, you might want to set the priority of this one by clicking High, Normal, or Low.

17. Click Next. The final wizard window appears displaying the information and settings you've entered.

18. Click Preview Fax. Both the cover page and document pages can be viewed here by using the Previous Image and Next Image buttons, and you can annotate the pages to add notes or drawing objects.

19. When you're ready to send your fax, click Close in the upper right corner to close the Preview, and click Finish to complete the Fax Wizard sequence. The Fax Monitor shown in Figure 7.8 appears, showing you the progress of your fax.

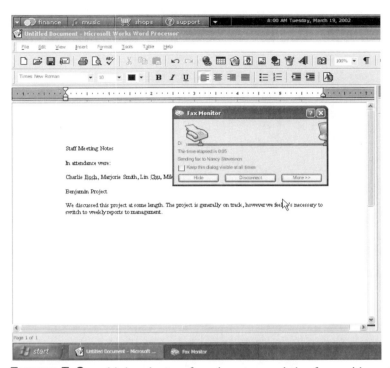

FIGURE 7.8   Make choices for when to send the fax and how to prioritize multiple faxes in this dialog box.

That's it. Your document and cover sheet are on their way to your recipient.

Address Book

We all have too many names, faces, email addresses, and fax numbers to remember these days. What to do? Take a look at Windows XP Address Book. Here's a central location where you can store all your contact information, and use it to easily address mail or even dial the phone for you.

You may have run into an address book feature in your email program. Programs such as Outlook and Outlook Express have an address book, which saves contact information in the Windows Address Book (.wab) format. If you don't have such a feature, or if you prefer to use an address book separate from a mail program, you can use the standalone Address Book feature in Windows.

tip **The good news is that you can import and export .wab files between Outlook and Address Book easily. Just open the program you want to copy an address book into and use the File, Import, Address Book (WAB) option. There is also an Other Address Book option on this menu to import Comma Separated Value (.csv) or Lightweight Directory Access Protocol (LDAP) Data Interchange Format (LDIF) files.**

✔ **To add contacts to your Windows Address Book, follow these steps:**

1. Select Start, All Programs, Accessories, Address Book. The Address Book appears.

2. Click New and select New Contact. The Properties dialog box shown in Figure 7.9 appears.

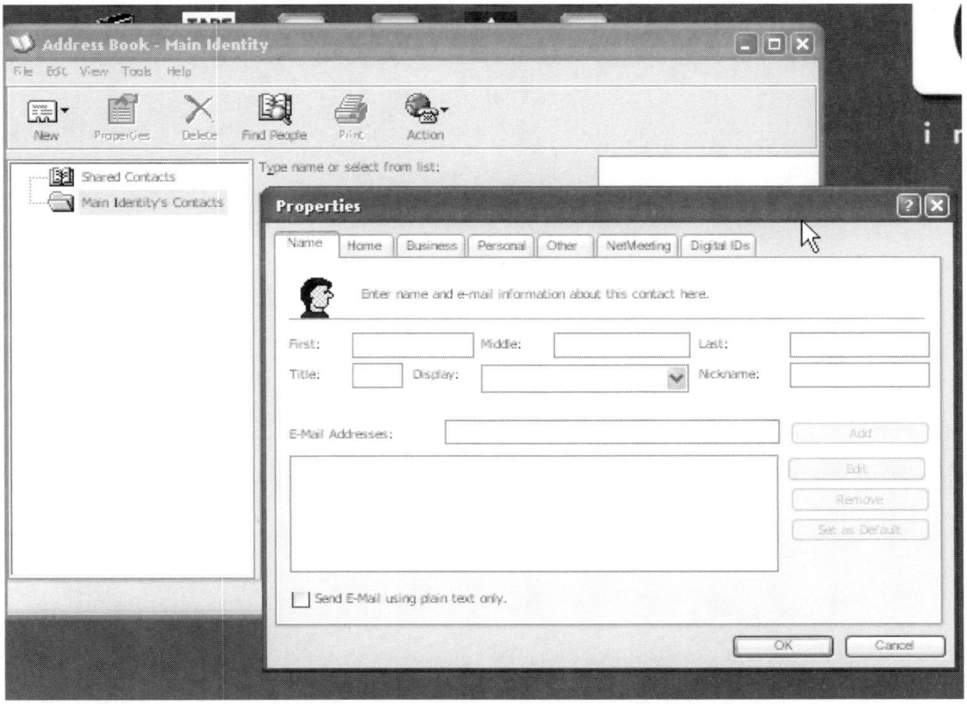

FIGURE 7.9 Seven—count 'em—seven tabs worth of information can be input in this little dialog box.

3. Enter information on the Name tab of this dialog box, including First, Middle, and Last names; Title; Display (the name that should be displayed in the list of contacts); and even a Nickname.

4. If you want to send e-mail to people, record their E-mail Addresses. If there are multiple e-mail addresses, enter one, click Add, then enter another, click Add, and so on until they are all entered.

tip **Be sure to set the email address you use most often as the Default address by clicking it in the list and then clicking Set as Default. That's the address that will be used whenever you select this name from the contact list in your email program.**

You can use other tabs in this dialog box to enter information, including the following:

- *Home tab*—Use this to enter home address information and even to have Windows display a map to the home address automatically.
- *Business tab*—Enter business information, such as address, job title, department, and company Web page.
- *Personal tab*—Here's where you can enter all that information that makes your next call or email more personal, such as the names of the contact's spouse and children, and special dates like birthday and anniversary. Sales people, take note.
- *NetMeeting tab*—If you're going to use Microsoft's online meeting feature, NetMeeting, you can enter connection information for conferences here.
- *Digital IDs tab*—If you practice secure emailing, you'll want to note any digital ID information for this contact's email address. Digital IDs allow you to identify and read protected information from this person.

When you've finished entering all the information for this contact, click OK. You can now click the contact in the Address Book list and use the Action button to send email or to dial the contact's phone number. In various programs, such as Microsoft Works, you can use commands, such as Insert, Address to open your Address Book and to select contact records to automate text entry.

Multimedia Madness

Now for the fun stuff! Without having to install fancy multimedia software, Windows allows you to work with sound, video, and photos with built-in, easy-to-use multimedia accessories. You can record and play voice and music files, edit video clips, and work with graphic images like a pro.

Windows Media Player

The Windows Media Player is an application that allows you to play back sound files, listen to the radio, and assemble play lists. You can copy music from a CD or the radio, or open any sound file on your computer or the Internet and play it back.

Sound files come in several formats, including Musical Instrument Digital Interface (MIDI), .wav, and so on, which Windows Media Player can handle with ease. Microsoft even provides several sample files you can use to learn your way around Windows Media Player.

✔ **Try opening and playing back a sample music file by following these steps:**

1. Select Start, All Programs, Accessories, Entertainment, Windows Media Player. The player window appears, looking like Figure 7.10.

2. Place an audio CD in your CD-ROM drive.

FIGURE 7.10   Play a variety of media formats from the Windows Media Player.

3. Click the Copy from CD link on the list in the blue bar along the left side of the screen.

4. In the CD contents list that appears, click the first item.

5. As the song plays, you can watch its progress as the Seek icon moves across the screen. To move through the song, drag the Seek button to the right to go forward or to the left to go back.

6. Use the Stop, Play, or Volume buttons to control the playback.

7. When the song has finished playing, you can continue to explore the Media Player window (check out the Radio Tuner or Media Guide). Click Close in the upper right corner of the player when you're done.

Note that you must have a sound card and speakers to play and hear sound from your computer. Depending on your computer/monitor setup, speakers might be integrated with your monitor, or you can plug external speakers into your monitor and computer. Every Compaq Presario and HP Pavilion comes with your sound card and speakers either already set up for you, or they will set up automatically when Windows detects new devices you add on, such as speakers. Therefore, you should have no problem getting sound going.

There is one final cool feature. Try using different 'skins' for your playback controls by clicking the Skin Chooser option in Windows Media Player. These are artsy versions of the control buttons pointed out on Figure 7.10. Figure 7.11 shows a preview of the Canvas skin. Take a look and figure out which graphic elements match the Play, Stop, Previous, Seek, and other controls in this image.

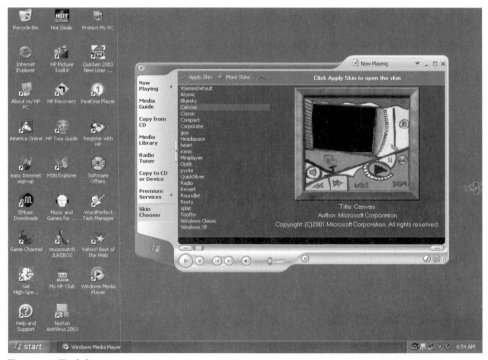

FIGURE 7.11 Several built-in skins offer cool playback controls. Click More Skins to access skins on the Net at WindowsMedia.com.

Windows Moviemaker

If you're a full motion kind of person, Windows Moviemaker is for you. This great little program lets you open video clips, edit them, organize them in collections, and even email them to friends.

caution   **Keep in mind that video files can be memory hogs. You might consider using the writeable CD or DVD drive that comes with many Presario and Pavilion models to store video collections and free up space on your computer.**

✔ **Take a look at Windows Moviemaker and play back a sample video by following these steps:**

1. Select Start, All Programs, Accessories, Windows MovieMaker.

2. Select File, Import.

3. If it's not already selected, locate the My Videos folder in the Look In drop-down list.

4. Click the Windows Movie Maker Sample File and click Open. The video sequence is opened in the Movie Maker window, as shown in Figure 7.12.

5. Click any one of the five segments displayed as a thumbnail and then click Play. That segment of the clip plays.

6. To play the entire segment, click the first segment and then, holding down Shift, click on the last one. Then click Play.

7. While the longer video is playing, if you want to have the video play back in a larger area, click Full Screen. When the video is done, press Esc to return to the Movie Maker.

8. You can string together several video clips in any sequence you like by using the Clip, Add to Storyboard/Timeline command. The

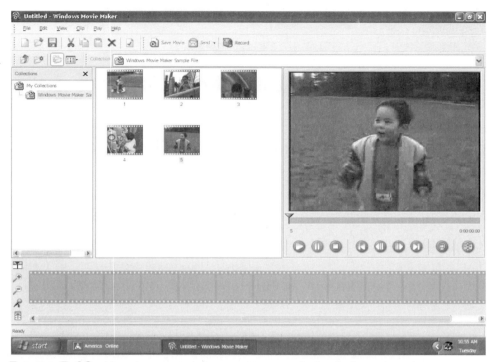

FIGURE 7.12   Use the controls here to stop or playback the video clip.

selected images are added to the film strip area at the bottom of the screen. You can also cut individual segments using Edit tools.

9. If you create a movie you want to save, click File, Save and save it to your computer or a writeable CD.

10. If you want to email a video clip, select Send, E-mail and complete information about the video attachment in the Send Movie Via E-mail dialog box.

11. When you're done, select File, Exit to close Windows Movie Maker.

There are plenty of features in this product you can discover by playing with the sample file and exploring the Microsoft Movie Maker on the Web site (select Help, Microsoft Movie Maker on the Web to get there). If you have your own digital camcorder, upload your videos to your computer. You're in for hours of fun editing, storing, and playing back home videos.

Paint

Paint has been around a while, and, if you've used a Windows-based computer before, you have probably encountered it. It's an easy-to-use graphics program that lets you open graphics files in several formats, edit and annotate the images, and save them.

Using the tools in Paint, shown in Figure 7.13, you can crop an image, draw on it, fill objects with color, and add text. You can work with a variety of file formats, from a Joint Photographic Experts Group (JPEG) photograph file to a Windows bitmap file containing drawn objects, or even an animation file in Graphic Interchange Format (GIF).

FIGURE 7.13 Use text and drawing tools to modify any image in Paint.

Project: **Designing a Family Crest**

If your family were to have a family crest, as families did in olden days, what would it look like? Use Paint to draw shapes and add colors to design a new family crest. Think of one image that represents each person in your family and include it in a sort of collage. For example, if someone plays music, draw a musical note or, if another person plays basketball, draw a circle with lines on it to indicate that.

✔ **To design your crest in Paint, follow these steps:**

1. Select Start, All Programs, Accessories, Paint.

2. In the Paint program, select File, Open and locate the graphics file you want to work with.

3. Use the various tools to draw on the document.

4. Click objects to select them and use the Eraser, Fill with Color, or other tools to modify them.

5. Click the Text tool and then type text directly onto the image.

6. Use tools such as the Brush or Airbrush to paint on your image.

7. When you're done, save the file by selecting File, Save and choosing the best file format for your purposes in the Save dialog box, Save as Type list.

Fun and Games

Windows XP provides almost a dozen games you might want to know about to help you while away those long boring hours at work or home. The games on offer include the following:

- FreeCell
- Hearts
- Internet Backgammon

- Internet Checkers
- Internet Hearts
- Internet Reversi
- Internet Spades
- Minesweeper
- Pinball (shown in Figure 7.14)
- Solitaire
- Spider Solitaire

FIGURE 7.14 Pinball offers a virtual pinball game, complete with flashing lights and bouncing ball.

As the names suggest, several of these games are played on the Internet. When you select one of these, you will be set up by Zone.com to play a match with somebody else who is logged on at the same time that you access the game. Who knows, you might find yourself playing checkers with a sheep rancher in Australia or back-gammon with a rock star in London.

You access games by selecting Start, All Programs, Games. Internet games will direct you to an online site to find your partner. Other games simply open at this point ready for you to play. Check each game's menus to get a demo of the game, rules, or to launch a new game with one or more players. Many also allow you to control sounds, music, and player functions

 tip **Read more about playing games in Chapter 10.**

Chapter Summary

In this chapter, you explored some of the settings you can make to Windows XP to make your computer more accessible and easy to use. You learned about the Files and Settings Transfer Wizard and how it can save you effort by moving files from your old computer to your new one. Then you discovered what programs are built into Windows XP Accessories, from faxing software and an address book to multimedia players and games.

part

3

Taking Advantage of Pre-Installed Software

8

Working with Computer Utilities

A computer is something like the human brain. It takes in a lot of different kinds of information and input from a variety of sources, and all that information has to work together. Conflicting information can cause problems. In addition, sometimes both the brain and your computer have to deal with an invading virus.

Just as a stressed-out person can go on overload, your computer can come crashing down if it's being pulled in too many directions. There are programs that you use to maintain your computer's health, and they're called utilities. In this chapter, you'll learn about utility programs on your computer that can help keep your computer going strong.

Keeping Your Hard Drive in Shape

Some utilities help to make your hard drive more efficient or test the setup of files for greatest efficiency. Disk Cleanup is included with your computer to organize your hard drive.

Your hard drive is essentially a large storage medium, but it doesn't always store files in one piece. It can put some bits of data from a file in one sector and then throw a few others in a different location. As time goes by, your hard drive is like a checkerboard with bits of data spread everywhere. Many little bits of data become obsolete and are just sitting there cluttering things up.

Disk Cleanup is a utility that goes through your hard drive and identifies ways to make it more efficient. For example, it can consolidate some data into adjoining slots or delete things like temporary files that were created while you were working, but that are not needed by any program anymore. By cleaning up how data is stored on your hard drive, you can improve your computer's performance.

To run Disk Cleanup, select Start, All Programs, Accessories, System Tools, Disk Cleanup. The dialog box in Figure 8.1 appears, indicating that the program is gathering data about your hard drive.

When the program finishes checking your hard drive, the dialog box in Figure 8.2 appears. This shows how much total space Disk Cleanup can save you by deleting certain files. If you want to see the files the utility intends to delete, you can click View Files.

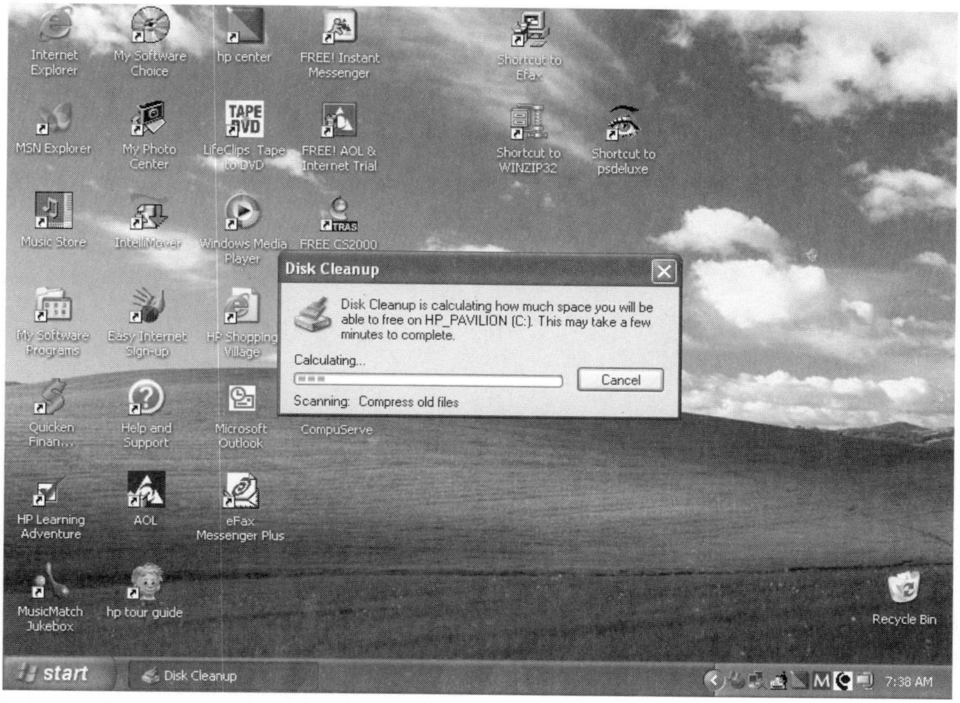

FIGURE 8.1   Disk Cleanup is taking a look at your hard drive.

Click OK. You get a confirming dialog box, asking if you're sure you want to complete the cleanup and to delete the files. That's all there is to it.

You should run Disk Cleanup every few months to keep your hard drive in order.

note **The More Options tab of Disk Cleanup offers other ways of clearing space on your hard drive, including removing optional Windows components, uninstalling programs you don't use, or running a System Restore. You'll read more about System Restore later in this chapter.**

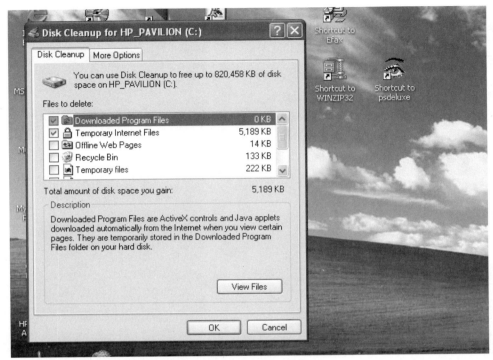

FIGURE 8.2   I had 820,458 kilobytes (kb) of junk on my computer to get rid of!

Recovering from Disaster

Most of the time your computing experience will be just great, with no crashes or disasters of any kind. However, I won't kid you; disasters do happen. Because of all the hardware and software on your computer, files you download from here, there, and everywhere (including destructive viruses) and new versions of software bringing new settings and files, conflicts occur that can cause you to lose data or, in extreme cases, not even be able to get your computer to function. Several programs are included with your computer that give you a disaster safety net.

Going Back in Time with System Restore

One utility that is part of Windows XP is called System Restore. You can use this program to restore your computer to some time in the past, for example, one hour ago or last Tuesday. System Restore creates automatic restore points, and you can select which one will suit your purposes or create your own. Then, you can go back to those computer settings to undo some change you may have made that resulted in a problem.

System Restore doesn't affect your documents or email, but it will change Windows XP settings for your system and hardware back to what they were before you started having trouble. In many cases, that solves the problem.

System Restore can also be a useful preventive method if you are considering making a change to your computer and you're concerned that action could cause a problem. You can create a restore point yourself just before making the change and restore to that point if you encounter a problem.

✔ **To restore to an automatically saved restore point, follow these steps:**

1. Select Start, All Programs, Accessories, System Tools, System Restore. The Welcome screen shown in Figure 8.3 appears.

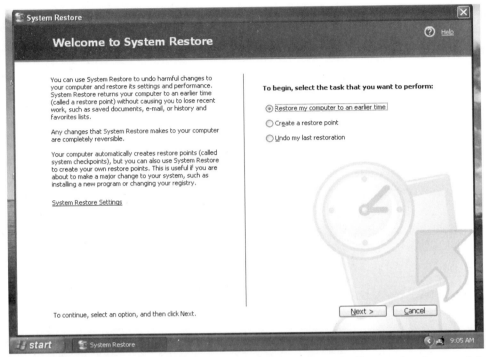

FIGURE 8.3   You have the option of using an automatically saved restore point or creating one of your own.

2. Make sure the Restore My Computer to an Earlier Time option is selected and then click Next. The Select a Restore Point dialog box appears.

3. Click a date with a bold number on it; these are the restoration points available to you. You'll see a listing of actions performed on each date that created a restore point, as in Figure 8.4.

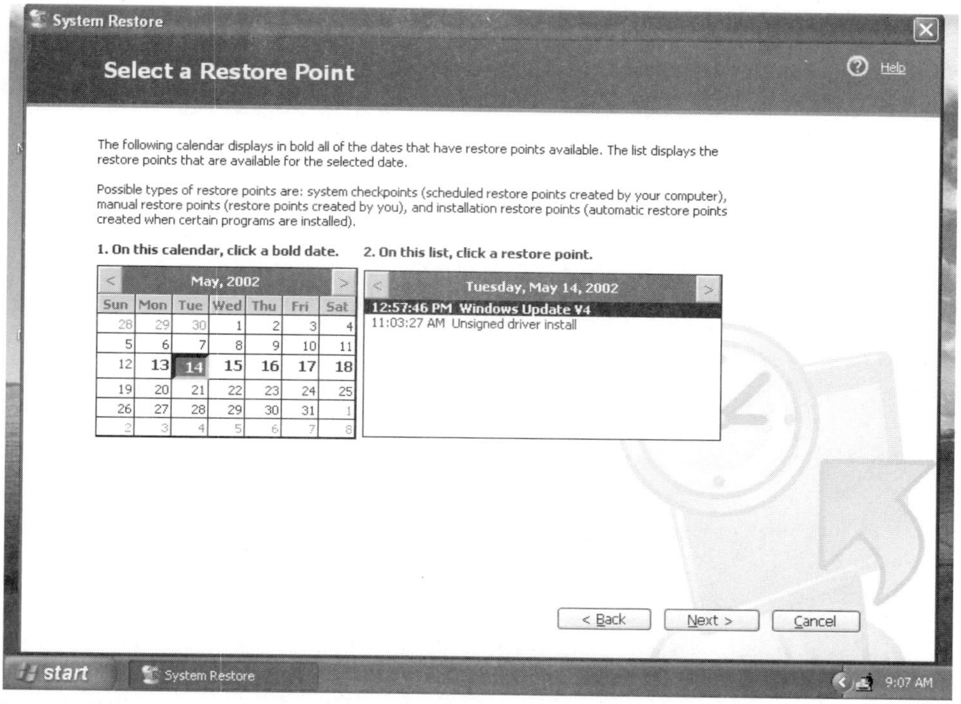

FIGURE 8.4   Find the action you want undone in this list.

4. Click a restore point and then Next. The Confirm dialog box shown in Figure 8.5 appears, explaining what will happen should you click Next to proceed.

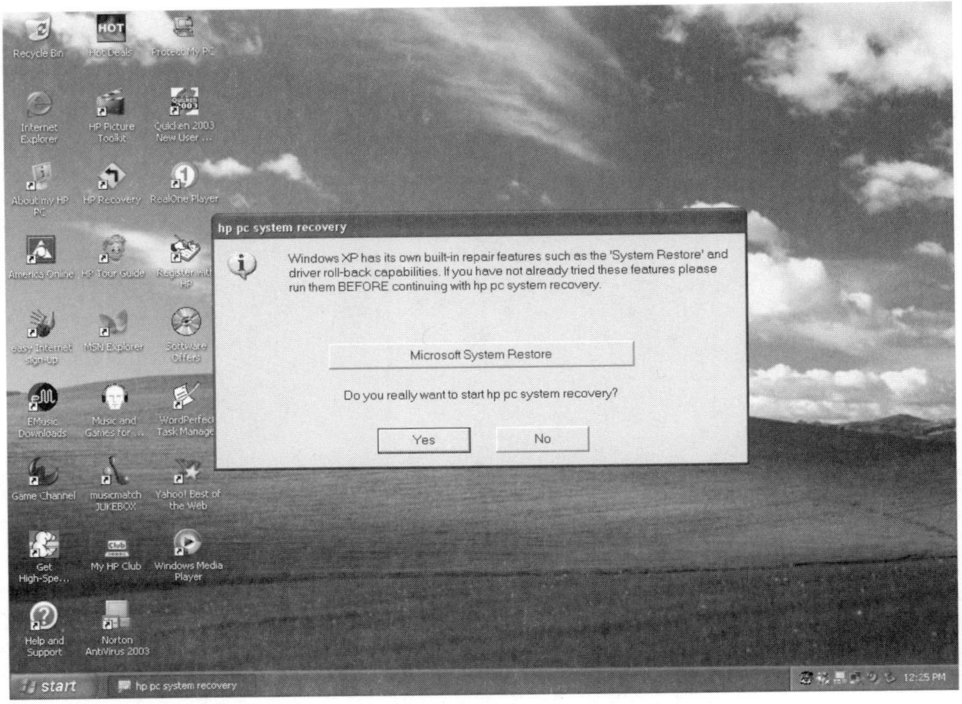

FIGURE 8.5   Warnings are in red in this descriptive dialog box.

5. Click Next. The System Restore runs, shutting down Windows and restarting. A Restoration Complete window appears, allowing you to view any files that were renamed.

6. Click OK to close System Restore.

> *caution*   If you run a System Restore to a point before you installed a piece of software, it doesn't uninstall the software; it just reverts any changes made to your system at the time of installation. You should still go to the Control Panel and run the Add or Remove Programs sequence to remove the program entirely.

How Application and System Recovery Work

Application Recovery and System Recovery are programs that restore factory settings to your computer. Application Recovery reinstalls any software applications that came with your computer when you first opened the box. System Recovery restores system settings. You can do a nondestructive recovery. This does not delete your documents and other files and does reinstall Windows and restore settings. You can also do a destructive recovery that gets rid of anything you've added to your computer since you first booted up. Destructive recoveries are used in case of severe computer problems.

Each program can be accessed through the PC Recovery Tools item on your Start, All Programs menu on Pavilions, or by selecting Start, All Programs, Compaq, Compaq PC Tools on your Presario. When you select Application Recovery from the Tools menu, you'll go through a series of windows, such as the one shown in Figure 8.6, to select the applications to recover.

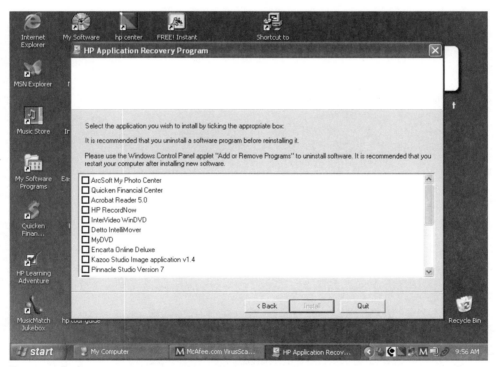

FIGURE 8.6   Click the checkbox for any application you want the feature to recover.

When you access System Recovery through the HP Tools menu, you see a message (see Figure 8.7) asking you if you're sure you want to run the recovery. Simply click Yes to proceed.

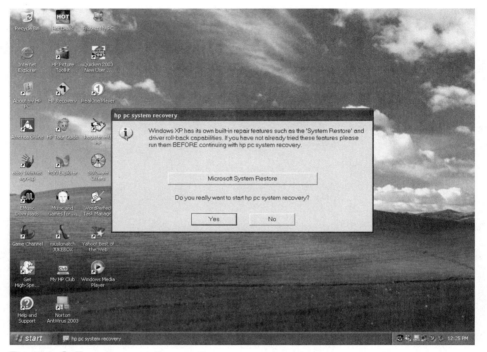

FIGURE 8.7   Because System Recovery makes changes to your computer, you are asked to confirm your choice to run it.

If you have experienced serious damage and your computer cannot load Windows, you can access System Recovery by turning off your computer. When you next turn it on and a blue screen appears, press F10 repeatedly to open the System Recovery program.

caution   **It is strongly recommended that you try using Windows XP's System Restore before using System Recovery to solve any problem because System Recovery can cause a more drastic change to your computer systems.**

Get Protected with Norton Antivirus

With so much time spent on the Internet today, people and their computers are at risk. Because it's often difficult to tell where downloaded files and email attachments originated, it's hard to keep potentially harmful material off your hard drive. That's where antivirus software comes in. It protects your computer settings and data from changes or damage.

What Is a Virus?

A virus is a small computer program, typically taking the form of an executable file, that runs and causes damage or performs an action on your computer. Viruses are created and spread by people who run the gamut from harmless pranksters to those wanting to cause serious damage.

Viruses have appeared that do a variety of things, including the following:

- Wiping all data from your hard drive
- Generating an email to everybody in your e-mail address book to spread the virus to their systems
- Causing a message or graphic to appear on your screen
- Making your CD drawer open and close continuously
- Causing files to be saved in a different format than you think you're saving to, for example, saving a word processing document as a template rather than a document

You get the idea. These things can be jokes, or they can ruin your whole day. Luckily, a good antivirus program can spot many viruses and stop them in their tracks.

What Options Does Norton Offer?

Norton Antivirus software is one of several popular antivirus programs, and it's included on your computer as a limited time trial.

Norton, like other antivirus programs, depends on you updating a list of virus definitions from their Web site frequently and scanning your hard drive to spot viruses included on that list. The definitions must be updated regularly because new viruses appear all the time. If you haven't updated your software and a new virus appears, you're not protected at all, no matter how many times you scan your computer.

When you've signed up for Norton's LiveUpdate service, it sends you notices when new viruses have been added so that you can keep up to date.

Norton Antivirus LiveUpdate provides protection through the Internet through a one year subscription. During that time, you get all updates to virus definitions and even upgraded Norton software for the subscription fee.

Scanning for Viruses

To run a scan for viruses using Norton, you select Start, All Programs, Norton Antivirus, Norton Antivirus 2003. Then you can run a Full System scan.

✔ **Follow these steps to run a virus scan:**

1. Select Start, All Programs, Norton Antivirus, Norton Antivirus 2003. The window shown in Figure 8.6 appears.

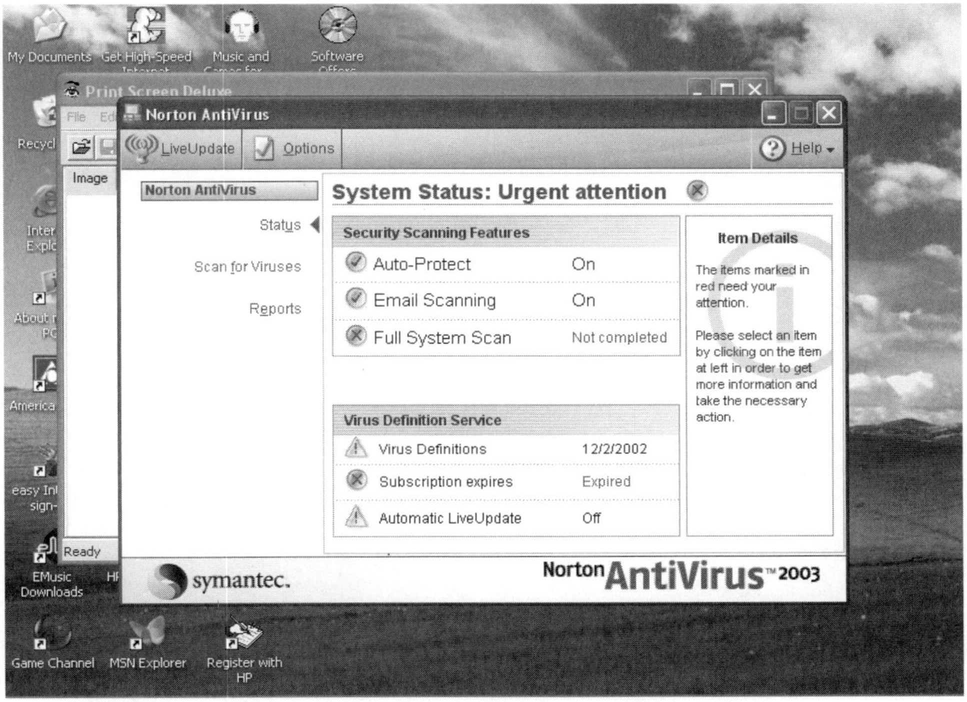

FIGURE 8.8   Choose where you want to scan from this window.

2. Click Full System Scan..

3. Click Scan Now. The dialog box shown in Figure 8.7 appears, showing the scanning in progress and any infected files that Norton locates.

4. If viruses are found, choose to Fix, Quarantine, or Delete them.

FIGURE 8.9 The scan may take a few minutes, but you can continue to use your computer while it runs.

5. When any repairs are complete, close the dialog box by clicking the Close button in the top right-hand corner.

 note **To update virus definitions, which you should do often, click the LIveUpdate button and follow the instructions there.**

Chapter Summary

In this chapter, you saw some of the utilities included on your computer that help you diagnose problems and keep your hard drive in shape. You learned about restoration utilities you can use in the event of disastrous system problems or data loss. Finally, you tried out Norton antivirus software to scan your computer for potentially harmful viruses.

9

Words and Numbers

In this Chapter

✔ Creating documents in Works

✔ Designing a flyer

✔ Organizing your finances with Quicken

If you have work to do, you'll be happy to hear that HP has included on your computer just what you need to write documents, design presentations, and run the numbers.

Depending on when you purchased your computer, you'll have some of these productivity tools:

- Suites of office software that allow you to design common documents, Microsoft Works and Corel WordPerfect Office
- A financial planning software package, Quicken

 note **If you purchased your Pavilion prior to September 2002, you have Works installed and a trial version of the WordPerfect Suite. If you purchased after that date, you will have a fully functional version of WordPerfect instead of Works. Quicken will be available on all models, but only Microsoft Money is available on earlier models.**

Working with Office Suites

Various software packages include several commonly used tools, such as word processing, spreadsheet, and presentation programs. These are called office suites because the programs they include are useful for getting your work done. Two such programs may already be installed on your HP Pavilion: Microsoft Works and Corel WordPerfect Office 2002. Microsoft Works comes with every Compaq Presario.

One nice thing about these programs is that they integrate the features and functionality of the various programs they contain. You can easily work with similar tools and menus, move information between documents created in the different programs, and find help.

 tip **You can also relatively seamlessly convert Works documents into WordPerfect documents and vice versa, because each recognizes several other program formats.**

Getting to Work with Microsoft Works

Works from Microsoft has several good things going for it. It contains word processor, spreadsheet (to work with numbers), database (to manage data), calendar, and address book components. In addition, it works with other Microsoft programs, such as Microsoft Money, MSN Photos, and Outlook Express.

One neat thing about Works is that it's designed to use wizards to easily generate commonly created documents. This makes it easy to use for people who have little experience using different types of software. Figure 9.1 shows the types of templates available in the Works Word Processor program.

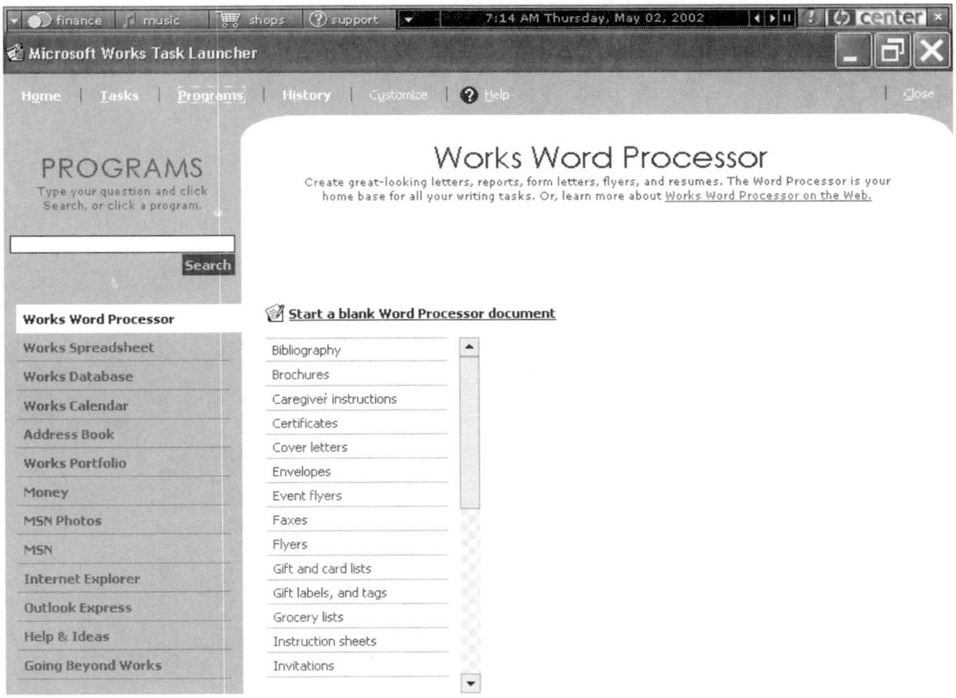

FIGURE 9.1   From brochures and event flyers to grocery lists, Works Word Processor makes designing polished-looking documents easy.

Working with Wizards

You get things done in Works by using simple-to-follow wizards. A wizard is a step-by-step walkthrough of the process involved in creating a document. Typically, with a wizard you will be asked to enter information or make choices from lists. Based on your responses,

Works builds the document you've chosen. Figure 9.2 shows the choices of themes that are offered by the Event Flyers Wizard from the Works Word Processor, for example.

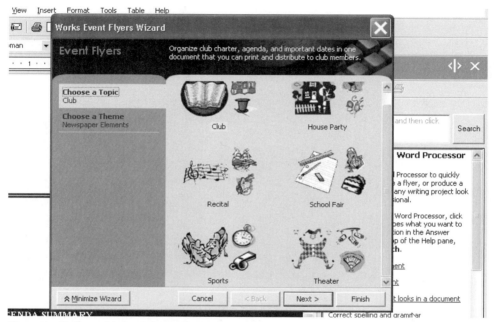

FIGURE 9.2   Microsoft has built in various common themes for your event flyer; all you have to do is choose one.

Project: **Designing an Event Flyer**

Using a Works Wizard, design a flyer for an upcoming theatrical event. Include a graphic image for the event that you find in Clip Art or download from the Internet, as well as information about where and when the event will be held.

✔ **Follow these steps to create your flyer:**

1. From the Windows desktop, select Start, All Programs, Microsoft Works, Microsoft Works Task Launcher.

2. Click the Programs tab.

3. If the Word Processor option isn't showing, click Works Word Processor in the list of programs along the left side of the Works window.

4. Click Event Flyers in the list of Word Processor documents and then the Start This Task link that appears. The wizard window shown in Figure 9.2 appears.

 tip **You can see additional types of documents by dragging the scrollbar along the right side of the list of document types.**

5. Click the Theater topic and then on Next. The Choose a Theme wizard box appears, as shown in Figure 9.3.

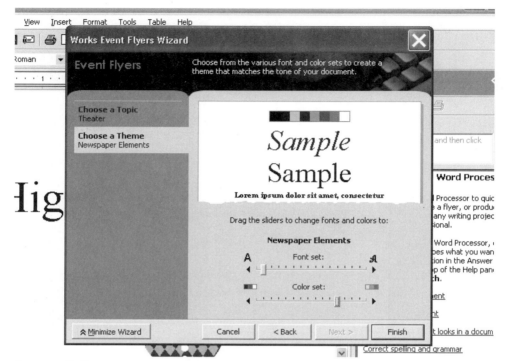

FIGURE 9.3   Easy-to-use sliders help you choose among preset fonts and color schemes.

6. Click the slider bar for either the Font set or Color set elements and drag it to a new position. You can also click any tick mark along the slider line to preview a sample of another format set.

7. When you're happy with your choices, click Finish. The event flyer shown in Figure 9.4 appears, using placeholder text and the font and color set you selected.

FIGURE 9.4 All the graphics and colors have been preset for you by the Works Wizard.

You can now edit the flyer as you like, entering the text you want included. You can also use any of the tools and menus of Works to modify the document in a variety of ways and then save it or print it.

Editing Works Documents

After you've generated a document in Works, you need to make it serve your specific purposes. Works has provided only placeholder text. You have to enter the specific information or data for your particular project. You can also move elements around on the page, delete or add graphics and text, or change the style of elements, such as making text bold or surrounding a graphic with a border.

✔ **Follow these steps to make some changes to the theater flyer you just generated to see how this works:**

1. Click your mouse to the left of the title "High School Drama Troupe" and drag to the right and down to highlight the entire phrase.

2. Type "Barnes Community Theater."

3. Click just above the address 55 Fourth Street and type "Presents TWELFTH NIGHT."

4. Click to the left of the line you just entered and drag to the right to select it.

5. Click the arrow next to the Font Size box on the Formatting toolbar (shown in Figure 9.5) and click 20 to enlarge the type size.

6. With the text still selected, click the Underline button.

Font   Font Size   Font color   Bold   Italic   Underline

Alignment
(4 buttons)

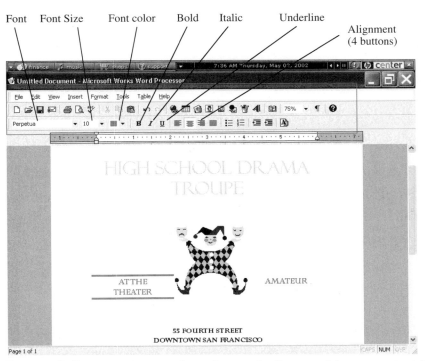

FIGURE 9.5   Use these tools to change the format of document text in a variety of ways.

7. Click just below the address and select Insert, Picture, Clip Art.

8. Click a piece of art, for example, one with two drama masks, and then click Insert to insert it into your document.

9. When the clip art appears, you may have to click a corner of the image and drag inward to make it small enough for all the flyer text to appear on a single page.

10. Click the Print Preview tool on the standard toolbar. The flyer should look something like the one shown in Figure 9.6.

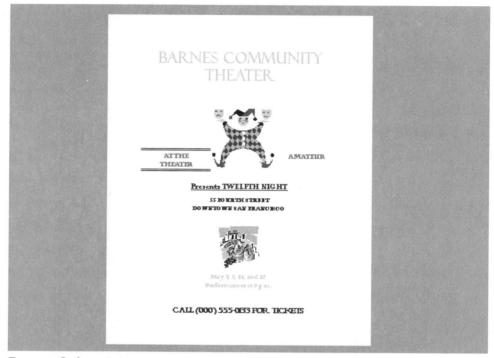

FIGURE 9.6   A few simple changes have produced a professional-looking flyer or poster for your event.

11. You can save the file by selecting File, Save. Locate a folder to save it to using the Save In feature and enter a file name. Click OK to save it.

 tip **You can see the names of various tool buttons on toolbars in Works by holding your mouse pointer over each tool.**

Performing Tasks in Works

Works has several other programs available, and most are as easy to use to generate documents as the Word Processor module you just worked with to create a flyer. However, Works also allows you to approach your work a little differently, by using a task wizard instead of a document wizard.

Where the Programs listing in Works gives you lists of common documents, such as invoices and flyers, the Tasks listing lets you choose from a list of common tasks, such as checking email messages or making hotel reservations on the Internet. Figure 9.7 shows the types of tasks listed in the Household Management category to give you an idea of what's offered. Some of these tasks lead you through a wizard to produce a document, much like the event flyer wizard you used earlier. Others lead you onto the Internet to display relevant sections of MSN.com.

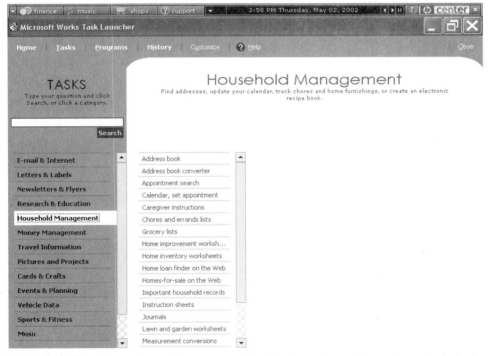

FIGURE 9.7   From home improvement to finding a home loan, these tasks help you to create documents or browse the Web.

To perform a task, you click the Tasks tab on the page that appears when you first start Works. If you select an option that involves a Web-based activity, such as Car Rental on the Web or Currency Converter on the Web, Works automatically opens your default Internet connection and takes you to the relevant Web site. If you click a task that involves producing a document, such as Caregiver Instructions or Party Planner, you'll be taken through a wizard to produce that document.

 tip **Use the History tab of the opening window of Works to look for documents you created in Works organized by Name, Date, and the Task or Program you used to create them.**

Crunching Numbers

Works also contains a spreadsheet program. A spreadsheet allows you to create complex financial documents that perform calculations and build formulas for anything from a simple household budget to a corporate profit-and-loss statement.

A spreadsheet looks like a large table. You can enter numbers and words in the various cells formed by the intersecting columns and rows. You can then perform calculations on the numbers and format the columns and rows to make polished-looking documents. The Works spreadsheet also has tools that help you build attractive charts that graphically represent numerical data.

Works also has typical financial documents, such as a personal budget, that have categories of information and formulas already in place. A personal budget, for example, lists typical household income and expense items. When you enter a number in the Amount column and press <Enter>, Works automatically calculates what percentage of your total budget that item represents.

Teaching you how to work with functions and formulas in a sophisticated spreadsheet program such as Works is beyond the scope of this book. However, take a look at some of the predesigned spreadsheets in the Works Task Launcher to give you an idea of how the program works.

Profiting from Financial Software

A popular type of application for home businesses and families is financial software. Financial software helps you organize your spending, track tax information, and even print out checks while keeping a record of every expense. One program is a leader in this field: Quicken from Intuit.

Quicken is one of the most popular financial management packages around, and you'll soon see why. With Quicken, you can manage banking, investments, family and business budgets, and loans. The beauty of the program is that you can enter all your financial information—from school loans to stock market investments and monthly household expenses—in one place and then use and track that information in a wide variety of ways.

note **The version of Quicken on your computer is the New User Edition, which does not have all the features of the full program. If you like, you can install the Quicken Deluxe version for $29.95. Do this by selecting Start, All Programs, Quicken, Unlock Quicken Deluxe and following the instructions there. (On Pavilions, Quicken is in the Finance folder on the Programs menu.)**

✔ **You have to run an installation program to be able to use Quicken. To do this, follow these steps:**

1. Select Start, All Programs, Quicken New User Edition Setup.

2. Click Next.

3. On the next window, click Yes to accept the license agreement.

4. On the final screen, make sure the Express installation is selected and click Install Now.

After it's installed, you can open Quicken by selecting Start, All Programs, Quicken, Quicken 2003 New User Edition. The first time you open the program you are asked to go through a New User Setup wizard. Complete this wizard by checking options that apply (such as whether you're married or own your own home) so that Quicken can build a basic financial profile of you. You'll then be presented with the main window shown in Figure 9.8.

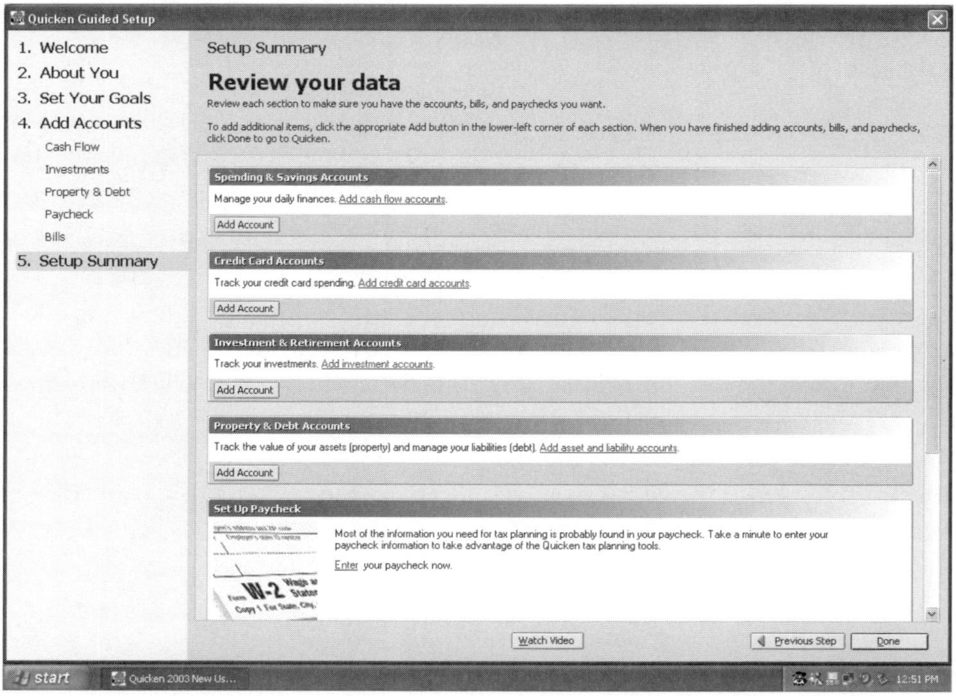

FIGURE 9.8   Quicken offers setup options for your various financial accounts.

To use Quicken effectively, you have to enter information about your various accounts, such as bank accounts, investments, loans, and regular expenses (see Figure 9.9). For example, you can enter information about your bank accounts by following these steps:

1. Click Create New Account in the Set Up Banking Accounts section of the Setup window.

2. Select a type of account, such as checking or savings.

3. Enter the last statement date and balance.

That's it. You can now connect with any institution that offers online access to your account and your online account information can be interfaced with Quicken. You can continue to create accounts and then use Quicken to write checks or to generate tax information.

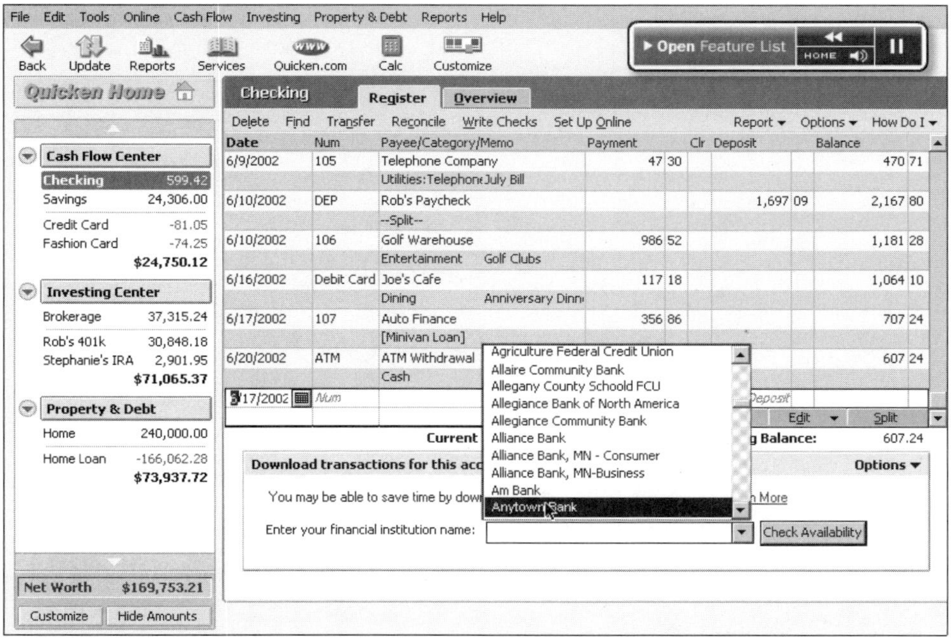

FIGURE 9.9   This sample account list from the Quicken 2003 Tour shows the kind of information you can obtain after you've entered data into Quicken.

caution   **It can take time to enter all your financial information into Quicken, but after you do, financial management will be much easier. However, do set aside a few hours to set Quicken up the first time you use it.**

After all your information is up to date in Quicken, you can use a variety of reports to review your financial status, such as your net worth or investment trends. Quicken can also generate charts and graphs that help you visualize your financial information.

Chapter Summary

In this chapter, you focused on software you can use to get your work done, from designing attractive documents to calculating numbers. You learned how to generate documents with easy-to-use wizards in Microsoft Works. You got a glimpse of the spreadsheet program included in Works, and you toured the money management features of Intuit's Quicken.

10

Fun and Games

In this Chapter

✔ **Playing games with Windows**

✔ **Playing games online**

A computer should do more than help you work; it should also help you play. Your computer does just that by making almost a dozen Windows XP games available for you to play.

Playing Windows Games

Windows XP comes with several games built in, from card games such as Solitaire and Hearts, to more strategy-oriented games such as Pinball and Minesweeper. In addition, you can access Internet versions to play games, such as Checkers and Reversi, with real opponents through Microsoft Network's (MSN's) *zone.com*.

Playing Cards

If your idea of heaven is sitting down with a deck of 52 cards and counting on the luck of the draw, you'll find Windows XP's card games to be right up your alley. You can play four card games: Hearts, Solitaire, Freecell, and Spider Solitaire. Each is played with a virtual deck of cards. In some cases, you click and drag cards to play. In others, you click the card you want to move and then click the location to move it to. In Hearts, the computer acts as the other player; in other games, such as Solitaire, you play against yourself.

Try a hand of Spider Solitaire to see how these games work. Spider Solitaire is played with 2 decks of cards and 10 stacks of cards, similar to regular solitaire. You can deal additional cards by clicking on the card decks in the bottom right-hand corner of the game area. In Spider Solitaire, you can move a card from the bottom of a stack to an empty stack. You can also move a card from the bottom of a stack to place it on a card with the next highest value. Color or suit don't matter. You can move a set of cards onto a blank stack. Keep in mind that, if a blank stack is on the screen, you can't deal more cards until you've placed something there.

✔ **Let's get started playing cards:**

1. Select Start, All Programs, Games, Spider Solitaire. A blank game appears with a Difficulty dialog box open.

2. Accept the Easy: One Suite difficulty level by clicking OK. The computer deals a set of cards, as shown in Figure 10.1.

FIGURE 10.1 Note the spider design on the cards.

3. Click any card and drag it to rest on another card that is one higher than it. For example, place the 9 in the figure on the 10. As you move the card from a stack, the computer flips the next card in that stack face.

4. Continue to move cards to stacks with the next highest card on them. Be aware that you can't move sets of cards that aren't consecutive. Therefore, for example, if you have a stack with 10, 9, 8, 3, 2, 1, you can't move the 10 and all the cards under it to another stack. You would have to move the 3, 2, 1 to another stack first and then move the 10, 9, 8.

When you have created a set of cards from King to Ace, the set folds up and moves off to the side. The goal is to make every possible set from the two decks of cards.

Before you finish the game, note some of the options for controlling the game, which are similar to options in other card games in Windows XP.

In the Game menu, shown in Figure 10.2, you have several commands:

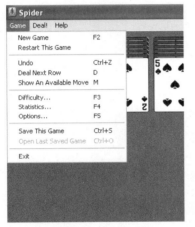

FIGURE 10.2 The Game menu provides controls for how the game works, as well as statistics about the number of games you've won (or lost).

- There are controls to start or restart a game.
- You can undo a move, deal the next set of cards (you can also do this by simply clicking the deck of cards on the screen), or get a hint (Show An Available Move).
- Use the Difficulty command to change the difficulty level.
- Click statistics (see Figure 10.3) to see how many wins or losses you have racked up.

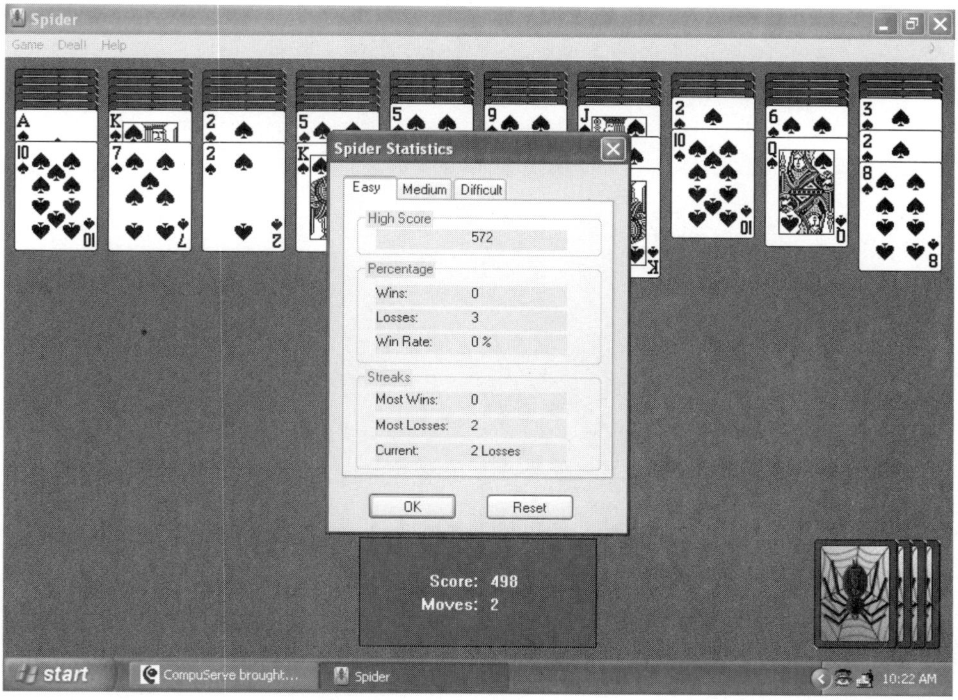

FIGURE 10.3 Don't worry. If you lose a lot like me, you can reset the statistics and get a clean slate.

- Open Options to control how sound, animation, and automatic dealing works.
- If you have a game going and have to leave, you can save it (Game, Save This Game) and finish it later, or you can exit (Game, Exit) without saving.

caution **Don't be fooled. The Deal button on the menu bar doesn't open a menu containing commands; it just deals the next row of cards.**

Clicking to Score

Minesweeper and Pinball rely more on your dexterity or ability to strategize than on the luck of the draw.

Minesweeper has you click on squares trying to avoid uncovering any mines, which ends your game (see Figure 10.4). The numbers that appear on clicked squares indicate how many mines are located within eight squares. If you think a square has a mine underneath, mark it by right-clicking it.

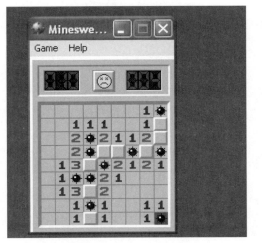

FIGURE 10.4   Use your noodle to figure out likely hiding spots for mines.

Pinball is a virtual pinball game with flashing lights and dinging bells. You can play pinball with up to four players. You control play with simple keyboard commands (see Figure 10.5). Using these commands, you can bump the table from different sides and swing flippers to stop the ball.

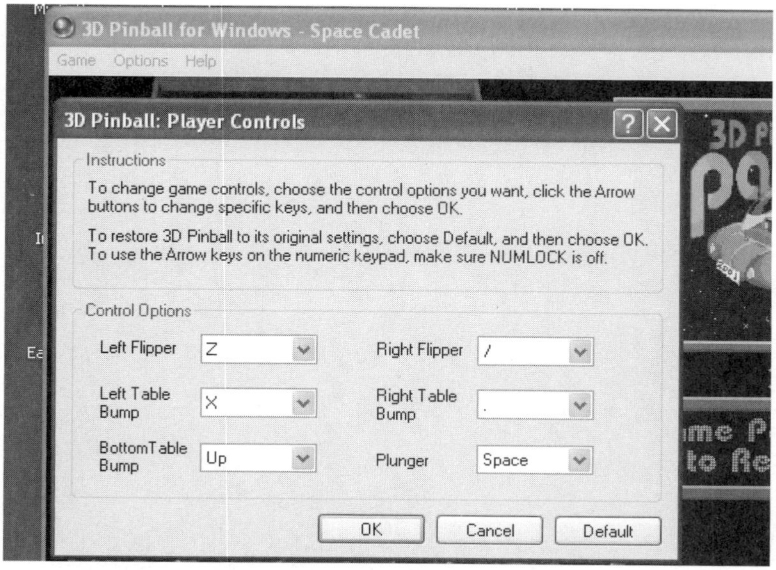

FIGURE 10.5 It won't take you long to memorize these keyboard controls.

caution **If you bump the virtual pinball table too hard (usually a matter of initiating the bump command too frequently), you can tilt.**

Project: **Challenge Your Friend to a Pinball Match**

Time to play some pinball. Get a few friends to come over for a pinball tournament. Remember, you can have up to four players with Windows Pinball. Decide the order of play and determine a prize for the winning player.

✔ **Follow these steps to play a game:**

1. Select Start, All Programs, Games, Pinball. A welcome screen appears while the game loads. Then, you'll see the pinball game shown in Figure 10.6.

FIGURE 10.6   Looking for all the world like an arcade game, this pinball machine even tilts.

2. Select Game, Launch Ball. After a few seconds, the ball is in play.

3. Use <Z> and </> to move the left and right flipper, respectively.

4. Use <X>, <.>, and <Up> to bump the table from various sides.

5. If you want to pause the game at any time, press <F3> and then press <F3> again to resume.

When the game ends, your score is displayed. You can explore the menu of the 3D Pinball game to set it up to play sounds and music, to select the number of players, and to review high scores.

Playing Online

Stuck for a playing partner? Through *zone.com*, you can be matched with another player to play a game such as Backgammon on the Internet. The game takes place in real time, that is, the other person is logged on at the same time you are and you have consecutive turns at play. Internet games included with Windows XP include Backgammon, Checkers, Hearts, Reversi, and Spades.

note **You need to get a .NET Passport, which is free. A .NET Passport allows you to log in with a single click to any Web site that displays the .NET Sign In button. Go to www.passport.com to get yours.**

✔ **To initiate a game of Internet Checkers, follow these steps:**

1. Select Start, All Programs, Games, Internet Checkers. The *zone.com* opening screen shown in Figure 10.7 appears.

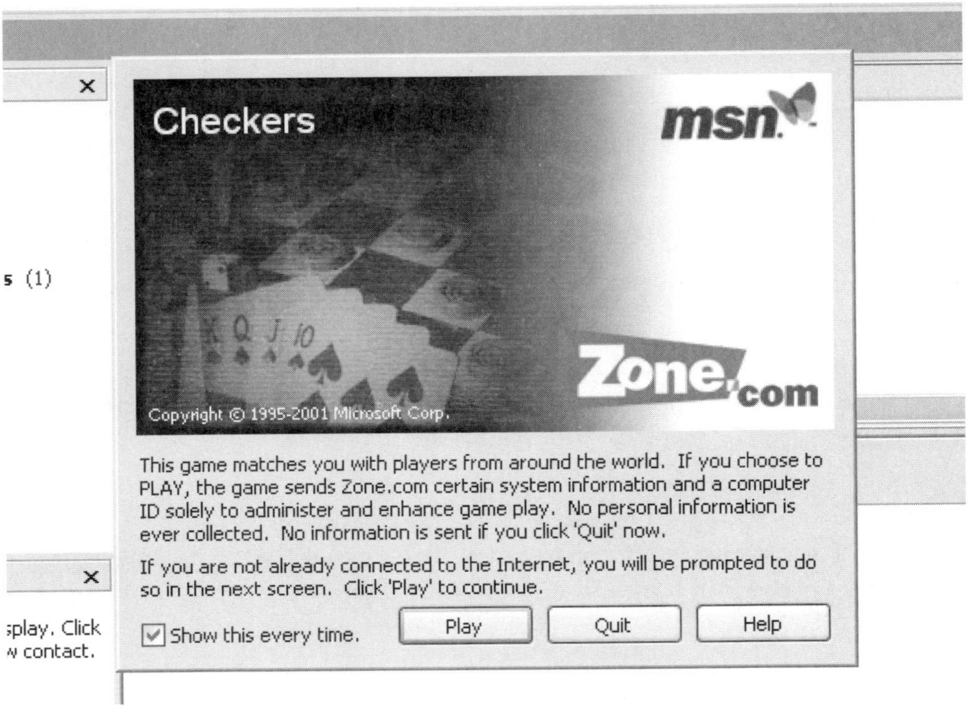

FIGURE 10.7 This screen explains how online games work.

2. Click Play. You are connected to another user on the gameboard.

3. If you want to chat with preset phrases while playing, leave the Chat on setting and click the arrow in the Select a Message to Send field (for example, "It's your turn" or "Good move").

4. When the display says Your Turn (see Figure 10.8), you can click a checker and then click the square you want to move it to.

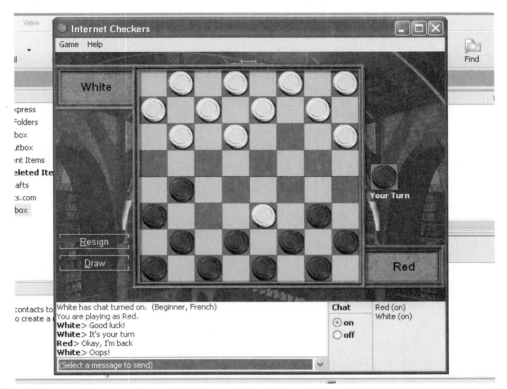

FIGURE 10.8 I lost this game, but had a lot of fun.

5. To jump a checker, click your piece and then on the square on the other side of the piece you want to jump.

6. When the game is over, if you don't want to play anymore, it's a good idea to send the message that you have to go now and then click Close to close the game.

Because you can only communicate with preset phrases, you don't have to worry about encountering anybody who will speak to you inappropriately. Also, there is no way the other player can contact you directly. Play as much as you like and enjoy.

Chapter Summary

In this chapter, you got to have some fun playing games both offline and online. You practiced a card game, played a virtual pinball machine, and got online to play a game of checkers with another game enthusiast.

chapter

11

Getting Down to Business with Presario Multimedia

In this Chapter

✓ Working with Intervideo WinDVD

✓ Personalizing your music experience with MusicMatch Jukebox

The world of multimedia includes media such as music, video, digital imaging, and graphics. In this chapter you'll work with a video playback and music programs that are included with your Compaq Presario. (Chapter 12 covers graphics and digital imaging for Pavilion users.)

Presario owners can take advantage of Intervideo WinDVD to play back their favorite video files, and Musicmatch Jukebox to play Internet radio, MP3 files, and music CDs. Whether you need this capability for work or pleasure, you'll find these programs expand the world of computing in some entertaining ways.

 note **Both of these products are also included on most Pavlion models.**

Moving Pictures with Intervideo WinDVD

Intervideo's WinDVD is a very popular application for playing videos from DVDs, or any video file you download to your computer from the Internet. If you have a video camera you can upload your own video files and play them back using WinDVD.

A limited version of this product is included on all Presarios. With this version you can open videos, play them, and use features to stop and pause playback, and adjust the volume of the audio.

Note that the full version of WinDVD, which you can easily upgrade to using the pop-up window that appears when you open the software, provides a much richer feature set. With the full version you can add video effects to sharpen the image or adjust colors; take advantage of pan, zoom, and speed settings; use features that allow you to take screen captures of video images; and do audio mixing and bookmarking so you can return to favorite sections of videos easily. Finally, the full version contains a feature called Movie Encyclopedia which reads the serial number from a movie DVD, and displays information about the movie, such as the year it was released, the director, and cast.

✔ **To open and play a video using WinDVD limited edition, follow these steps:**

1. Select Start, All Programs, Intervideo WinDVD 4, Intervideo WinDVD4.

2. Click on the arrow underneath the word WindDVD to open the Playlist menu shown in Figure 11.1.

FIGURE 11.1 This menu allows you to open and play video files.

3. Click on Open File.

4. Locate the file you want to play; if you like you can use the sample video file located in the My Videos folder inside the My Document folder.

5. Click the Play button (the large right pointing arrow) to play the video (see Figure 11.2).

> *tip* **You can also play a video by pressing Enter on your keyboard.**

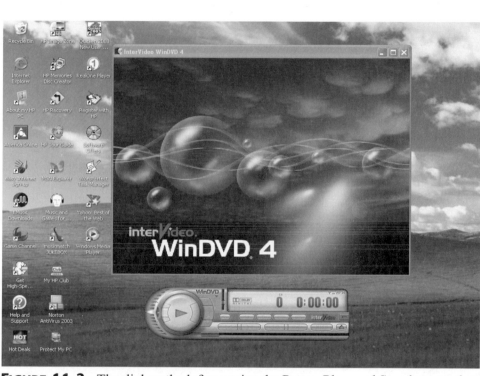

FIGURE 11.2 The dial on the left contains the Pause, Play, and Stop buttons that control video playback.

6. Click on the slider and move it up or down to adjust volume.

7. Click the Pause button to the left of the Play button to pause playback, or click the Stop button to the right of the Play button to stop the video.

Music to Your Ears

If you're like me, you love to sit at your computer working or playing while listening to music. Well, now you can forget the DVD player or FM radio set. You've got both built into your Presario. With Music-Match Jukebox, you can tune into radio, play CDs, and even build music libraries that match your tastes.

Tuning Into Radio Stations

From country to jazz, you can pick and choose radio stations that match your musical interests. You can mix and match different catego-ries of music to create a personal radio station. The Music Matching feature allows MusicMatch Jukebox to observe your listening habits and to provide a personalized radio experience based on your prefer-ences. You can also view a list of broadcast stations and tune into any one of them at any time. To listen to radio stations, you must first be connected to the Internet (see Chapter 13 of this book if you need help getting connected).

✔ To tune into a broadcast station, follow these steps:

1. Double-click the MusicMatch Jukebox shortcut on your desktop or select Start, All Programs, Music, MusicMatch, Musicmatch Jukebox.

2. Click the Radio tab in the top pane of the jukebox. The program takes a moment to connect to the MusicMatch Jukebox site, and then the information shown in Figure 11.3 appears.

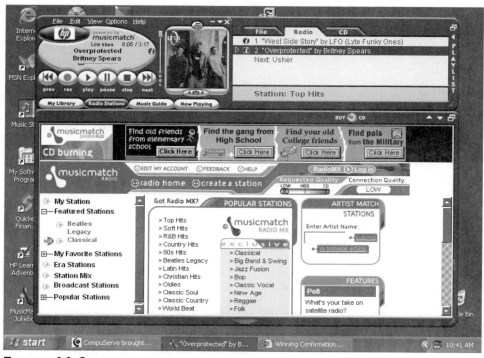

FIGURE 11.3 A wide variety of broadcast radio stations is accessible through the Jukebox.

3. Click the Broadcast Stations link in the left-hand pane. A list of categories appears.

4. Click a category name and then click a station. A listing of that station's Web address is shown.

5. Click the link to go to the station. You may have to click a listen button when the station Web page appears.

Project: Create Your Own Radio Station Mix

Next time you have a party coming up, you can create your own station with a mix of music that matches your friends' tastes. You might even create a logo for your own "audio station" and put it on your party invitations (see Chapter 9 for more about designing documents).

✔ **Identify at least four stations that play the type of music you and your friends like and then follow these steps:**

1. From the Radio window in Figure 11.3, click Create a Station.

2. When prompted to save the station in the mixer window, click the mixer window link. The window in Figure 11.4 appears.

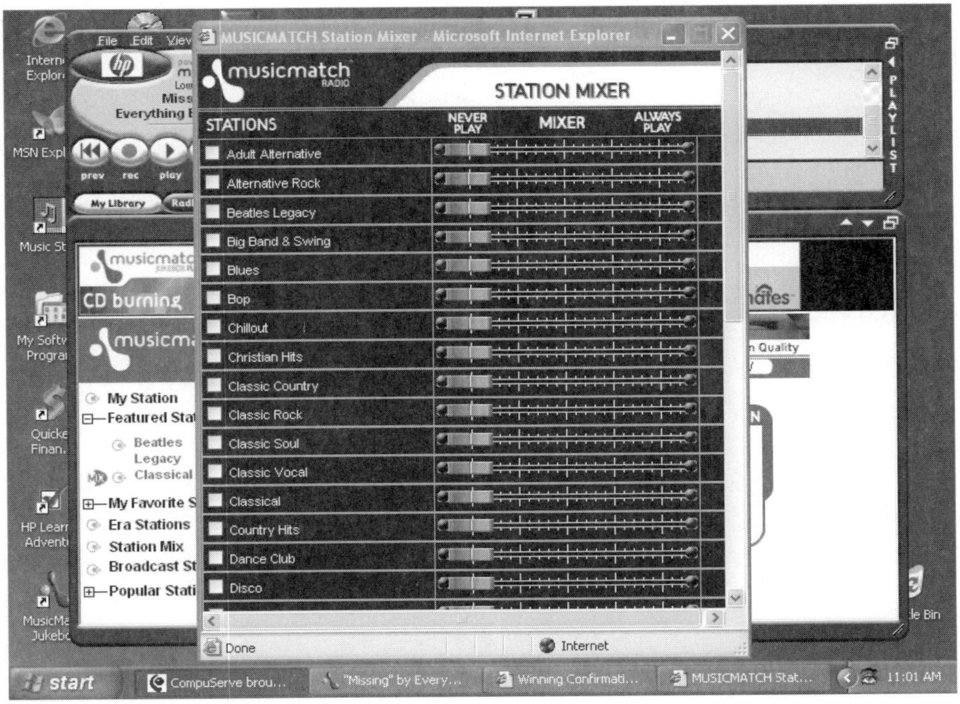

FIGURE 11.4 You can mix and match various kinds of music using the tools on this screen.

3. Select the categories of music you'd like to hear by clicking the appropriate boxes and moving the slider to the right to represent how much of that type of music you'd like your music mix to include.

4. Scroll to the bottom of the list, enter a name for your personal station, and then click Save & Exit.

 tip **Try the Era Radio feature. With this, you specify a date range, say 1950 to 1960, and MusicMatch plays only music from that era.**

Playing CDs

Man does not live by radio alone, so I'm sure you'll want to be able to play your own CDs now and then. You can do that with MusicMatch Jukebox, which provides controls for playing, pausing, and jumping easily to any song on the CD. You don't even have to have a CD player cluttering up your computer workstation.

✔ **To play a CD, follow these steps:**

1. Double-click the MusicMatch Jukebox shortcut to open the program.

2. Place a CD in your CD/DVD drive.

3. Click the CD tab in the top pane of the Jukebox. The CD begins playing, and you see the title list, such as the one shown in Figure 11.5.

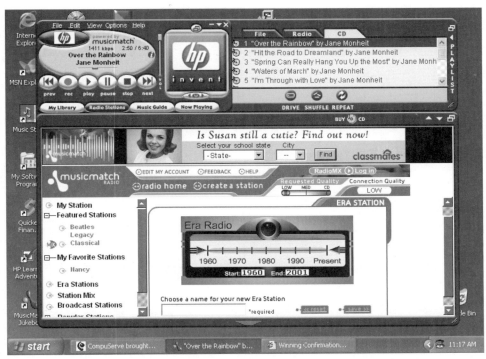

FIGURE 11.5   Click another title in this list at any time and click the Play button to play it.

You can use the playback controls to the left of the title list to play, pause, stop, or move to the previous or next title on the CD.

 tip   **You can switch among your radio stations, audio files, and CD by just clicking on the appropriate tab at any time.**

Adding to a Music Library

A music library is a customized list of audio files you build in Music-Match Jukebox. You may find music to include in these libraries any place, for example, downloaded from the Internet or from a CD. You can mix and match titles from different sources and play them in any order.

✔ **To create a music library playlist, follow these steps:**

1. Click My Library. A list of any existing music libraries appears, as in Figure 11.6.

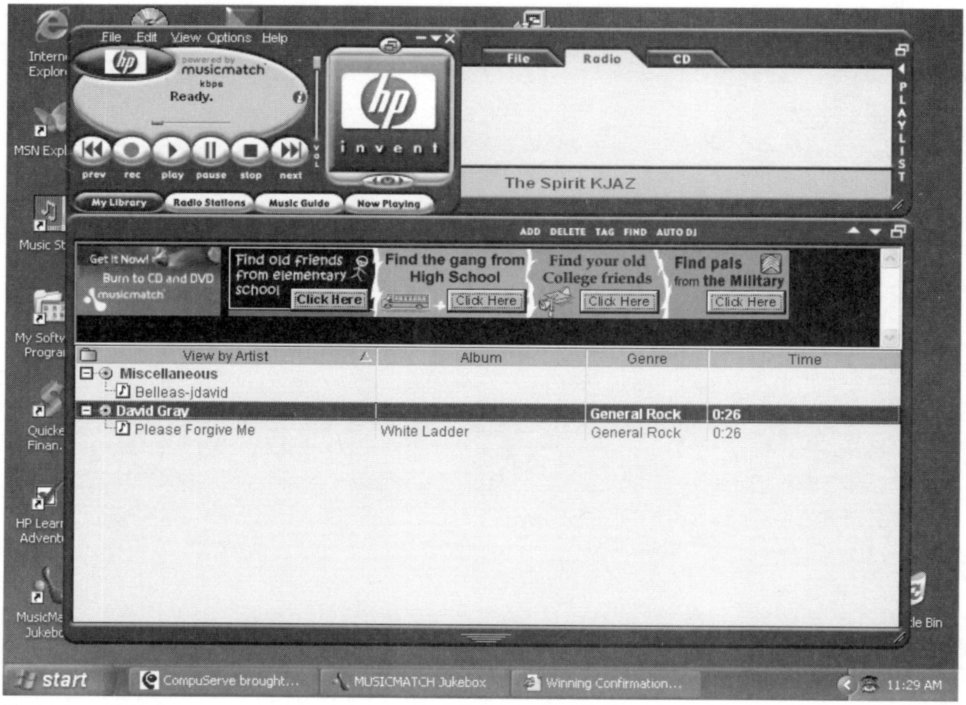

FIGURE 11.6 You can build multiple music libraries.

2. Select Options, Music Library, Search and Add Tracks from All Drives. The Search for Music dialog box appears.

3. Locate an audio file that you have stored on your computer by selecting a drive to search in the Look in drop-down list or using the Browse feature. For these steps, you should find a few music samples that are included with Windows XP (such as the Windows welcome music) by searching all drives.

4. All the audio files that were found are listed in your playlist.

5. Double-click a file, and it plays.

Chapter Summary

In this chapter, you got to explore a video editing program that comes with Presarios to play back a video file. You explored the world of digital music with MusicMatch Jukebox to use radio, CDs, and personalized playlists.

12

Having Fun with HP Pavilion Graphics and Digital Imaging

In this Chapter

✔ **Getting lost in the Funhouse**

✔ **Being creative with Greeting Card Creator**

✔ **Discovering HP Image Zone Digital Imaging Software**

Working with images is one of the most fun ways to use your Pavilion. From images you find online to photos you upload from your digital camera, you'll find hours of entertainment organizing and editing your images to share with others.

or Pavilion users the HP Image Zone provides a sophisticated digital imaging application that lets you work with, organize, and edit photos. Pavilions also come loaded with two graphics programs from ArcSoft that are strictly for fun.

> *tip* **If you own a Presario and want to purchase either of the ArcSoft products, visit their Web site at www.arcsoft.com.**

Greetings from Greeting Card Creator

There's nothing like a greeting card to make friends and family smile on a special occasion or when they need cheering up. It's even better if you can create a personalized greeting that will have the recipient grinning from ear to ear.

Now, if you own an HP Pavilion, there's no reason not to send this kind of customized greeting every day if you like. Greeting Card Creator from ArcSoft provides a simple-to-use format for combining photos and text greetings into a greeting card you can email to anybody instantly.

Project: Create Your Own Greeting Card

Next time a holiday rolls around, why not send an audio greeting card? Gather the family around and brainstorm what you'd like to say, both in text and in an audio greeting, and then get going. Note that you'll need to connect a microphone to your computer to record the audio message.

1. Select Start, All Programs, Pictures, ArcSoft Greeting Card Creator, Greeting Card Creator.

2. At the opening window click OK to accept the Letter Size greeting card format.

3. Click on the Select Design button. The window in Figure 12.1 appears.

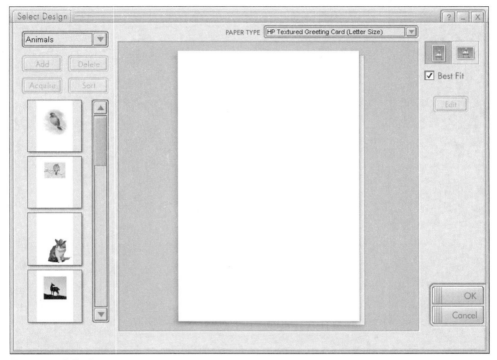

FIGURE 12.1 The first step in creating a greeting card is to choose a design.

4. Scroll down in the design previews along the left side of the card and click on the Hum3 design, or another of your choosing. The image appears in the design pane.

 tip **If you want to select from another category of design, such as Birthday or Flowers, choose the category from the drop down list at the top of the thumbnail previews.**

5. Click OK.

6. Click on the Add Title button. The Write Message dialog box shown in Figure 12.2 appears.

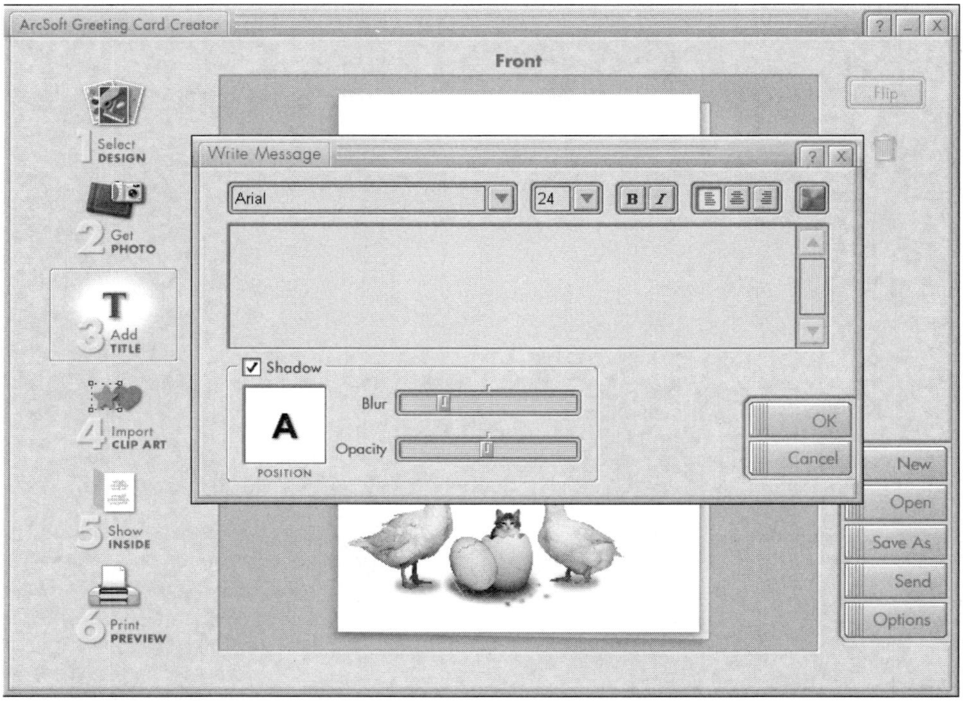

FIGURE 12.2 Use various font formatting tools in this dialog box to make your message stand out.

7. Type this message (or another one to fit the design you chose): "Spring is here!"

8. Click the arrow on the Font drop down list and select the Allegro BT font.

9. Click OK.

10. Click Import Clip Art.

11. Click the arrow next to the first box to display different categories of clips, and click on Festive Clips.

12. Double click on the eas_1 clip, then click OK.

13. Resize the clip (drag inward on one of the corner handles that appear when you click on the object) and drag it to move it to the left of the text "Spring is here!"

14. Click the Show Inside button. The window in Figure 12.3 appears.

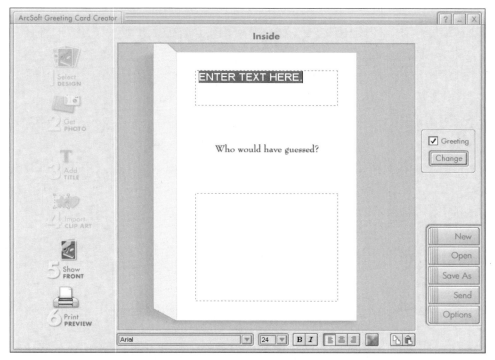

FIGURE 12.3   A standard message will appear here, but you can change it.

15. Click the Change button.

16. Scroll to the right until you locate the message: "Wishing you a Happy Easter;" click on the text, then click OK

17. Select the placeholder text "Enter Text Here." and type: "There's a holiday hatching."

18. Enter your name or names in the second text box at the bottom of the page.

19. To email the card click Send.

20. Click OK to accept the default Windows file format.

21. Fill in your email message and click Send.

Your card is on its way. If you want to send it again save it to your My Pictures folder before closing the program.

Into the Funhouse

ArcSoft's Funhouse is a photo graphics program that's strictly for fun. With this program, which comes with all HP Pavilions, you can put your cat on a $10 bill, put your daughter's head on your dog, use more than 150 predesigned templates to insert your own photos, and then share the images using email. You can add text to images and can modify the font, size, color, and the style.

With Funhouse, you can take a couple of photos and blur them together into a collage. You can easily resize, rearrange, and b lend your image with the template to get a clean, seamless look.

One other great feature of Funhouse is that you can capture images from a video device connected to your computer, if it's compatible. Funhouse's easy and fun interface lets you use all these features with ease (see Figure 12.4).

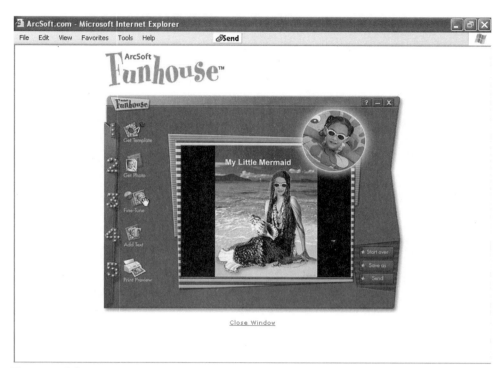

FIGURE 12.4 Funhouse makes it easy to print or email your final photo to friends.

✔ Here are the simple steps to create a Funhouse image:

1. Click on Get Template.

2. Click on a template, then on OK.

3. Click on Get Photo.

4. Click on a photo, then on OK. This will be the face that will appear in the template. If you'd rather use a photo of your own, click the Open button and browse for it on your hard drive.

5. Click on Fine Tune. The window in Figure 11.5 appears.

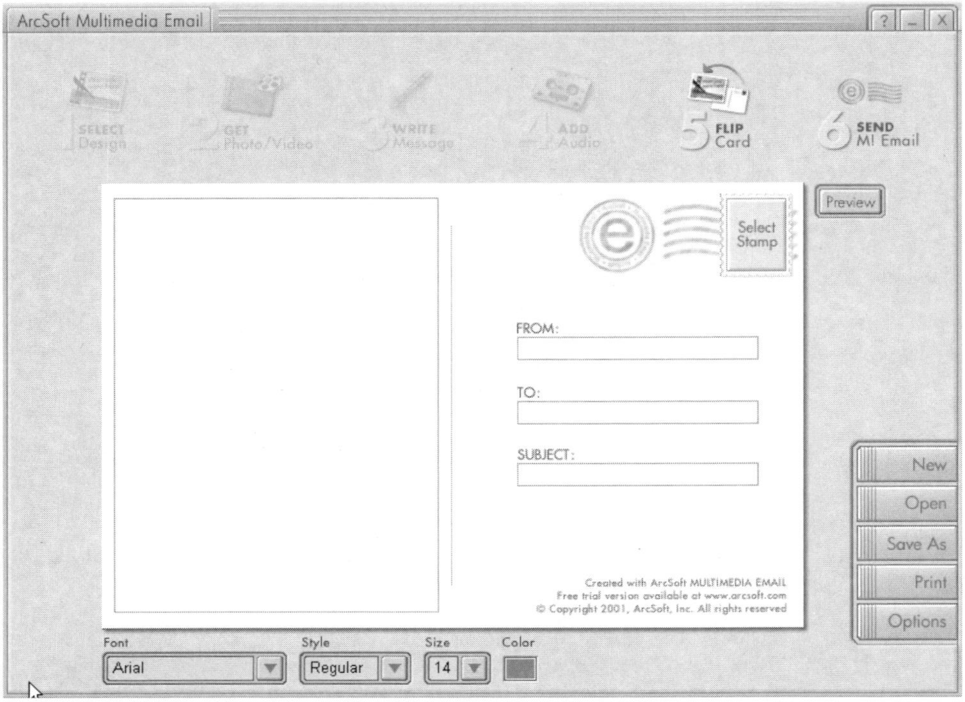

FIGURE 12.5 Here you can adjust size, location, rotation, and color attributes of the inserted image.

6. In the second set of images click the larger photo (the one on the left) to enlarge the inserted image until it fills the space. You can also use the top and bottom set of pictures to change the orientation of the image, or rotate it to the left or right.

7. Use the four directional arrows to move the image within the template.

8. Use the three sliders at the bottom of the dialog box to adjust color and brightness.

9. Click OK.

10. Click Add Text.

11. Enter text appropriate to the image you selected, then click OK

12. Click Print Preview to see how your graphic will look when printed, or Print to print a copy.

Exploring HP Image Zone

If you own an HP Pavilion you have an amazing digital imaging package built right in (see Figure 12.6). HP ImageZone provides features that allow you to organize, back up, edit, and share digital images, including photographs and videos. With Image Zone you can also use templates to create projects such as a collection of images about your vacation or a holiday and to save what you create to disc or share it via email or online with online albums.

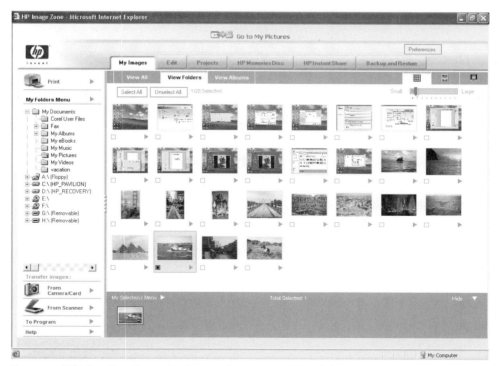

FIGURE 12.6   On these 6 tabs you have a wealth of digital imaging features.

tip You can even use the HP Instant Share feature to order professional quality prints of your images.

Other tools in Image Zone you can explore on your own allow you to create slide shows of images, sort your images by filename or date created, and search for images. You can even work with video clips.

Editing Images

Using HP Image Zone you can modify any image in a variety of ways. For example, you can remove red eye from pictures of people, crop photos to get rid of unneeded portions, rotate or resize an image, or modify the color or brightness to make the image crisper in appearance.

✔ **Follow these steps to practice some of the tools you can use to modify an image:**

1. Double-click the HP Image Zone icon on the Windows desktop. The main Image Zone screen, shown in Figure 12.6, appears.

2. Click on the photo you want to edit (several sample photos are included in you're My Pictures folder which you can use).

3. Click on the Edit tab,

4. Click on the Crop item in the list of tools on the left; the choices shown in Figure 12.7 appear.

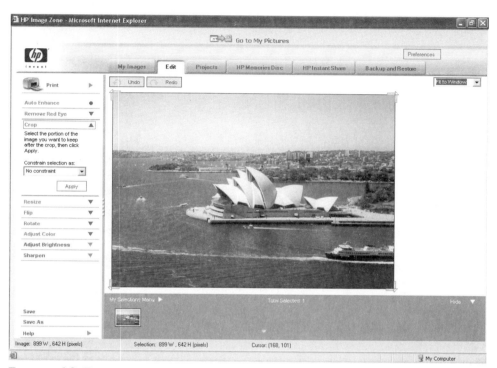

FIGURE 12.7 Clicking on any item in this list reveals additional controls for each tool.

5. Move your mouse over the image; the cursor will appear as two crossed lines.

6. Click and drag to select the portion of the image you want to keep.

7. If you're pleased with your cropping, click Apply in the Crop menu to complete the cropping.

8. Click the Resize tool. The choices in Figure 12.8 appear.

FIGURE 12.8 You can adjust the resolution or resize for common photo sizes with these tools.

9. Click the arrow on the Resize for item and select 4 x 6 in photo.

10. Click Apply. The image is resized.

11. Click the Adjust Color item (note that you may have to click the Resize item to close that area first).

12. Adjust the Hue or Saturation by clicking on each slider and moving it right or left. Note the effect this has on the image.

13. You can save the image to save any changes you have made to it by click the Save or Save As items and providing a file name.

 tip You can reset the image to its original color settings by clicking the Reset button before you save the image.

Using Project Templates

Projects are documents you create using your photos. HP Image Zone provides several project templates that get you started. For example you might choose a Birthday template that provides background including balloons and a gift artwork, as shown in Figure 12.9. When you select one of these project templates the selected photo or photos are added to it, with placeholders for text which you can use to add captions or comments.

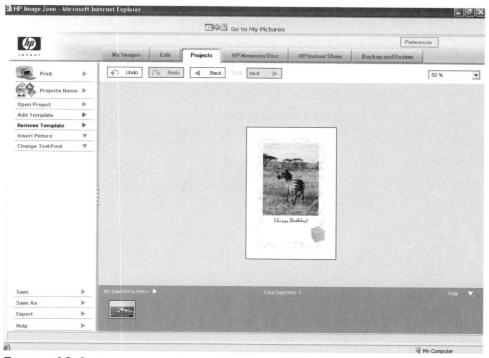

FIGURE 12.9   Project templates provide attractive designs you can place your photos in.

Project: **Create a Birthday Card**

You can use a project template to create an attractive birthday card or party invitation. First, find a photo you'd like to use in the card. It may be a photo of the person who is having a birthday, or a photo that would go along with a humorous caption you'd like to include. Then follow these steps to create a birthday card:

1. Open HP Image Zone, and select your photo on the My Images tab.

2. Click on the Projects tab.

3. Click on Cards, then on Index Card 4 x 6. The Select Theme choices shown in Figure 12.10 appear.

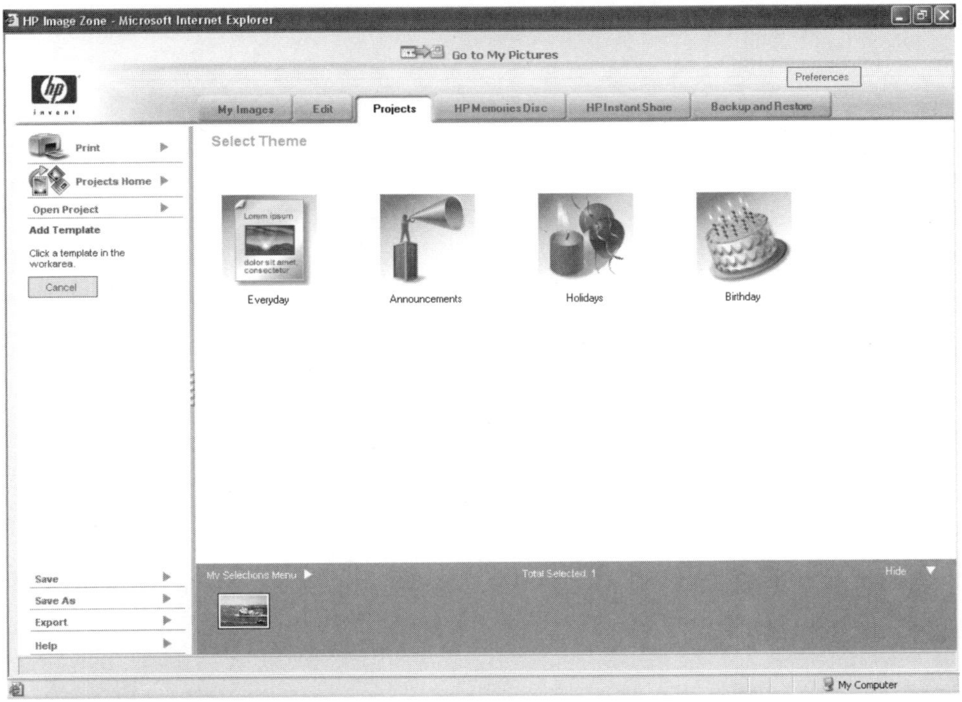

FIGURE 12.10 Here are four categories of projects offered here.

4. Click on the Birthday category. The templates shown in Figure 12.11 appear.

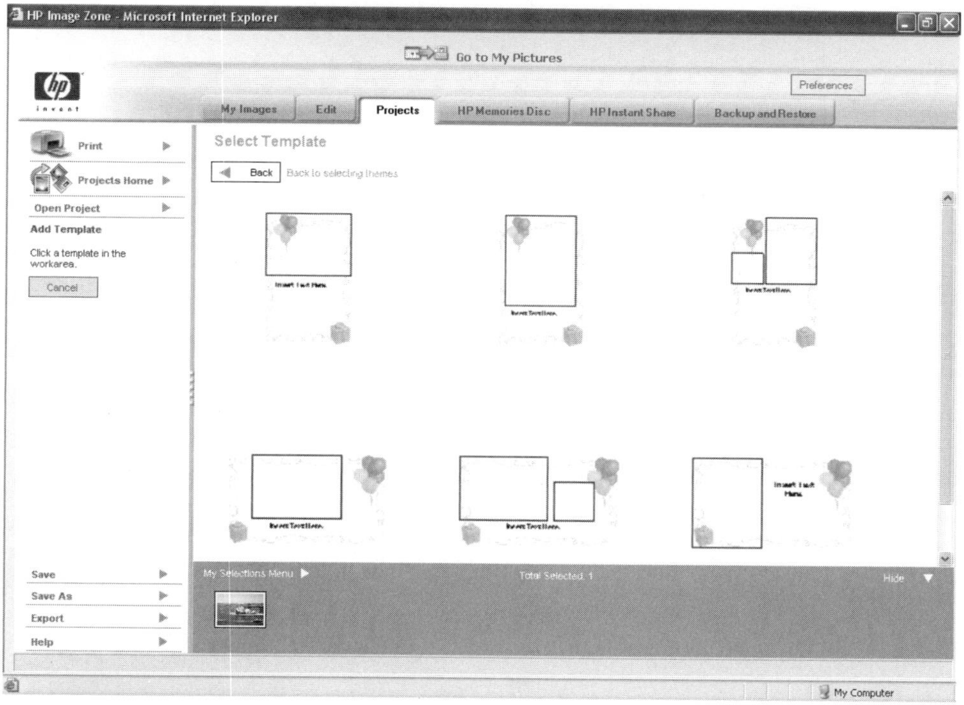

FIGURE 12.11 Templates with more than one box accommodate more than one image.

5. Click on any template you like. It appears with your selected photo in place and a text placeholder.

6. Double-click on the text placeholder; it opens for editing and the Text/Font tools become available as shown in Figure 12.12.

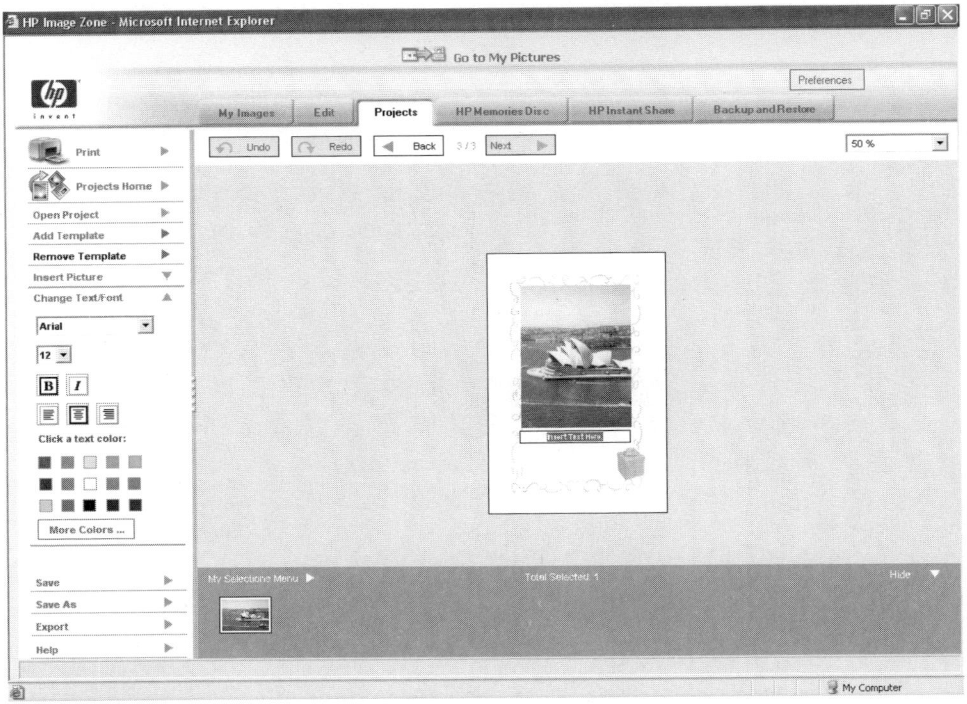

FIGURE 12.12 Text/Font formatting tools appear automatically whenever you select text for editing by double-clicking it.

7. Type this caption: "Happy Birthday!"

8. Use the font drop down list on the left to change the font to BernhardFashion BT.

9. Select a dark green color for the text by clicking on a color block in the Click a text color area.

10. Save the project by clicking on the Save item, entering a name, and clicking Save.

 note To open text for editing at any time and display the Text/Font tools, just double-click the text again.

Sharing Images

HP knows that while you can spend hours having fun with modifying images or placing them in documents, sharing images is the whole point. For that reason they've provided several tools to help you do that.

First, HP Image Zone offers ways to save images or video files or a combination to a CD with the HP Memories Disc Creator. This feature allows you to save images in an album which creates a slide show. You can add a title or description, add music files, build a slide show, and write the album to a CD or DVD disc.

HP Instant Share includes features to insert images in e-mails, post online albums, or order professional quality prints of still images online.

✔ **To creat a disc using HP Memories Disc Creator, follow these steps:**

1. Place a CD in your writeable CD/DVD drive.

2. From the HP Image Zone main screen, click on the HP Memories Disc tab. The dialog box shown in Figure 12.13 appears.

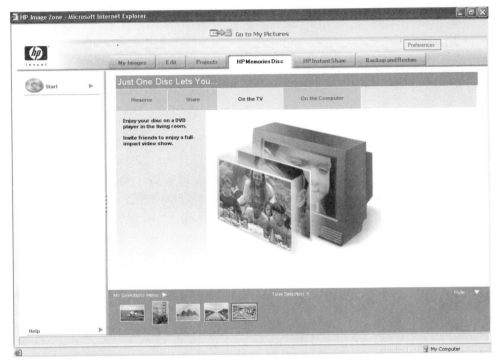

FIGURE 12.13 Any images you had selected will appear here.

3. Click under each picture and type a caption, if you like.

   tip If you want to add images to the album at this point click the Add button and locate other files to include. To remove an image click on it, then on the Remove button.

4. Click on Next.

5. In the dialog box shown in Figure 12.14, enter a title for your image slide show (which will also be printed on the CD label and jewel case insert).

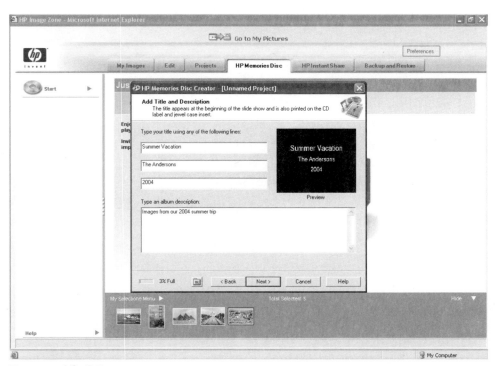

FIGURE 12.14 Help those viewing your images to appreciate what they're looking at by adding descriptive text here.

6. Click on Next. The Add Music Files dialog box appears.

7. Locate an audio file from a CD using the Select music from an audio CD drop down list.

8. Click Add to add music to your slide show. (You can add more than one piece of music to your show.) You can also select songs that are provided by Image Zone by clicking the Sample Songs tab, or locate audio files on your computer with the Computer tab.

9. Click Next. The Preview Slide Show dialog box shown in Figure 12.15 appears. Use the Play and Stop buttons to play the slide show.

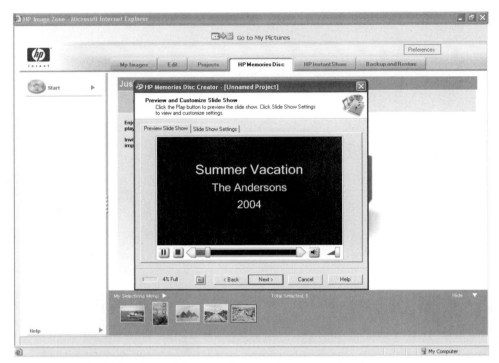

FIGURE 12.15 Play your slide show here before saving it.

10. Click on the Slide Show Settings tab and make any settings you like for how the slide show plays, including how long to display each image, whether to fit the slide show timing to the music, and whether to use audio annotations and print captions.

11. Click Next. A summary of your project and CD writer settings appears as shown in Figure 12.16.

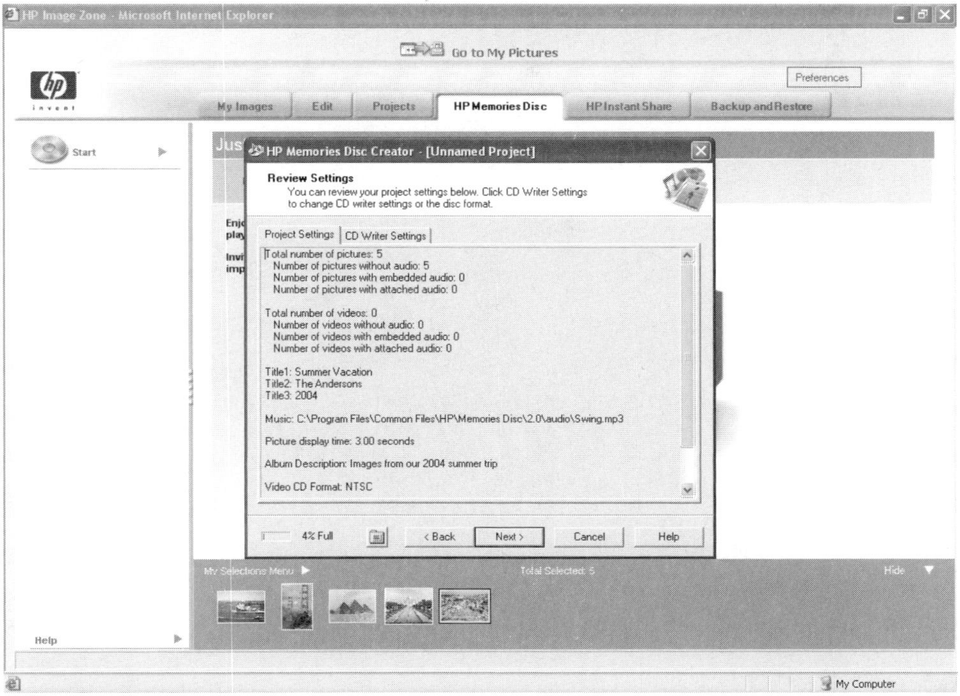

FIGURE 12.16 Review your settings; if you want to make changes click the Back button to go to the appropriate dialog box.

12. Use the CD Writer Settings tab to change the recording speed or destination drive.

13. Click Next. When the Make a Memories Disc screen appears, click the Make Disc button to write to your disc.

note You can play back a Memories Disc on either a computer or DVD player as long as it supports Video CD format (VCD).

Chapter Summary

In this chapter you learned about using software included with your Pavilion to work with photo images. ArcSoft Funhouse and Greeting

Card Creator are fun and easy to use graphics programs, while HP Image Zone, installed on all recent model Pavilions, provides a simple, complete solution for working with digital images.

Connecting to the Internet

chapter

13

Get Online Today!

In this Chapter

✔ How the Internet works

✔ What you need to get connected

✔ Signing up for an Internet account

✔ Choosing a browser

For many people, it's hard to imagine life without the Internet. It's a wonderful research tool for students and professionals, and it's a fast and easy way to communicate with people around the world. You can find the nearest location of a retail store, read restaurant reviews, build the ideal price and feature set for your car before you go to the dealer, and buy almost anything. You can chat with people from Calcutta to Rio who have common interests and interesting stories to tell. In short, if you're not online now, you should be. This chapter tells you how.

What You Need to Get Online

Getting connected to the Internet is a pretty easy process after you know what you need in the way of hardware and what service you want to use to get online. For a Compaq Presario or an HP Pavilion user, most of that is taken care of. You have an internal modem built in, you have installation files for several major Internet service providers, and you have a wizard to take you through the process step by step. About the only thing you need to supply is a credit card.

What's an Internet Service Provider (ISP)?

ISPs are companies, such as America Online (AOL) or Earthlink, that maintain servers (computers) that you use to access the Internet and to exchange email with others using the Internet. You usually pay a monthly fee for unlimited access to these services.

Most ISPs offer an email account and a Web site with informational services such as weather reports or news, as well as links to other sites. You can use your ISP site as your home page (the page that appears when you first log on to the Internet), or you can set another page as your home page (see Chapter 14 for more about setting your home page).

All About Modems

If you've recently purchased your computer, you'll be glad to hear it comes with an internal modem built right in (probably a 56 kilobits per second [kbps] modem or faster). A modem is the hardware that allows your computer to connect to an Internet server using a standard phone line to transmit data. If you want to connect by a standard phone line, you've got everything you need already set up when you unpack your computer.

tip Although most people are able to get online with their computer with no problem, modems are one of the most common problems encountered by people contacting HP Technical Support. To make sure your experience with your modem is smooth, check Chapter 2 for information about setting up your computer, Chapter 17 for information about updating drivers, and Chapter 19 for more about getting Help from HP.

note You can also get a cable modem, which enables your computer to transmit data across a cable television line. If you want to use a cable connection, you'll have to contact your local phone, cable television company, or ISP to sign up for their service and to purchase a cable modem.

Phone Lines and High-Speed Access

There are several options for connecting to the Internet today, from your regular phone line to high-speed phone and cable connections, and even completely wireless connections using a laptop or handheld computer. Speed is the name of the game here because connecting to the Internet at slower speeds can be a very frustrating experience. With a slow connection, files take forever to download, and you could go make a sandwich while waiting for a Web page with graphics to appear.

In the world of high-speed Internet access, here are some of the technologies and terms you'll encounter:

- *Broadband* refers to any connection that allows data to be transmitted at higher speeds than a standard phone connection (sometimes called narrowband).
- *Cable* access transmits data using a cable modem and uses the same type of cable across which you get your cable television signal. A cable connection means you don't tie up a phone line when you're on the Internet, and you don't have to log on to get online. Turn your computer on, and you're there.

- The *Digital Subscriber Line (DSL)* has several variations, such as Asynchronous Digital Subscriber Line (ADSL), and probably others by the time you read this book. Both DSL and cable modems use broadband technology, which means they can handle a lot of data faster than a standard phone line. However, DSL works using a telephone line, and cable modems run across cable. DSL is generally faster than cable, but it may or may not be available in your area. Check with your phone company or ISP to find out.

- *Integrated Services Digital Network (ISDN)* is a technology that provides data and voice transmission across the same line. The technology is most often sold to businesses that integrate network features with it or that connect to telecommuting employees in their home offices. However, you might use ISDN if you're interested in setting up a home network. Your house must be wired to use ISDN lines.

What Will It Cost You?

Connecting to the Internet through your standard phone line will cost you a monthly fee to an ISP, averaging around $20. You'll use a local access phone number to log on, so you shouldn't incur any toll call charges.

caution **If you have limited local message units on your present calling plan, you may incur additional costs on your phone bill. If you're going to use the Internet at all, it's worth upgrading to unlimited local calls.**

If you want high-speed phone or cable access, you'll have to pay for service installation and will probably pay a higher monthly fee to your phone or cable company. What kind of service you need and what you want to pay for it should relate to how often you use the Internet. If you're a casual user and not a home business owner, you can probably tap into the cheaper alternative of a simple phone-line connection.

Signing Up

The first step to getting online is to select an ISP. Hundreds of them are out there. Some, such as AOL and MSN, are online services with special member benefits, shopping malls, and research tools. Others, such as Earthlink and Leapfrog, focus on Internet access, Web hosting, and support. Your phone company and cable TV company probably offer Internet access as well.

Both Presarios and Pavilions offer an online item on the Windows Program menu (Start, All Programs). Here you can select a service such as AOL, Compuserve, or MSN, and a wizard will walk you through the set-up for the ISP you select.

If you own a Pavilion, HP has made it easy for those who don't care to go hunting for an ISP by building in an Easy Internet Sign-Up wizard (see Figure 13.1) and by providing what you'll need to connect to several of the major Internet service providers. (Note that Presarios don't currently offer this sign-up feature.)

tip **If you'd rather find an ISP on your own, visit *thelist.internet.com* to see listings of hundreds of ISP providers across the United States and Canada to compare their offerings.**

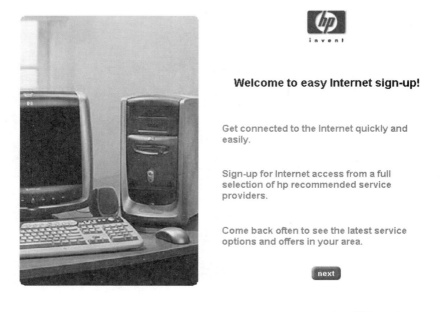

FIGURE 13.1   This easy-to-follow process gets you online quickly.

Project: **Getting Online with HP's Easy Internet Sign-Up**

If your family doesn't have an online account yet, it's time to get one. First, go the library or a friend's house and use their connection to visit the Web sites for AOL, CompuServe, MSN, and Earthlink, four of the services offered by the HP Internet Sign-up. (Tip: use a search engine to locate each service's publicly accessible Web page, or enter the addresses as *aol.com*, *msn.com*, and so forth.) Make a list of the features you like about each and then vote on which service you'd like to use. Consider price, ease of use, interface (what the Web site looks like), and features offered to members.

✔ **Then, use the Easy Internet Sign-Up feature to set up your account on your new computer:**

1. Make sure your computer is connected to a phone line.

2. Select Start, All Programs, Easy Internet Sign-Up. A Welcome screen appears.

3. Click Next, and the startup screen in Figure 13.2 appears.

 easy Internet sign-up

To download the latest service options and offers for your area, please complete the information below, and press the connect button:

Country   [USA ▾]

Zip/Postal Code   [98368]

*Telephone   area code   prefix
([360]) – [555] – [XXXX]

Purchase   where latest hp product purchased.
Location   [Circuit City ▾]

Press connect when done.

*Enter your area code and the first 3 digits of your phone number.

All information remains strictly private. All fields are required.

[privacy] [clear form] [skip form] [connect] [exit]

FIGURE 13.2 Start working with the wizard by entering details about your location.

4. Enter your phone number and zip code.

5. Click Connect. The wizard searches for and downloads service options and offers for your area The Sign-Up Options window appears (see Figure 13.3).

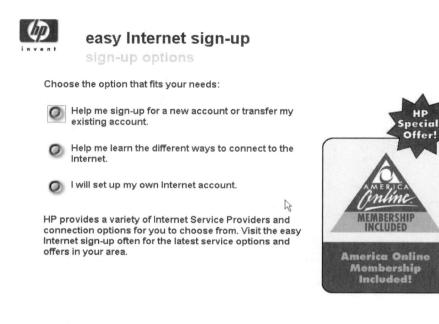

FIGURE 13.3   If you want more information about how to connect to the Internet, you can click the second option.

6. Click Help me sign up for a new account or transfer my existing account. The Select Service window shown in Figure 13.4 appears.

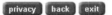

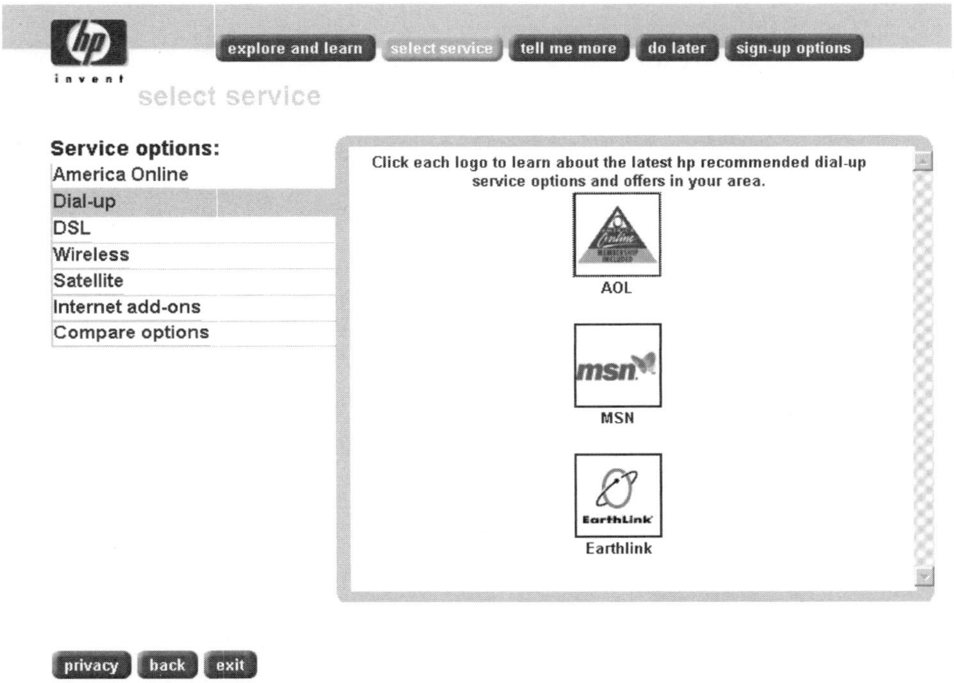
explore and learn
select service
tell me more
do later
sign-up options
invent
select service
Service options:
America Online
Dial-up
DSL
Wireless
Satellite
Internet add-ons
Compare options
Click each logo to learn about the latest hp recommended dial-up service options and offers in your area.
AOL
msn
MSN
EarthLink
Earthlink
privacy
back
exit

FIGURE 13.4 What's offered here depends on service and options available in your location.

7. Assuming you're using a standard phone line, click Dial-Up. (If you're using a DSL connection, click DSL). Providers such as AOL, MSN, Earthlink, GoAmerica, or DirectTV will be shown, depending on what's available where you live.

8. Click a logo to find out what the terms and cost of each plan are.

9. If you are ready to order one, click Setup on the plan terms window.

Depending on which plan you choose, you will be taken through a series of windows to run the installation procedure for that service's software and then to sign on and provide payment information (a credit card and billing address). During this process, you will have to select an email account name.

note **An email account name is important because it should be easy for you and others to remember. However, it's not always easy to get the name you want. Your own name (depending on how unique it is) is probably taken by somebody else. Your first name and last initial are also probably in use. Names like BestMom or SmartCookie are likely to have been used before. My advice is try to get your favorite name, but, just in case, have some backup names in mind or be willing to add a number or two to your name to make it unique.**

After you've finished the installation, you can log on by selecting Start, All Programs. Click the ISP's name in the list of programs, and, when the software opens (for example AOL's opening screen shown in Figure 13.5), enter your user name and password. Click Connect, and you'll be connected in moments.

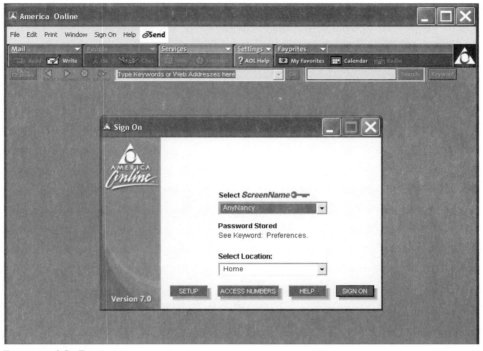

FIGURE 13.5 AOL's opening window asks you to enter your name, password, and then click the Sign On button.

tip Most ISPs allow you to save your password so that you don't have to enter it each time you log on (which is the case for the account shown in Figure 13.5). This can save time, but be aware that anybody who can get to your computer can log on to your ISP and access your email.

What Providers Are Already on Your Computer?

If you already have an account with AOL, CompuServe, Earthlink, or MSN, you'll be glad to hear that the files for installing those applications are already on your computer.

✔ Here's all you have to do to install them:

1. Select Start, All Programs, Online Services.

2. Click the ISP with whom you have an account. The installation program runs.

3. Click any confirmation windows that come up to proceed.

After it is installed, the software for the service should be available on your Start, All Programs menu. When you run that software for the first time, you will probably be asked to log on to retrieve local phone access numbers (see Figure 13.6). After you've selected a local number to dial in on, you're all set.

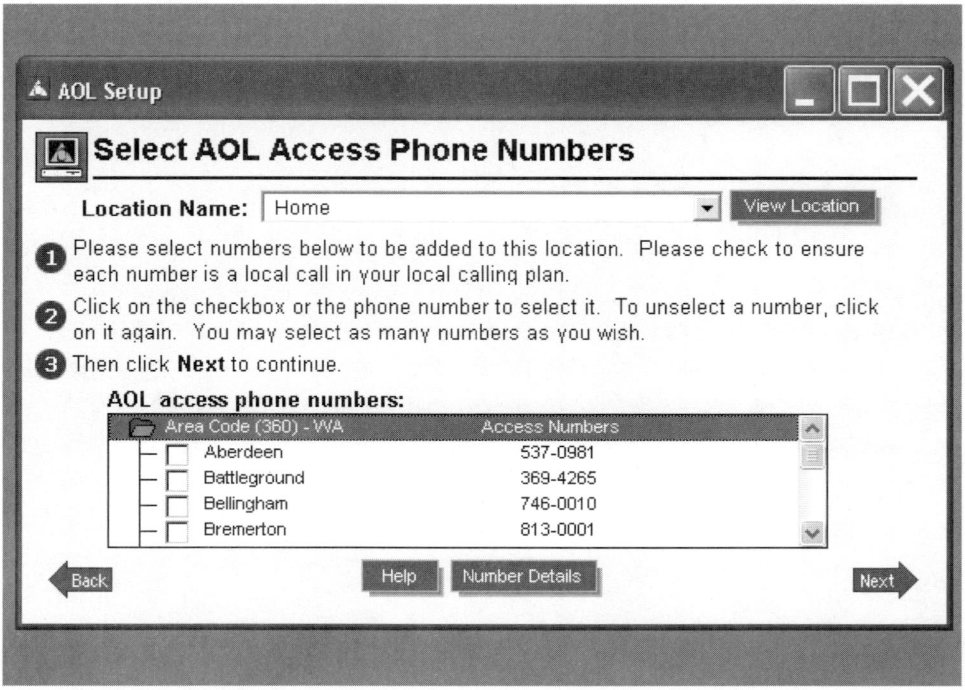

FIGURE 13.6 Your service will suggest several phone numbers in your area to use for dial-up.

tip It's recommended that you set up a couple of access numbers. If there's a problem with one or it's busy, the other number is used as an option automatically. Try to pick two that fall within your area code that are not toll calls, if available. Also note that some access numbers only allow slower modem access speeds.

Choosing a Browser

Browsers are software programs that enable you to move around the documents on the Internet and keep a record of your browsing activity and favorite sites.

Internet Explorer from Microsoft comes preinstalled with Windows XP on your computer (see Chapter 14 for how to get around using a browser). There are other browsers, including Netscape Navigator installed on many Presarios and the browser functionality that probably comes with your Internet service.

Browsers all offer similar features, but with a slightly different look and feel, so try out your ISP's browser and Internet Explorer to see if either of those will fit the bill. You will have to be logged onto the Internet through your service provider first; then, when you open your browser, it will go through your connection to access the Internet.

note See Chapter 15 for more about using a browser.

Chapter Summary

In this chapter, you were introduced to the Internet and what you need to get connected to it. You walked through HP's Easy Internet Sign-Up process and considered the options available in browsing software.

chapter
14
Security and You

In this Chapter

✔ Setting passwords

✔ Making security settings in your browser

✔ Protecting yourself against viruses

✔ Keeping kids safe online

✔ Avoiding spams and scams

The Internet can be a wonderful place, but, when you set foot online, you are opening yourself and your computer up to millions of people. Some of these people are nice, and some are...well...not so nice. Some transmit viruses, commit credit card fraud, pelt you with junk mail, or sell your name and contact information to other people who may or may not be nice themselves. There are abuses of your privacy and several sites out there that you would probably prefer your kids not see.

The good news is that there are protections built into Windows and your browser software that you can use to keep safe. You can also use Norton Antivirus (you get a free limited subscription to this software with your computer purchase) to stop damaging viruses from doing your computer any harm.

Passwords

The system that has been developed to identify people as they roam around the faceless Internet is password based. When you create an account with an online retailer, you pick a user name and password. If you sign up to use a research site, there's another password to enter. You can even use a password to protect your computer when you're away, ensuring that nobody can access the information stored there if they should happen to have physical access to your machine.

How you come up with passwords and make settings for using them can make them useful, or, if you do it wrong, not so useful.

A note about encryption, digital certificates, and signatures

Today many sites are going beyond simple passwords, which are a somewhat flimsy form of security because they depend on the human element to protect them. Digital certificates are used to authenticate software that you download and ensure that the source is reputable. Digital signatures can be used in sending messages from one place to another on the Internet. A digital signature consists of two keys: one that encrypts (or codes) the message before sending and one that decrypts (or decodes) it on the other end. Because only the recipient has the decrypting code, this should ensure some level of security for the message. Visit the PC Security and Performance area at *www.myhpclub.com* for more about keeping your computer and information safe.

Choosing Passwords Wisely

Most people know that you should avoid using passwords that would be easily guessed, for example, your last name, your street address, or your birthdate. If you choose such a password and your wallet is lost, all a clever computer hacker would have to do is run through a few bits of personal information until he discovered the right password.

Therefore, what makes a good password? Pick a password that is:

- The most random one you can think of (words you can look up in the dictionary are not good choices)
- One that uses a combination of letters and numbers
- Changed periodically
- Not used for every account and site you sign up for

A good password would be 56UN880PW5. However, that would be really hard to remember, and, if you had a unique password for every account and Web site similar to this hodgepodge of numbers and letters, you'd need to carry a book around to remember them all. So what's the solution? Try to find a middle ground between the completely obvious personal word or name and random gibberish that's impossible to remember. Simply adding a number to the beginning and end of a word can make the password more secure, for example.

Most important of all, never give your passwords to anybody else or leave a record of them lying around near your computer.

caution **Nobody from any Web site or Web store has any business asking you for your password to their site, so, if they do, don't give it to them. Immediately email the company about the incident. It's very easy for people to assume the role of somebody else online, even pretending to be an employee of a company with which you regularly do business.**

Setting Passwords

You can set passwords to online stores and other sites by simply following the registration process on each site. Some sites have strict requirements for passwords, for example, that they have at least six characters and use a combination of numbers and letters. Most require at least four characters. When you enter your password, you'll be asked to confirm it. That's in case you've introduced a typo when you first typed it.

 tip **If you forget your password, most sites have a feature that allows you to enter your email address, and they will email you your password.**

✔ **To set a password for Windows XP to protect your Pavilion from being accessed by others, follow these steps:**

1. Select Start, Control Panel. The Control Panel appears.

2. Click User Accounts. The User Accounts dialog box opens.

3. Click Change an Account.

4. Click the account you want to change (probably Owner if you haven't set up other accounts).

5. Click Create a Password. The dialog box shown in Figure 14.1 appears.

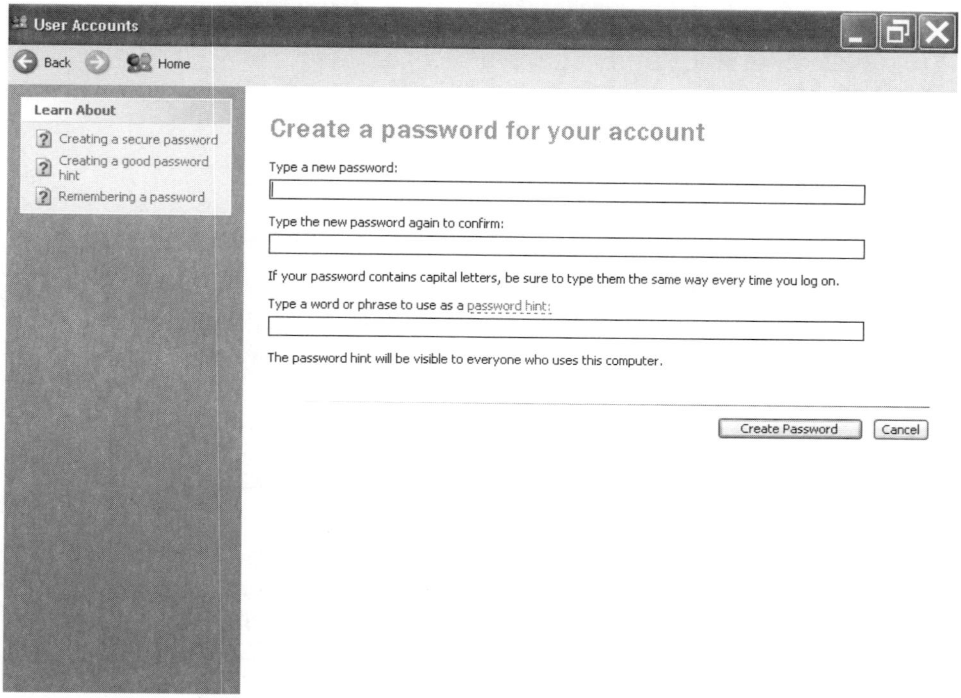

FIGURE 14.1 The password you enter is case sensitive, meaning that capital and lowercase letters must be entered the same way each time.

6. Enter your new password in the Type a New Password box.

7. Press tab.

8. Enter the password again in the second box.

9. If you like, you can enter a password hint. If you forget your password, you can use this hint to remember it.

10. Click Create Password and close the User Accounts dialog box.

caution People can log on to your computer as a guest. Don't leave the Guest account unprotected if you're really concerned about security. Be sure to set a password for it as well.

Cookies, Hold the Milk

Cookies may be good with milk, but computer cookies are not always so good for your privacy. A cookie in computer terms is a small bit of data that's sent to your computer whenever you visit a Web site. Cookies are used to identify you. For example, if you log onto a site such as *Amazon.com* and you're greeted with a cheery, "Hi, Joe! Here are our recommendations for you," that's made possible because your computer has provided data about you to that site. This can be very convenient because it can save you from having to reenter information about yourself, such as your billing address, each time you visit a site or place an order. However, it also means that information about you is being pulled from your hard drive whenever you're online.

note The term "cookie" comes from the original name for this feature, fortune cookie. This name was a result of a program for UNIX computers that sent out a unique message every time it ran, just as you get a unique message every time you open a fortune cookie.

You can set up how cookies are handled in your browser. With most browsers, if you have set your browser for high security, cookies are not allowed to be stored on your computer. That's more private, but it means you may not be allowed to use features of some sites, such as being able to download software. Most people are okay with a medium security setting

In Internet Explorer 6.0, which is probably the version on your Presario or Pavilion, you can actually control cookie settings separately from your security setting, which means you can keep your security levels strong and still allow cookies so you can access site features.

✔ **Follow these steps to set your security level and make settings for cookies:**

1. Open Internet Explorer.

2. Select Tools, Internet Options.

3. Click the Privacy tab (see Figure 14.2).

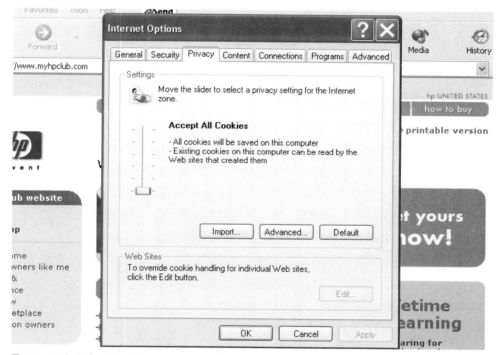

FIGURE 14.2 The Privacy tab is devoted to cookies.

4. Click the slider bar and move it up to higher levels of security (which allow less and less cookies to be saved to your computer).

5. Click Apply when you find a setting description you feel comfortable with.

6. Click the Security tab and then the Custom Level button (see Figure 14.3).

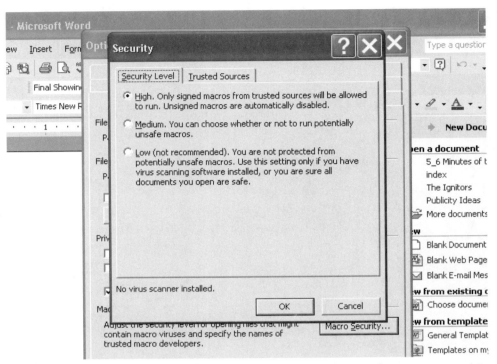

FIGURE 14.3 You can modify individual settings, but the simplest way to use this is to set a level of security you feel comfortable about.

7. Click the arrow on the Reset to field and select a setting from the drop-down list that appears.

8. Click Reset. A message appears confirming that you want to change security settings.

9. Click OK twice to close all dialog boxes.

tip **If you want higher security, you can keep a higher setting for security and cookies. If you come across a site that requires that you accept cookies to perform a certain function, change the setting. When you're done, just be sure to change the setting back to higher security.**

Avoiding Viruses Like the Plague

Computer viruses are the snake in the computing garden of Eden. Why people create them is beyond the understanding of most of us, but they do. A virus can play havoc with your computer's performance, making software crash or weird messages appear. The bottom line is that you don't want to catch this kind of virus.

How Viruses Work

Viruses are little programs called *executable* files that are set to run on your computer and perform some activity. Computer viruses can do a number of things. They can destroy data on your computer hard drive. They can generate an email to everybody in your Address Book and send the virus to their computer to do similar damage. Some initiate immediately when you open the file, and others are set to run on a particular date or when you perform some specific action.

You can do a couple of things to avoid viruses. First, don't open attachments to email messages from people you don't know or if you consider it odd that a particular person you do know sent you this attachment. Second, you can adjust the macro security level of many software programs on your computer, such as Word for Windows (see Figure 14.4). Macros are often the carriers of viruses. Finally, you can run an antivirus software on a regular basis.

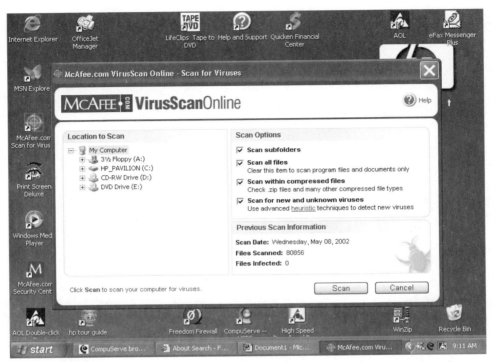

FIGURE 14.4 Most software programs in which you open documents can be set to warn you if a macro is attached to a document you're trying to open.

Using Norton Antivirus

Norton Antivirus (see Figure 14.5) is one of the most popular antivirus software products. Your Presario or Pavilion comes with a limited-time subscription to Norton. When you run the program for the first time (Start, All Programs, Norton Antivirus, Norton Antivirus 2003), you are asked to enroll in a subscription and register the software. When you install antivirus software, the latest virus definitions are downloaded; simply run a full system Scan from the dialog box in Figure 14.5 to check your computer for viruses.

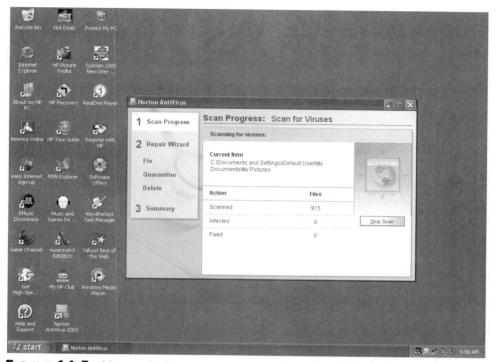

FIGURE 14.5 Norton lets you scan a floppy, CD/DVD drive, or hard drive.

However, because new viruses come out all the time, you must update your definitions on a regular basis. After you've subscribed to Norton, you'll get regular prompts to update whenever new definitions become available.

Protecting Your Kids Online

One of the wonders of the Internet is the sheer amount of information, software, and graphics that are available. You can research, exchange information, read articles, get pictures, chat with others in real time, and more. However, one of the dangers of the Internet is the type of information you can encounter. Although some organizations offer approval ratings to some sites and refuse approval to others, nobody is out there policing the Internet and removing objectionable content. That's because nobody has legislated a right to censor the content of the Internet. As parents, it's up to you to proactively control what your children can and can't access online.

You can do a few things to help keep your kids safe, and the first thing is to educate them. Rules that you lay down offline, such as not talking to strangers, should pertain online as well. Kids should not respond to email or instant messages from people they don't know. If they see something offensive or somebody continues to attempt to contact them, encourage them to report it to you right away.

 tip You can use the history listing on your browser to review the sites that have been visited in the past several weeks to monitor where your kids are going online.

Another thing you can do is to look for rating systems that approve the type of content you want your kids to see and then only allow them to visit sites that display that approval symbol. Finally, you can use your browser settings or third-party software to create lists of approved sites.

Project: Creating a Family Online Safety Pact

Every family is different, with kids of different ages and interests. Sit down with your family and create a Family Online Safety Pact. Agree on what types of sites the family wants to avoid and make sure everybody understands why certain sites can be dangerous or disturbing.

✔ **Then, set up Internet Explorer Content Advisor for your family, following these steps:**

1. Select Tools, Internet Options and then click the Content tab.

2. Click Settings for the Content Advisor and be sure the Ratings tab is displayed. The dialog box shown in Figure 14.6 appears.

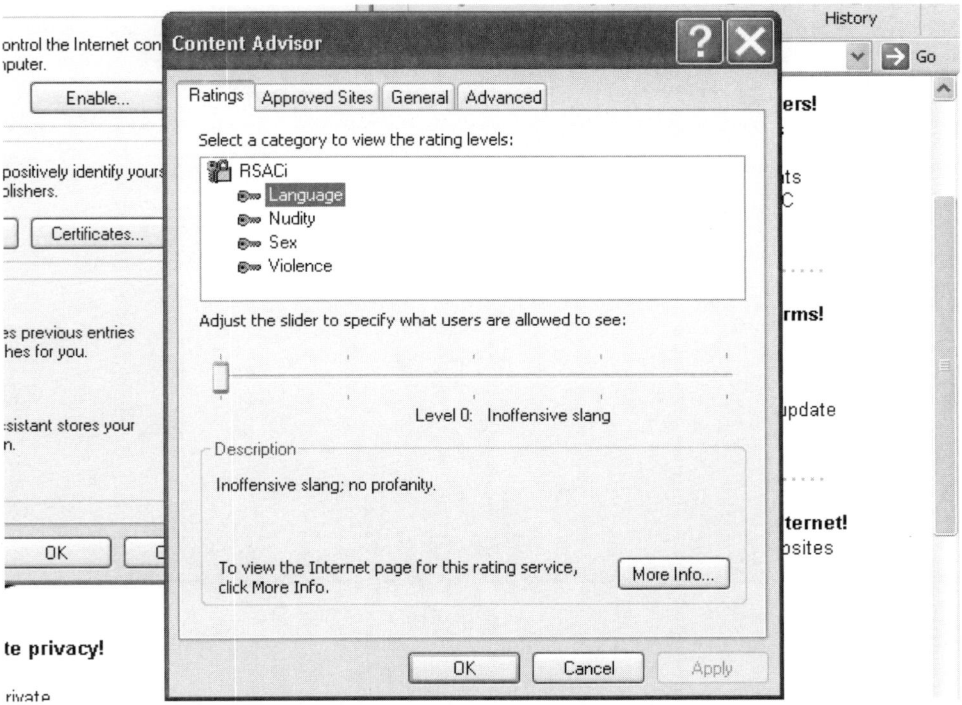

FIGURE 14.6 Although different things offend different people, one of the settings here is probably a match for your standards.

3. Click a category such as Language or Violence and then adjust the slider bar to a setting that you prefer. The further to the right you move means the more explicit the content that is allowed.

4. Click Apply.

5. Click the Approved Sites tab to create a list of sites you approve or disapprove of (see Figure 14.7).

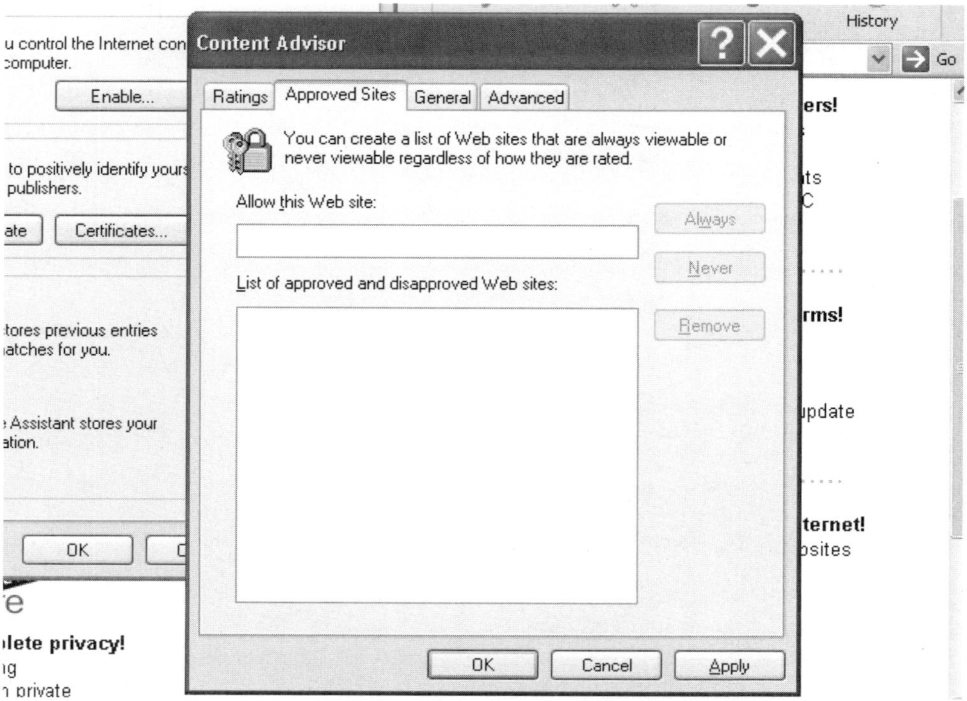

FIGURE 14.7 If there are sites you never want your kids to see, add them to the list of not viewable sites here.

6. Enter the address of a Web site in the Allow this Web site box.

7. Click Always to allow it to be viewed or Never to never allow it to be viewed.

8. Click Apply.

9. Click OK twice to close the Content Advisor and then the Internet Options dialog box.

note If you want to specify that a rating system from some organization must be present to view sites, you can use the General tab of the Content Advisor.

Steering Clear of Spams and Scams

Another assault on your privacy and security comes from the realm of email. One form of abuse of your privacy is spamming. This is when a company or individual sends you frequent emails promoting a product, site, or service when you haven't requested such email. Some of this email can be offensive in nature.

The other worry about email is that you'll get an offer for something—a free gift or lucrative career opportunity, for example—that is really just a come-on from a shady business or individual. The variations on how these people trick you, from getting you to give them your credit card number, which they then use for their own purposes, to selling you something that is not as they represented it, are many.

Avoiding Spam

Spam can proliferate and fill up your email inbox faster than weeds in spring. Your time is too valuable to waste deleting these, let alone worrying that the messages might introduce viruses to your computer.

Use these methods to avoid spam:

- When you register for anything on a Web site, from simple access to the site to membership to a retail account, look for any option that allows that site to share your information with others. Often, the selection to allow sharing is the default, and you have to uncheck that option.
- If you get mail you didn't ask for, DON'T send a reply asking to be taken off their list unless you know that it's a very reputable business. Most disreputable spammers use your reply as confirmation that your email account is indeed active, and they spam you even more.
- If you're being harassed repeatedly, you might try reporting the sender to an organization such as *bbbonline.org*, an online better business bureau.

tip　Many email programs, such as Outlook Express, allow you set up rules on what kinds of email you accept. For example, you can set up a rule that email from a particular sender should always be moved directly to your Deleted folder.

Staying Out of Trouble Online

Avoiding online con artists can be tricky because their methods and approaches are so various. Some good rules of thumb, however, would be these:

- Don't buy anything from anybody you don't know. Stick with companies you trust and that you know are likely to be around tomorrow to deal with if you have some problem with their service or product.
- If somebody's trying to sell you something online, they should have a business Web site you can visit. When you do, review their policies relative to returns, guarantees, and customer privacy. Look for seals of approval from organizations such as *bbbonline.org*.
- Never give out your passwords, credit card numbers, or contact information to anybody you don't know.
- Don't believe anybody who tells you you'll get rich quick, get something for nothing, or look 10 years younger. It doesn't happen, and it's a red flag that you're dealing with a less-than-reputable person.
- If somebody tells you someone you know provided your contact information, confirm with your friend that that's so before dealing with anyone online.

If you follow some common sense rules of conduct online, the Internet can be a safe and fun place to be.

Chapter Summary

In this chapter, you've seen ways to protect your privacy and security when you go online. You've learned about how to use passwords and how to avoid viruses. You've discovered some browser settings that keep you safe from objectionable material and that help you control how cookies can be stored on your computer. Finally, you got some advice about keeping safe online and protecting your privacy by minimizing spam.

15

Exploring the Internet

In this Chapter

The Internet, which began in the 1960s as a way for government and academic researchers to share information among themselves, has today become a venue for shopping, learning, investing, playing games, listening to music, getting the news, and communicating with others.

247

In this chapter, you get to explore the Internet and the World Wide Web. The Internet is a large collection of networks of computers, while the Web is a set of documents stored on those networks in the form of Web sites and Web pages.

note **People use terms like riding the Internet highway and surfing the Web somewhat interchangeably. For the most part, most of what you'll see online consists of Web documents stored on the Internet.**

Using the Internet Explorer Browser

Internet Explorer is a browser program from Microsoft that is included on your computer as part of Windows XP. A browser is a program used to navigate around the Internet, taking you to various Internet addresses called Uniform Resource Locators (URLs) or following hyperlinks you click with your mouse to go from one Web document to another.

Browsers also have features that allow you to go quickly to sites you visit often, to review the history of sites you've visited recently, and to help to ensure your online privacy. In this chapter, you'll use Internet Explorer to browse the Internet. If you end up using a different browser, for example, one provided by your ISP, you'll find that most browsers offer features similar to the ones you'll see here.

note **Presarios also include the Netscape Navigator browser. Navigator offers many features similar to those in Internet Explorer.**

Getting Places

One of the main functions of a browser is to get you from here to there on the Internet. It allows you to do that in several different ways. Take a look at Internet Explorer in Figure 15.1 and note the following features:

- The address line allows you to enter an Internet address, such as *www.myhpclub.com*; you then press <Enter> or click Go to go to that site.
- The Favorites feature lets you save favorite sites and return to them anytime by picking them from the Favorites list.
- The History button displays a list of sites you've visited during the past several weeks.
- The Search button opens a Search window where you can enter keywords and search for sites.

FIGURE 15.1 This simple set of tools makes browsing the Internet easy.

You'll also see hyperlinks on many Web pages; these provide another method of navigation. A hyperlink is a feature of a programming language called Hypertext Markup Language (HTML), which is used to design Web pages. Text coded as a hyperlink is usually a different color from regular text on a Web page. When you click a hyperlink (also referred to as "following a link"), your browser takes you to the linked Web document. This document might be on the same Web site or might be on another Web site entirely.

✔ **To go to a specific Web address, follow these steps:**

1. Click in the Address box of the browser; this highlights the address of the currently displayed site.

2. Type the address you want to go to, for example, *www.amazon.com*.

3. Click Go to the right of the Address box or press <Enter>.

   It may take a few moments, but the page should display shortly.

 tip In many cases, you don't have to type a full URL (which normally takes the form *http://www.myhpclub.com*). You can simply type the site name and .com and press <Enter>. If the site name isn't recognized, a search feature opens in Internet Explorer to help you find the site.

caution You may have difficulty going to some addresses. In that case, a message displays that the site is unavailable. This could mean that the Web site no longer exists, the URL for it has changed, or the Web server that it runs on is busy. You may also have typed the address incorrectly. If you get this message, enter the address again to be sure you have it right or try again later.

Navigating Around

Browsing is mostly about moving from one Web page to another. You can do that by entering URL addresses as you did in the previous section, or you can use the Back and Forward buttons on your browser to move backward or forward through pages you've recently viewed, one page at a time.

Here's how this works. If you open *MyHPClub.com*, then go to *Amazon.com*, and then you move on to *Microsoft.com*, clicking Back moves you back to *Amazon.com*; then clicking Forward moves you forward to *Microsoft.com*.

You can also use the Address list and History features to go to a previously viewed page. The Address list is a drop-down list of addresses you've visited in your current Internet session. The History feature keeps track of all the Web sites you've visited for the last four weeks.

✔ **Follow these steps to use the Address list:**

1. Click the downward-pointing arrow on the right end of the Address box. Recently visited sites like the ones shown in Figure 15.2 are displayed.

2. Click on any one of these site names to return to that site.

PCs Made Easy

FIGURE 15.2 *All the sites you've visited during your current Internet session are displayed here.*

✔ To locate a site from the History listing, follow these steps:

1. Click History. You'll see the History window shown in Figure 15.3. This displays all sites visited today, as well as sites visited during the past several weeks.

2. Click a week to display all the sites from that week.

3. Click any site to return to it.

FIGURE 15.3 Having trouble remembering the site you visited last Tuesday? Check out your browsing History.

Saving Favorites

In addition to the record of sites that you've visited that are kept automatically by Internet Explorer, you can save your own record of favorite sites so that you can jump back to them at any time. The Favorites feature is found on most browsers.

✔ **You can save a Web page to your Favorites collection and visit it again by following these steps:**

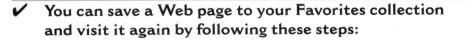

1. Display the Web page you want to add to Favorites.

2. Select Favorites, Add to Favorites. The dialog box in Figure 15.4 appears.

about.com/

Add Favorite   ? X

WHAT
TO

Internet Explorer will add this page to your Favorites list.   OK

☆   ☐ Make available offline   Customize...   Cancel

Name: What You Need to Know About™   Create in >>

the new Honaa Civic Hybria.   offenaea migraine sufferers.   top aigital cameras.

FIGURE 15.4 Adding a favorite is as easy as naming it.

3. Enter a Name if you want to locate the page by a name other than its URL (for example, if you wanted to name the Hewlett-Packard site HP or Pavilion).

4. Click OK to save it.

5. To go to a Favorite page, click Favorites.

6. From the list that appears in the Favorites window, shown in Figure 15.5, click the site you want to visit.

 tip **Are your Favorites getting a little full? Have a favorite site that's not in favor anymore? Simply display the Favorites pane, right-click a favorite site, and then click Delete from the shortcut menu that appears to remove that site from your Favorites list.**

Setting Your Home Page

You may have heard the term "home page" before. There are actually two varieties of home pages. There are Web site home pages, and then there's your browser home page.

Web sites, which are typically made up of several individual Web pages, will have a single home page, which is their command central.

FIGURE 15.5 Click any folder to display sites within them or any site to go directly to it.

You can typically get an overview of site contents and move to any page on the site from the home page.

On the other hand, your home page is like your home base for browsing the Internet. It's the first page that your browser displays whenever you go online, and you can return to it at any time by clicking the Home button on your browser.

Project: **Picking Your Perfect Home Page**

By default, Microsoft has set *MSN.com* as your Internet Explorer home page, but you might want to set your favorite search engine, such as Google or Ask, or your school Web site or a news channel as your home page.

✔ **First locate a Web page that you think you'd like to use as a home page. Then, just follow these steps:**

1. Select Tools, Options. The Internet Options dialog box shown in Figure 15.6 appears.

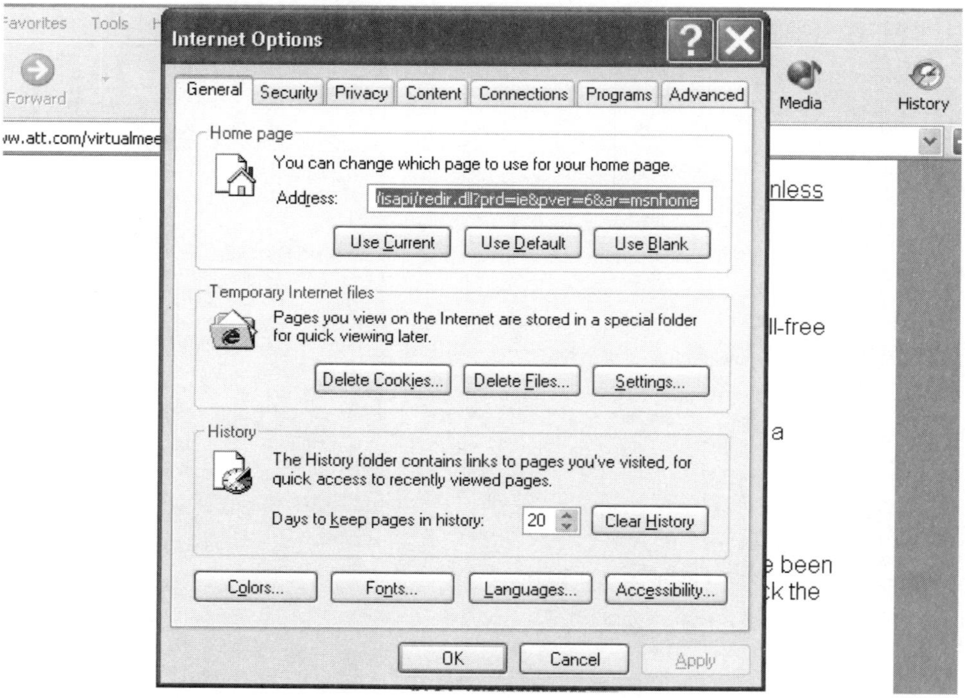

FIGURE 15.6 The seven tabs on this dialog box contain a wealth of settings for how Internet Explorer takes you around the Internet.

2. If you have the page you want to use currently displayed, click Use Current to set it as your home page. If you don't have the page you want to use displayed, type its URL in the Address box, and click Apply.

3. Click OK to close the dialog box.

   Now whenever you log on, your home page will be displayed.

Going Shopping

You can enter the URL of any online store, such as www.amazon.com, to go to that site and shop. When you enter the URL, you are presented with some form of shopping cart feature. A shopping cart, such as the one shown in Figure 15.7, is like a folder where you can save the items that you want to buy. You then go through a checkout process to enter your address and payment information to complete your order.

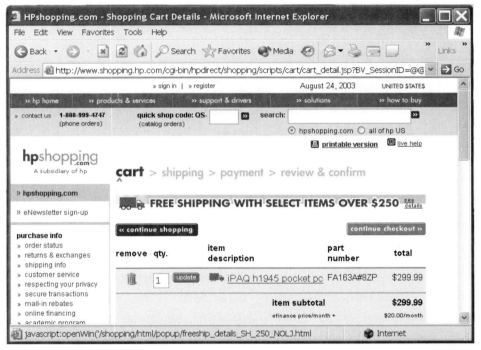

FIGURE 15.7 Look for a button labeled Checkout or something similar to finalize your purchase.

Both HP Pavilions and Compaq Presarios offer a Hot Deals icon on their desktops. When you click this icon, you're taken online either to the My HP Club (shown in Figure 15.8) or the My Presario Club Web sites.

PCs Made Easy

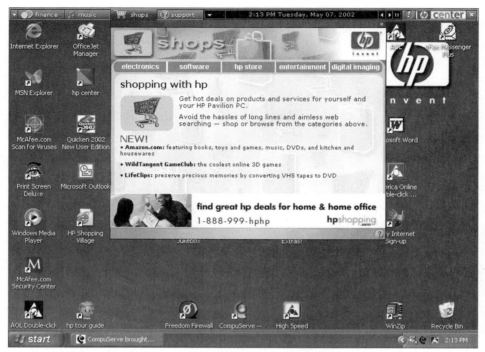

FIGURE 15.8 Shopping sites gather links and deals in one spot.

These sites offer the following features:

- A link to HP or Compaq Shopping where you can purchase computers, computer supplies, and peripherals, such as printers, fax machines, and networking accessories, as well as handheld computing devices and DVD players.
- A link to Club Zones where you can get free music downloads; PC security, maintenance information, and tools; and special offers on everything from digital photography products to online classes.
- Feature articles that provide information about software that might help you get more out of your Pavilion or Presario. These club sites also have special how-to articles that help you with topics, such as how to move all your files to a new computer and how to be the most productive with Windows XP.

Shopping Online Safely

Shopping online is generally a safe way to do business, but here are a few things to check for. There should be a privacy statement on store sites that ensures that your name and contact information will not be given out to any other business. Also, a security statement should include the use of Secure Sockets Layer (SSL) software, which protects information that you send online. Finally, look for a little icon of a padlock in your browser window. If the padlock is closed, the site is secure; if it's open, think twice about purchasing anything on that site.

Shopping online requires a credit card and sometimes involves shipping charges. Have your credit card and shipping information ready before you go shopping. Most sites use the metaphor of a shopping cart or shopping bag where you place items, and you then go through a checkout process where you provide your credit card and shipping information.

Check out return policies before you buy. If what you get isn't what you wanted, it can be a hassle to make returns if the site doesn't make the process easy for you.

Learning Online

Whether you own a Pavilion or Presario, you have a resource for learning available to you. Pavilions offer an online version of Encyclopedia Britannica, while Compaq provides a free one-year subscription to Encarta Online, a virtual encyclopedia and learning resource.

note **If you purchased your Pavilion before the fall of 2002, you'll get Encarta. If you purchased your computer more recently, you have Britannica available to you.**

Exploring Encarta Online Deluxe

Your computer includes a one-year subscription to Encarta, Microsoft's online encyclopedia. The first time you select Start, All

Programs, Encarta Online Deluxe, you will be asked to sign on with a .NET Passport. If you don't have a .NET Passport, follow the on screen instructions to obtain one. When you've activated Encarta, you'll see the opening window shown in Figure 15.9.

FIGURE 15.9 Encarta Online Deluxe includes a dictionary, atlas, and more.

Here's what Encarta includes:

- A searchable English dictionary that includes an audio feature so you can hear words pronounced correctly.
- A challenge trivia game. Note that you have to install Macromedia Shockwave Player to run the game, but don't worry. A window pops up when you open the game offering to download the player automatically and for free.
- An online atlas you can use to search for maps of any country and can zoom in to view details of different regions.

- A comprehensive encyclopedia that covers a wide variety of topics with articles, activities, and Web links.

- Terraserver, which contains views of the Earth from a satellite out in space.

- Schoolhouse provides a page that contains lesson plans that students and teachers can use for free.

Getting around Encarta essentially involves clicking a link, then entering a search term to retrieve an article or definition (see Figure 15.10), or making choices from lists, such as the region for which you want to retrieve maps in the atlas.

FIGURE 15.10 The Physical Science and Technology category offers articles on several scientific disciplines.

Learning Made Fun

A one year subscription to Britannica Online is included with all Pavilions shipped after September 2002. It's a wonderful resource to help kids do homework and to provide a wealth of material for everybody from the college-bound student and home businessperson to the soccer mom or dad.

When you log on to Britannica, you'll see the main window shown in Figure 15.11. Britannica doesn't just offer the renowned encyclopedia in an online format. There is also the Merriam-Webster dictionary on the site and headlines from *The New York Times*.

FIGURE 15.11 Browse the encyclopedia, read about current events, or shop in the Britannica store.

The World Atlas (Figure 15.12) includes data on culture, economy, history, major cities, and geography all in one easy-to-search format.

With the world changing so quickly these days, an online resource that is kept up to the minute is the best way to get information for your family or business.

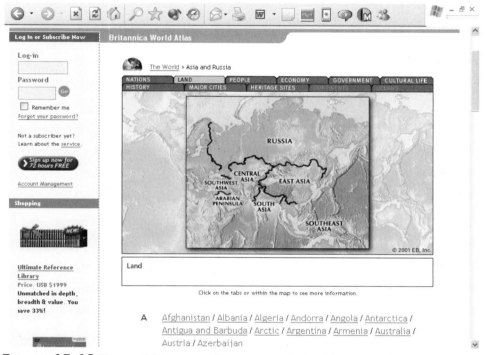

FIGURE 15.12 The world is at your fingertips with the Britannica Atlas.

To search the huge amount of information on Britannica, you can use the Search feature on the Britannica home page. Using the Search drop-down list, you can choose what to search: the entire Britannica site; the full encyclopedia; or just the concise or student editions, video and media collections, dictionary, or thesaurus. You can also search for other Web sites related to your search term.

Here are some tips for performing searches that find what you need:

- Select as specific a keyword as you can. If you're looking for information about sports cars, instead of entering the keyword "automobile," use "sports car."

- If you want a phrase (such as "sports car") searched exactly, rather than having the search engine look for results including either sports or car or both, enclose the words in quotes.

- Sometimes searches are case sensitive, meaning that, if you enter "Catholic," you may get very different results than if you entered "catholic."

- You can use wildcard characters to open up your search. For example, precede the word "boat" with an asterisk (*boat), and you can find information about various kinds of boats, such as sailboats, tugboats, rowboats, and so on.

- A search involving Boolean characters allows you to narrowly define a search. "Music and (piano or organ) not Bach" will get results about piano or organ music, but not results that include Bach.

✔ **To perform a search, follow these simple steps:**

1. Click the arrow on the Search box and choose a source for the search.

2. Type your keyword with any punctuation or Boolean operators you require.

Click Go. Your results will list all the applicable sources, as shown in Figure 15.13.

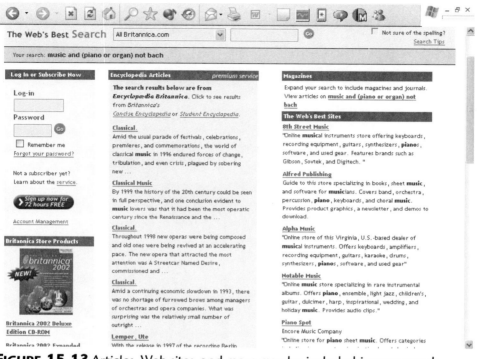

FIGURE 15.13 Articles, Web sites, and more may be included in your search results.

Chapter Summary

In this chapter, you learned the basics of browsing the Internet using Internet Explorer. You learned to navigate using your browser, set up a home page, and save favorite Web sites. You explored links to online sites providing education, shopping, and support opportunities.

16

Getting in Touch with Email

In this Chapter

✔ Selecting an email program

✔ Using Outlook Express to send and receive email

✔ Downloading attachments

✔ Organizing email folders

✔ Using email etiquette

It's hard to believe that email wasn't around a dozen or so years ago. Today, many of us check our email several times a day, sending and receiving hundreds of messages a year to family, friends, business associates, and online businesses. Email is also used to send files around the world, helping us to do business and to communicate in the blink of an eye.

In this chapter, you'll use Outlook Express, which comes installed on your computer, to learn about the basics of email.

Choosing an Email Program

There are many email software programs out there, including the one that's typically provided by your ISP when you get an online account. They all do things somewhat alike, but some are more feature rich than others. Before you can decide which program is for you, you need to understand a few basics about email itself.

How Does Email Work?

Email is simply the sending and receiving of text messages, Web content in HTML format, and sometimes computer file attachments in an electronic form from one computer to another. Email can be sent across a home or office network or it can be sent to others across the Internet.

You must have an email address, such as anyusername@aol.com, for people to send email to you. You must know a person's email address to address email to him. You need an email client, that is, a service that sends and receives your email and that is usually provided by your ISP, but that is also available through services such as Hotmail. You will also use some form of email software to receive, read, send, and manage your email.

Selecting an Email Program

ISPs, such as AOL or Earthlink, provide an email account with your Internet connection. You can use their email program from their home page, or you can set up another program, such as Outlook Express, to access those email accounts.

Not everybody needs all the same features in his or her email program, but, in deciding which e-mail program to use, consider whether the program you think you'd like to use has these features:

- When you save copies of sent and received messages is it easy to manage the stored messages? Can you create and rename folders to store them in, and can you find stored messages easily? Can you set up the program to save sent messages for a certain length of time automatically?
- Can you modify the appearance of emails by changing fonts or adding graphics. (See Figure 16.1 to see how Outlook Express allows you to do this.)

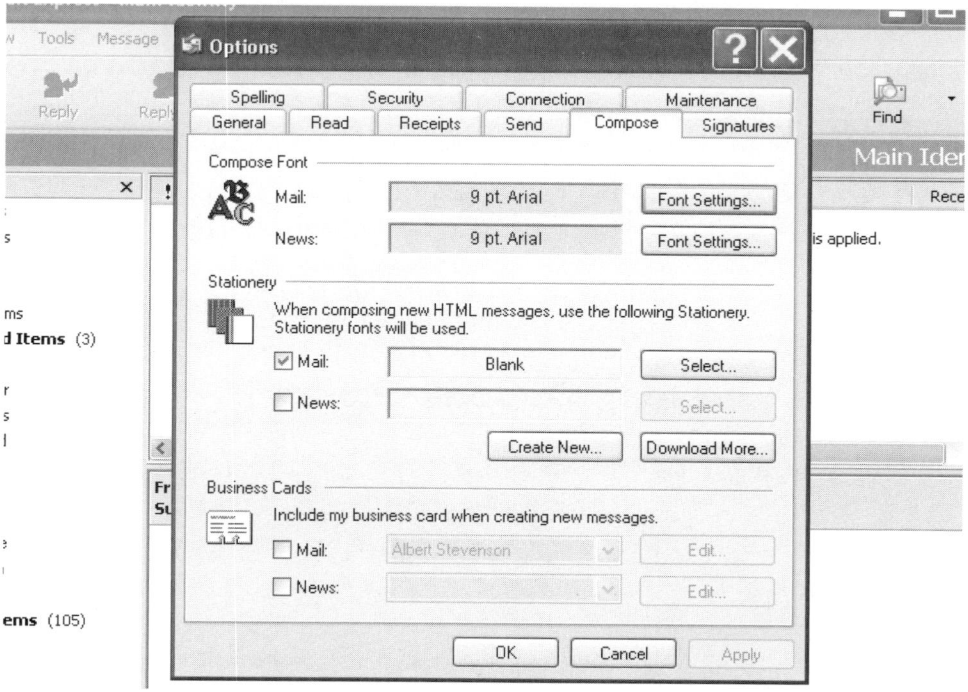

FIGURE 16.1 You can even create a stationery design for your email messages using these settings.

- Does the program include a good download management feature that lets you control where files are downloaded to and whether they open after download?
- If you go out of town, does the program offer a feature to send a reply automatically letting people who email you know you're away?
- Can you set up the software to forward email to another address in case you have two accounts and want to redirect messages temporarily?
- Does the software provide tools to block email from certain sources to help you avoid spamming or harassing email?
- Will the software allow you to download email and read it offline?
- Can you easily sort messages by sender name, date, or subject?
- Does the program offer ease of use in addressing, forwarding, and copying people on messages?
- Can you add a signature (for example your name, address, and phone number) to be attached to every outgoing email automatically?

Using Outlook Express

Outlook Express is an email program from Microsoft that is included on your Compaq Presario or HP Pavilion. It is a slightly less robust version of Microsoft Outlook, which you may have used at work or on a previous computer.

 tip Although Outlook Express lacks a few features of Outlook, it takes up less memory when it's running than Outlook. This can help alleviate some problems with computer memory when you have to send or receive very large files.

Setting Up Your Email Account in Outlook Express

To allow Outlook Express to retrieve your mail, you have to tell it something about your email account. You can get that information from your ISP, so contact them first and tell them what you want to do. They'll provide you with a protocol to use for your incoming email server (such as Internet Message Access Protocol [IMAP] or Post Office Protocol [POP]), along with incoming and outgoing mail server addresses.

✔ **To set up the account, follow these steps:**

1. Select Tools, Accounts.

2. Click Add, Mail.

3. On the Internet Connection Wizard that appears, enter the name you want to appear on messages when you send email and click Next.

4. In the dialog box that appears, enter your email address and then click Next. The E-mail Server Names dialog box shown in Figure 16.2 appears.

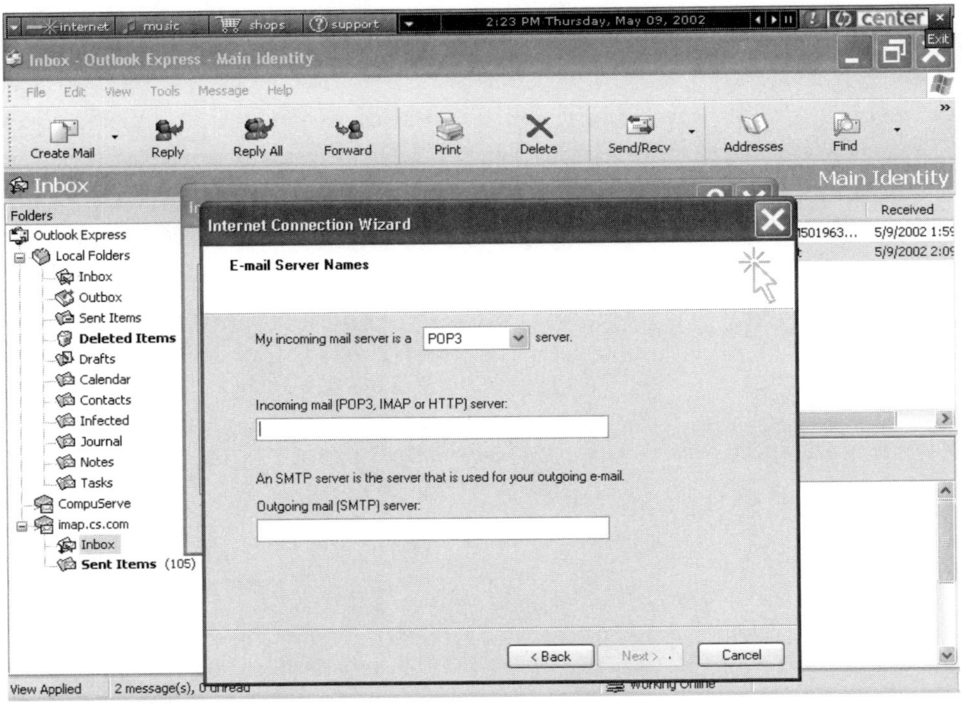

FIGURE 16.2 This is where the information from your provider comes into play.

5. Click the arrow to display a choice of server types and select the correct one for your provider.

6. Enter an incoming mail server address and an outgoing mail server address.

7. Click Next.

8. Enter your Account Name and your Password in the appropriate field.

9. Click Next, and you've finished the wizard. Click Finish to return to the Internet Accounts dialog box.

10. If you want this account to be your default email account, click Set as Default and then click Close.

If you have set this account as your default account, when you are connected to the Internet through your ISP and you click the Send/Recv button, Outlook Express goes out and retrieves your mail from that account.

Setting Up the Address Book

You can send messages by simply entering an email address for a recipient in a new message form. However, emailing becomes much easier when you've stored addresses of people you frequently contact in Outlook Express's Address Book.

Project: **Building Your Online Address Book**

Create a form and make enough copies of it for everybody in your family. Include on this form a column for First Name, Last Name, Email Address, and Home Phone. Have each person in the family fill out a sheet for people they want included in your online Address Book. Designate somebody to create the contacts in Outlook, and somebody else to assemble the sheets in a binder to keep in case something damages your computer and you lose your email addresses someday.

Then, you can address messages by choosing a contact from a list. You can also simply begin typing a name, and Outlook will recognize it and enter the full email address for you.

✔ **Follow these steps to add contacts to your Address Book:**

1. Click Addresses. The Address Book dialog box opens, as shown in Figure 16.3.

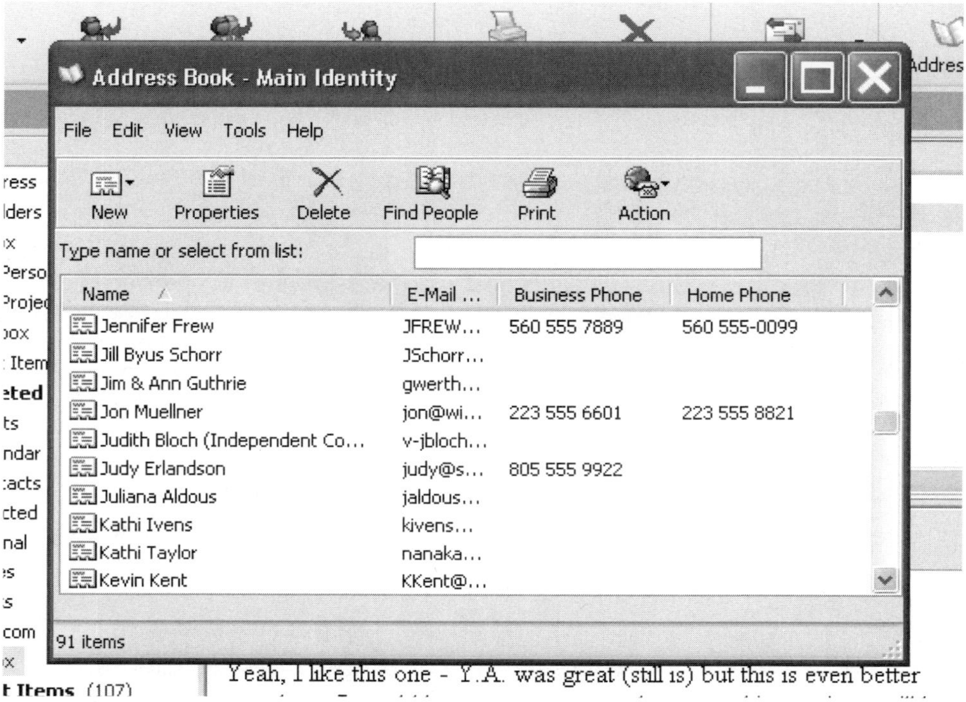

FIGURE 16.3   You can address a message to somebody from this dialog box or even initiate a phone call to them using choices on the Action button.

2. Click New and then New Contact. The Properties dialog box shown in Figure 16.4 appears.

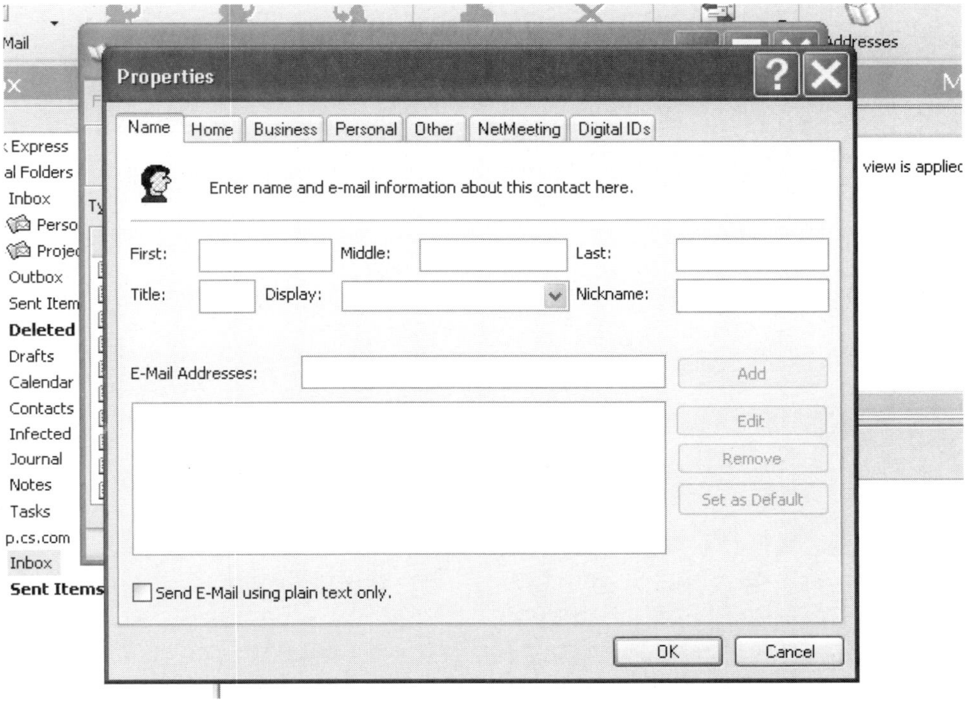

FIGURE 16.4 You can enter a wealth of information about your contacts on the seven tabs in this dialog box.

3. Enter the contact's first, middle, and last name, a title such as Mr. or Dr., and an email address.

4. Click Add to add the e-mail address. If you want to add a second e-mail address, type it in the now blank E-Mail Addresses box and click Add again.

5. Click the Home or Business tab and enter contact information, such as address, phone, fax, Web page, or mobile phone number.

6. If you want to enter personal information, such as the contact's spouse's name or birthday, go to the Personal tab.

7. When you're done entering information, click OK to add the contact to the Address Book.

tip You can use the New, New Group command in the Address Book to create a group of email addresses so you can send messages to everybody in the group with a single action. This becomes useful to communicate with everybody on a project team at work or the neighborhood carpool, for example.

Creating and Sending Messages

Creating an email message is a simple matter of entering a recipient's address, a subject, and the text of your message. You can address an email to as many people as you like and can also copy or blind copy people. A blind copy involves sending a copy of the message to somebody without letting the recipient know that that person has been copied.

note As an email courtesy, try to create a subject line that makes it clear what the message is about. People who get lots of email will find it much easier to prioritize and deal with each message that way and won't have to read a message to discover its topic.

✔ **Follow these steps to create a new message in Outlook Express:**

1. Click Create Mail. The blank New Message form shown in Figure 16.5 appears.

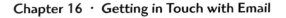

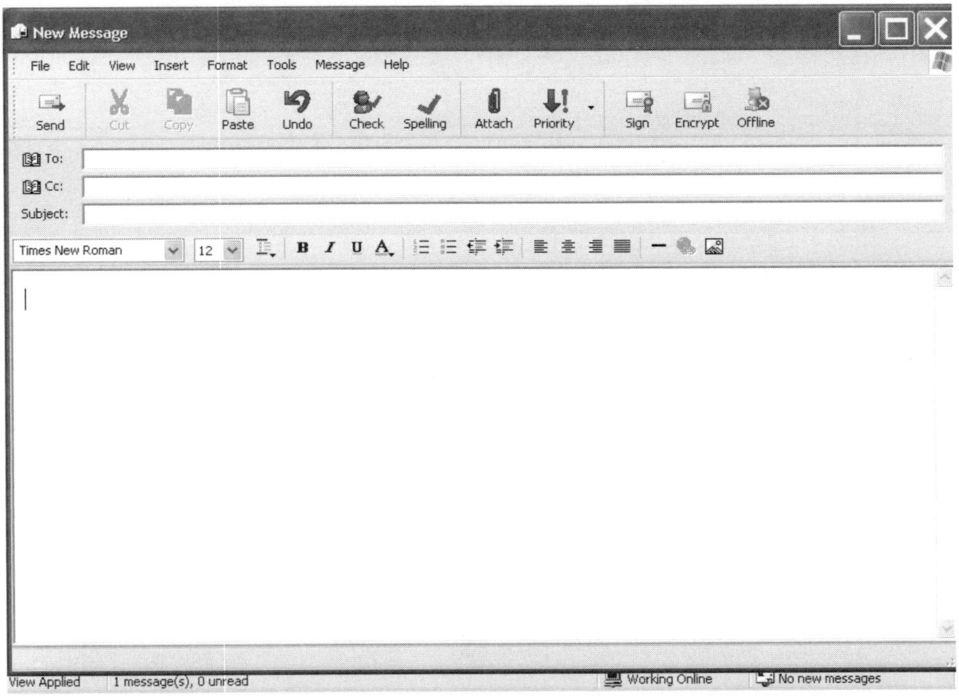

FIGURE 16.5 The formatting tools in this form don't become available to you until you've clicked in the message area.

2. In the To: field, you can enter an email address (such as Smith@aol.com).

3. If you have stored contact information, you can click the To: button to display the contact list, shown in Figure 16.6. If you have created contacts for your address book, they are listed here. You can then click a name in the list and click the To:, Cc:, or Bcc: buttons to address the message to as many people as you like. Click OK to close the dialog box and return to the message.

Copy   Paste   Undo   Check   Spelling   Attach   Priority   Sign   Encrypt   Offline

Select Recipients   [?] [X]

Type name or select from list:

[   ]   [Find...]

Main Identity's Contacts   [v]

Name /	E-M:
Patricia Thomas	pthon
Paul Levesque	PLev
Playwrights Festival	
Richard Graves	RGra
Rick St. Onge	rsaint
Rick St. Onge	rsaint
ronperson@expertnotes...	ronpe
Sarah Ohman	mts2C
SUE GILLARD	sgillar
Susan Colby	susar

[New Contact]   [Properties]

Message recipients:

[To: ->]

[Cc: ->]

[Bcc: ->]

[OK]   [Cancel]

FIGURE 16.6 Address your message to as many people as you like from this dialog box.

4. Enter a topic for the message in the Subject box.

5. Click in the message area and type your message.

6. When the message is ready to go, you just click Send to send it on its way.

 note You can control whether emails are sent immediately (which can slow down your work a bit while you wait for each one to go) or sent all at once when you exit Outlook Express. You make this setting by selecting Tools, Options, and displaying the Send tab. Select or remove the checkmark from the Send Messages Immediately checkbox to control this.

Controlling the Look and Feel of Your Email

You can format your email in a variety of ways. You can use predesigned stationery to add an attractive background to your message, or you can use the text formatting tools available to you in a New Message form.

Project: **Pick a Stationery for Family Email**

Stationery can make your emails look special, adding color or graphics to every message you send out. Have your family review the stationery available in Outlook Express and pick one that appeals to you all. Consider changing the stationery you use with each season of the year.

✔ **To specify stationery to be used on all your email messages, follow these steps:**

1. With no new message open, select Tools, Options and then click the Compose tab, shown in Figure 16.7.

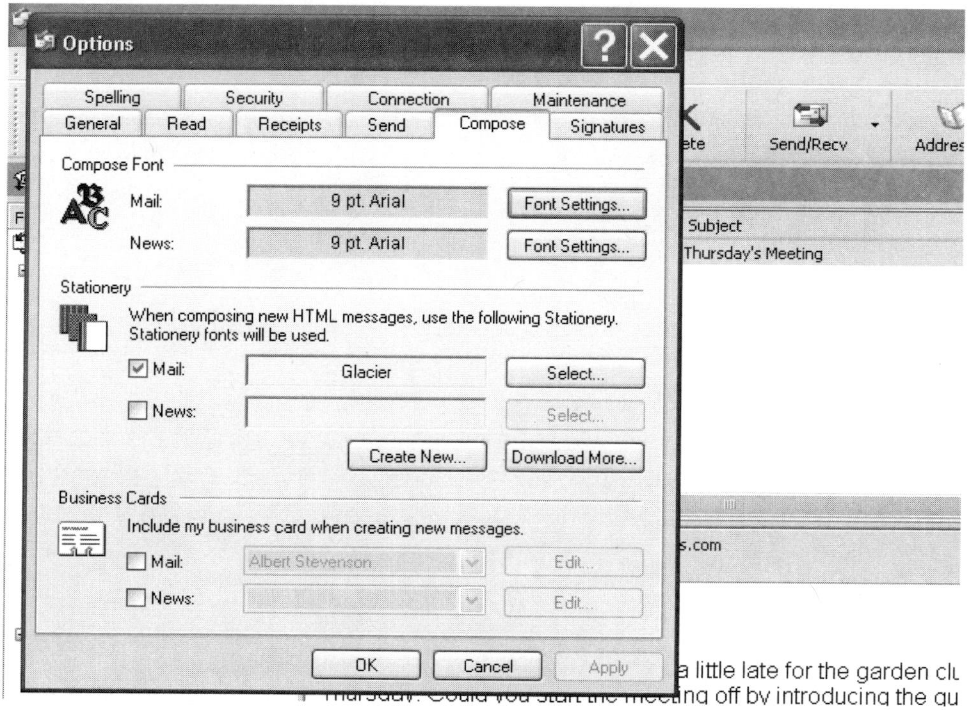

FIGURE 16.7 *Set defaults for font and stationery here.*

2. Click Select in the Stationery section of this dialog box. The Select Stationery dialog box opens.

3. Click any stationery listed here and then click OK.

4. Click Apply and then OK again to close the Options dialog box.

note **You can also change the stationery you're using as you create an email message. With a new message open, click Format, Apply Stationery, More Stationery to make a different choice for that message only.**

You can use the formatting tools in a new message to format selected message text, or you can use the Compose tab of the Options dialog box to set default formatting for all message text. Settings you can apply include which font to use, font style (bold, italic, and so on), font size, color, and effects, such as underlining.

> *caution*   **Not all email programs can read background graphics and font styling. Be aware of this if you use formatting for emphasis in your message, such as making a phrase bold or underlining it. Some people might not get it.**

Receiving and Forwarding Messages

When you receive emails—and you will—they appear in your Inbox. Double-click the Inbox to open it. Messages are listed in the order they were received by default, with the most recent on top of the list.

Double-click any message to read it. It will open, looking like the message in Figure 16.8.

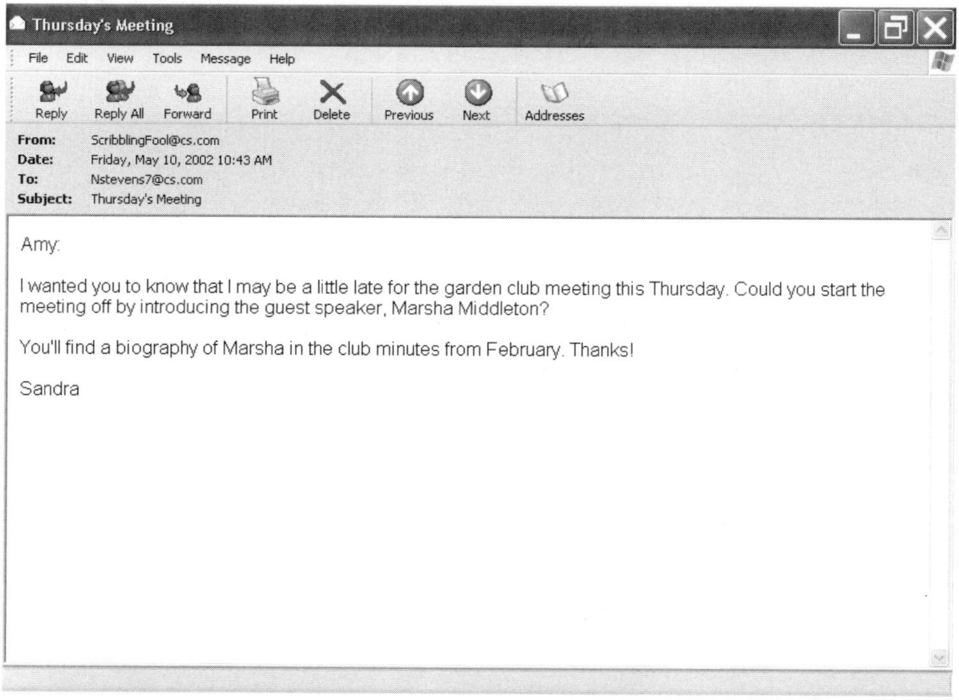

FIGURE 16.8 Information about who sent the message and when will appear at the top of each message.

At this point, you have a few options:

- You can reply to the sender of the message or reply to the sender and all other recipients (if any). If you use the Reply or Reply All options, your response is automatically addressed for you with a subject line that starts Re: and includes the original subject line text. All you have to do is enter your return message and click Send.

- You can forward the message to somebody else. If you click Forward, you'll have to enter an address or addresses to forward to and add a comment, if you like. Note that the recipient of a forwarded message will see notations of the original sender's name in his or her copy.

- You can print the message, using the standard Windows print dialog box.
- You can delete the message. If you make this choice, the message is moved to your Deleted folder, where you can retrieve it (but only for a short period of time) if you change your mind.
- If you want to store the message, you can select File, Move to Folder, or Copy to Folder. (You'll learn more about managing message folders shortly.)

If you don't want to take any of these steps, you can either click the close button in the upper right hand corner, or click Previous or Next to view another message in the Inbox. The message you were viewing remains in your Inbox.

Working with Attachments

Attachments are computer files that you include with an email. The two processes that you need to learn about related to attachments are how to attach a message to your emails and how to view and download files others attach when they email you.

caution **Email attachments may slow down the transmission of your email, especially if they are large files, such as graphics. Some email programs may actually block receipt of very large files.**

✔ **When you create a message, you can attach a file by following these steps:**

1. In the new message form, click Attach. The Insert Attachment dialog box shown in Figure 16.9 appears.

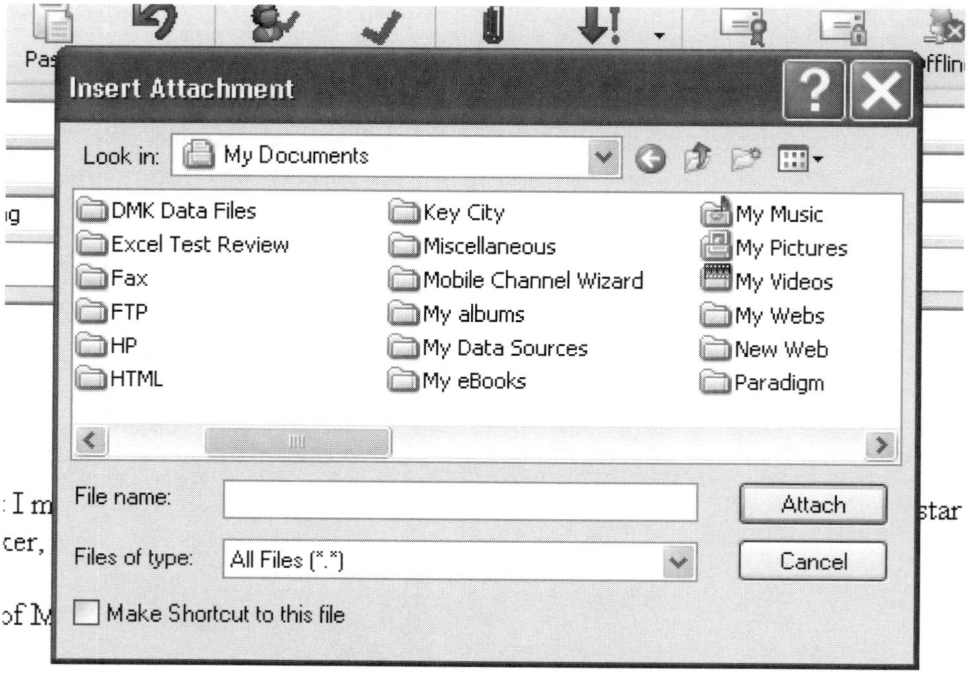

FIGURE 16.9 Locate the document you want to attach on your computer or a floppy disk.

2. Use the Look in drop-down list to locate the folder where you've stored the file.

3. Click the file name and then Attach.

That's it. When you send the message, the attachment will go along with it.

When you receive a message with an attachment, the symbol of a little disk will appear on the message icon in your Inbox.

✔ **To open an attachment you receive with an email, follow these steps:**

1. Double-click the message in your Inbox to open it. The Attach line under the Subject lists the name of the document that's attached and its size.

2. Double-click the attached file. The Open Attachment Warning dialog box opens (see Figure 16.10).

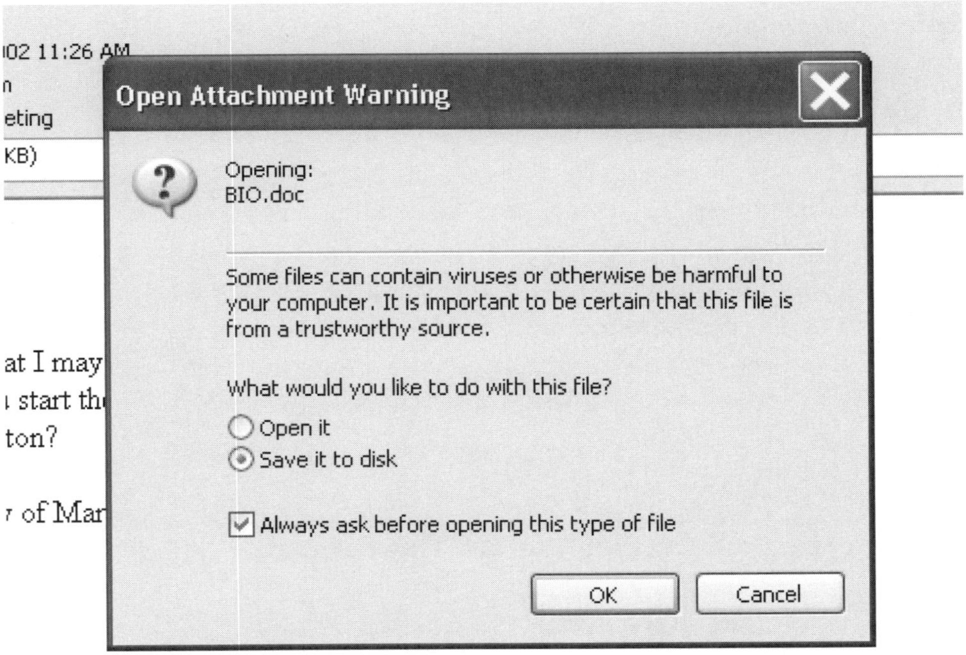

FIGURE 16.10 Note the warning about files containing viruses and consider the source before opening any attachment.

3. If you want to open the attachment in the program it was created in, such as Works, click the Open it option. If you want to save the file to a folder on your hard drive or a floppy disk, select the Save it to disk option.

4. Click OK.

Depending on your choice in Step 3, the document will open for you to read it, or the Save As dialog box appears so that you can select a place in which to save the file.

 note **If the program that the file was created in is not installed on your computer, you won't be able to open the file. There are programs such as Adobe Acrobat (which is included on your Presario or Pavilion) that can open files created in any format, as long as the files were saved in Adobe Acrobat and you have Adobe Acrobat on your system to open them.**

Organizing Email Folders

Outlook Express is organized with folders. Your Inbox is a folder and so are your Sent Items, Contacts, and Deleted Items. When you send a message, a copy is automatically filed in your Sent Items folder. When you delete a message, it is moved into the Deleted Items folder. However, you can also create folders of your own and move messages into them at any time. For example, you might create a folder for each person in your family or folders for Family Finances or School Projects.

✔ **To create a new folder, follow these steps:**

1. Click the folder where you want the new folder to appear. For example, if you want to create a subfolder in your Inbox, click the Inbox folder.

2. Select File, New, Folder. The New Folder dialog box shown in Figure 16.11 appears.

3. Enter a name in the Folder Name field.

4. Click OK to create the folder. It now appears in the list of folders along the left side of the Outlook Express window.

FIGURE 16.11 Enter a folder name that's descriptive of the contents you intend to place there.

To move a file into a folder, you click the message in your Inbox and drag it to the folder. Alternately, you can select Edit, Move to Folder, or Copy to Folder and specify the folder in which you want to place the file.

Email Etiquette

Just as it's polite to end business letters with "sincerely" and to answer phone calls with "hello," email communication has its own newly minted rules of conduct called netiquette. Paying attention to netiquette will help you not only come off as a polite emailer, but also make sure your communication or the feeling behind it isn't misunderstood.

Here are a few rules of netiquette to live by:

- When you use all capital letters in your message, it's called shouting because it gives a sense of larger-than-life urgency that fairly shouts at the reader. Capitalize all the letters in a word occasionally for emphasis, but never leave your Caps Lock on for the duration of a message.

- If you have email, you should check it regularly and reply promptly. People who send you a message and then wait a week for a reply will be frustrated. Even if you can't deal with typing a lengthy response right away, send a quick reply acknowledging that you got the message and will be replying in a day, a week, or whenever you think you can get to it.

- Repeat portions of the original email you reply to so the person receiving your message will remember what the original comment is that you're referencing. Many email programs will format the original text differently from your reply text automatically, but, if not, you can use the << and >> symbols to set off original lines of text in your reply.

- Double-check who each message is addressed to before sending and be sure that you want all those people to read what you have to say, especially if you're replying to all the original addressees of a message. Email is so instant that, after you've clicked Send, there's no turning back.

- Keep your head. If you are angry or upset, take time before sending an email. Remember, your anger will be frozen in text forever and can be forwarded to anybody. If you think you might regret what you're saying later, wait until you calm down to review and then send the message.

Chapter Summary

In this chapter, you've learned all about email and how to create, send, forward, and reply to messages. You've explored the features of Outlook Express and walked through the process of setting up an email account and formatting email messages. Finally, you learned about email netiquette so you can be a good citizen of the Internet.

part

5

Upgrading Your Computer

chapter

17

Managing Computer Memory

In this Chapter

✔ Understanding how computer memory works

✔ Checking your available memory

✔ Freeing up hard disk space

✔ Adding memory

Computer memory has come a long way in recent years. It wasn't that long ago that your computer came with 4 megabytes (Mb) of memory. Today, 256 Mb is pretty average. However, somehow we humans use up what we've got, whether it's our paycheck or our computer memory. When you're feeling the pinch of a full hard drive, you'll be glad to know your Pavilion or Presario is easy to upgrade. Before you do, though, you should understand what memory is.

What Is Computer Memory?

The type of memory called Random Access Memory (RAM) is essentially the available space on your computer that can be used to run programs. Windows can also use your hard drive space to create temporary memory called *virtual memory* that serves the same purpose as RAM. In addition to the program you are working in at the moment, your computer will try to keep recently used programs available in RAM memory so you can access them quickly as you work. Unlike the files stored permanently on your hard drive, when you turn your computer off, whatever was in RAM and virtual memory is lost.

Sometimes you can solve a temporary RAM memory issue by simply closing some programs on your computer if you have too many running at one time. However, if you have to do this all the time, you probably don't have enough RAM. In that case, you may find that your programs run slowly, or you may experience computer crashes on a regular basis. That's when it's time to upgrade.

RAM memory comes in modules that you can buy and install in your CPU by opening it up and slotting the modules into place. Those memory modules come as different types. In fact, today, you need a good memory just to remember all the different types of memory. There are options such as Single Inline Memory Modules (SIMMs) that are generally found on older computers, Rambus Dynamic RAM (RDRAM), Rambus Inline Memory Module (RIMMs), Dual Inline Memory Modules (DIMMs), and Double Data Rate Synchronous Dynamic RAM (DDR SDRAM). These are different types of memory based on the chip set (such as a Pentium or Celeron chip) in your computer. HP Pavilion and Compaq Presario models differ somewhat in the type of memory modules they use (see Figure 17.1) .

In addition to RAM, there is a certain amount of storage space on your hard drive where you save all your software programs and files. Where RAM can be upgraded by adding memory modules, if you don't have enough hard disk space to store all the files and software you want on your computer, you will either have to remove some files or

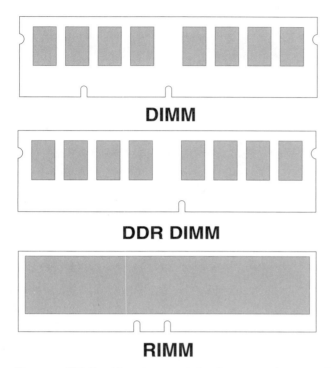

DIMM

DDR DIMM

RIMM

FIGURE 17.1 Memory modules fit into sockets inside your computer.

programs or replace the hard drive. (Replacing the hard drive is covered in Chapter 18.)

Check Your Available Memory

Before you can determine the best way to manage your memory needs, you need to know how your system is using your current memory. First, you can check on how much RAM you have in use when you're running the programs you typically work in. Then, you can check the space on your hard drive and take some steps to clean it up to free up some storage memory.

Checking Out Your RAM

Adding to RAM is easy, but it does mean spending the money to buy memory modules. Before you do that, you should know how much RAM memory you have and how much of it is being used. The best way to do this is to use some of the system information reports in Windows XP.

✔ **Follow these steps to review system information:**

1. Select Start, All Programs, Accessories, System Tools, System Information.

2. Scroll down in the right-hand pane.

3. The information shown in Figure 17.2 appears.

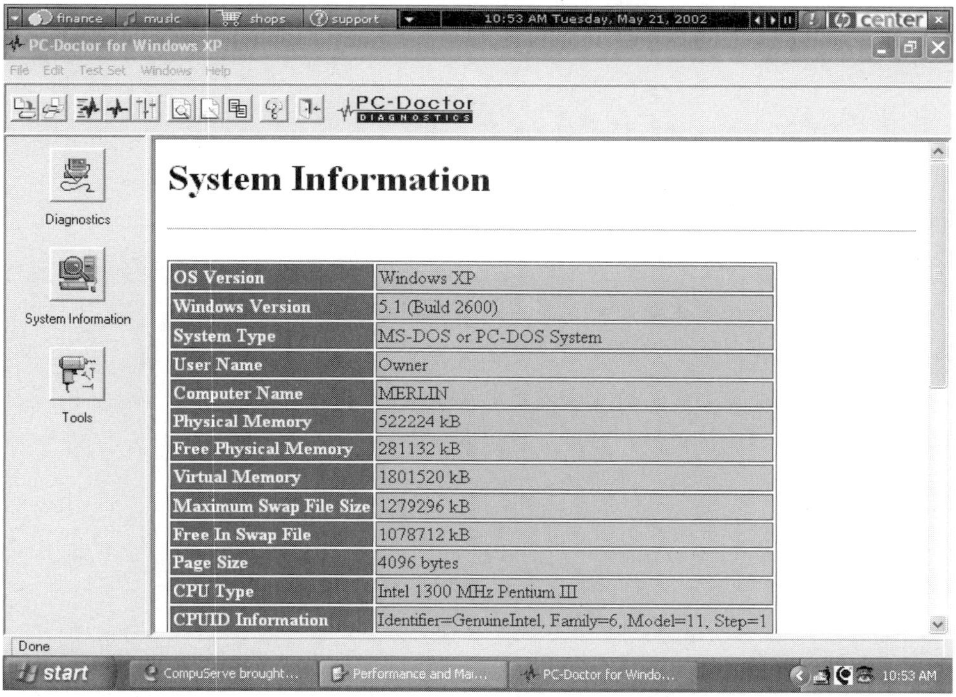

FIGURE 17.2 You can learn all about your computer's specifications here.

According to this system information listing, I have 522,224kb (or about 512Mb) of physical memory, that is, RAM. Of that, I have 9 Mb free, or almost half. Any problems I might have shouldn't relate to available RAM. However, if you notice that free physical memory is very low on your system, it may be time to upgrade.

Freeing Up Hard Disk Space

If you need hard disk space because you don't have enough available to install a new piece of software, for example, you can try these two things to free up more disk space:

- First, remove any programs you don't need and archive any files you don't use on a regular basis. See Chapter 6 to learn about uninstalling software.

- Second, run a utility called Disk Cleanup, which suggests deletion of files no longer used by your system and which optimizes the storage of other data on your hard drive. Chapter 8 tells you how to run the Disk Cleanup utility.

Adding Memory Modules to Your Pavilion

If you've decided that what you need is more RAM, it's time to go shopping and buy your memory modules and then install them. First, check the HP At Home Web site (*www.hp-at-home.com*) and search for your system to view its technical specifications, like those shown in Figure 17.3 for the Pavilion 520N.

Frontside Bus	100MHz
Memory	512MB SDRAM with up to 32MB allocated to video memory
Hard Drive	60GB* Ultra DMA; *Gigabyte(GB) is defined as 1,000,000,000 bytes (accessible capacity may vary)
CD-RW drive	hp CD-Writer (16x/8x/40x) 16x max. speed write 8x max. speed re-write 40x max. speed read
Multimedia Drive	16x max. speed DVD-ROM
Video Graphics	Integrated Intel® Direct AGP 3D graphics with up to 11MB of dynamic video memory
Data/Fax Modem	ITU V.90 K56flex modem, data/fax only (33.6Kbps send/download up to 56Kbps/14.4Kbps fax)
Total Drive Bays	External (1) 3.5", (2) 5.25"; Internal (2) 3.5"
Available Drive Bays	Internal (1) 3.5"
Total Expansion Slots	3 PCI
Available Slots	2 PCI
Total External Ports	4 USB; 2 serial; 1 parallel; 1 game port; 2 PS/2
Available External Ports	4 USB; 2 serial; 1 parallel; 1 game port
Total Memory Slots	2 DIMM
Available Memory Slots	0 DIMM
Memory Speed	133MHz

Registration and profiling → subscriber's choice: driver notices, support alerts & e-newsletters

FIGURE 17.3 My system has two DIMM slots.

Your HP documentation will tell you what kind of memory module you must use for your Pavilion or Presario. From the information on this site, I know my system uses DIMM slots, and my documentation tells me that DIMM modules have to be 168-pin unbuffered SDRAM compliant with Intel PC SDRAM Unbuffered DIMM Specification and that I can install 64Mb, 128Mb, or 256Mb modules. Now don't be intimidated by this string of technobabble! It's just information you have to take with you when you go shopping for memory. The store where you buy the memory should be able to provide the right type of module to fit these specifications.

 caution **Putting the wrong kind of memory module into your Pavilion or Presario could cause damage to the computer, so check carefully for the proper specifications.**

tip **You can add memory modules, but you can also replace the memory modules that come with the computer with higher capacity modules.**

Safety First

To install memory, you have to open up your computer. Before you go digging around your CPU with a screwdriver, remember that you're dealing with expensive equipment that has many small parts and that can hold an electrical charge even when it's turned off.

There are several safety procedures you should know about:

- Disconnect everything from the system, including phone lines, network connections, and power connections.
- It's a good idea to wear an antistatic wrist strap when working with electronic equipment and to use a foam pad of some sort to conduct any electricity away from you.
- Beware of sharp metal edges when removing the cover to your computer.

- If you don't feel comfortable working with electronic equipment, consider having a service technician do it for you.

Opening Your Computer Up

If you have your new module in hand, it's time to open up your computer. This is really a very simple process, so, if you've followed the safety precautions in the previous section, you'll do fine.

✔ **Follow these steps to open your computer:**

1. Turn off the computer and disconnect it from any power source, phone or network lines, and peripherals, such as a mouse or monitor.

2. On the right side of the back of your CPU, loosen the two screws (see Figure 17.4) with a flathead screwdriver. Note that the screws do not come out of their slots. They should just be loosened.

3. Standing behind the back of the computer, put one hand on the top to hold it steady.

4. Grab the handle on the right side panel (see Figure 17.4) and pull it toward you.

5. Finally, lift the panel up and remove it from the CPU.

With some HP models, you also have to remove the fan duct to get at your memory slots. To do so, place the computer on its side and press the two tabs shown in Figure 17.5 down. Then, just push the fan (B) down and out.

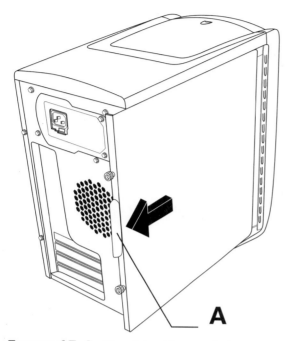

FIGURE 17.4 The right side panel gives you access to your computer workings (A).

Adding Memory Modules

Now that you have your computer open, adding memory modules is a snap. The number of memory sockets will vary depending on which Pavilion or Presario model you have, but you can recognize memory sockets and modules by taking a look at Figure 17.6.

✔ **To add a memory module, follow these steps:**

1. Locate an empty memory socket and push down the retaining clips on either end.

C

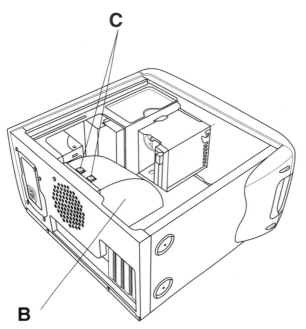

B

FIGURE 17.5 Push the tabs marked C in this illustration to remove the fan duct (B).

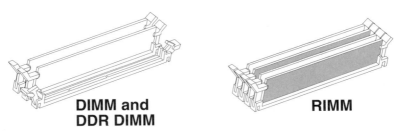

DIMM and DDR DIMM   **RIMM**

FIGURE 17.6 DIMM and RIMM sockets look similar.

2. Hold the module you want to insert by its edges (try not to touch the gold contact points) and line up the notches on the lower edge with raised areas in the socket (see Figure 17.7).

3. Push the module into the socket until it is tightly in place. The clips at either end should click into place when it is inserted correctly.

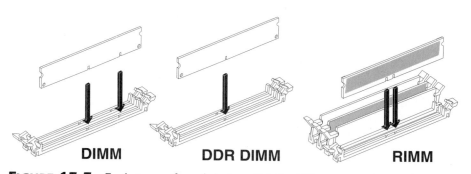

DIMM   **DDR DIMM**   **RIMM**

FIGURE 17.7 Each type of module has slightly different notches to line up with the memory socket.

That's it. Now you can replace the fan duct and side panel and reconnect your computer. When you reboot, Windows will recognize the additional memory.

Chapter Summary

In this chapter, you learned about how computer memory works. You checked your system to see how much memory you have available and learned about how you can free up hard disk space on your computer. Finally, you walked through the process of installing additional memory modules in your computer.

18

Upgrading Your Hardware

In this Chapter

✔ Replacing a disk drive

✔ Changing the optical drive

✔ Replacing the battery

When you have been using your computer for a while, you may find that a piece of hardware in your CPU wears out, or you may want to replace an item with a newer technology. You can, for example, put in a new disk drive, change the CRW optical drive, or replace the battery that provides backup power to keep your computer's date and time calculations functioning.

Upgrading and Repairing

Upgrading or repairing your computer when there's a problem, rather than replacing your computer, makes as much sense as keeping your car in good repair rather than trading it in whenever you come across a mechanical problem. It can be even more cost-effective when you do it yourself, rather than taking it to the nearest computer shop. Knowing you can handle these functions yourself can also be satisfying, like the first time you figured out how to change the oil in your car.

Most common upgrades and repairs are really pretty simple to do, as long as you take a few simple safety precautions and avoid forcing delicate electronic parts to do things they don't want to do. Typically, all you need is a single screwdriver to remove the outer panel of your CPU and perhaps to remove some internal pieces. Most elements inside your computer simply pop into and out of place in sockets, though occasionally you'll have to remove and then reattach cables.

Opening Up Your Computer

In Chapter 17, I outlined safety precautions you should use whenever opening up your computer. I'll repeat them here because they are very important:

- Remember that you're dealing with expensive equipment that has many small parts and that can hold an electrical charge even when it's turned off.
- Disconnect everything from the system, including phone lines, network connections, and power connections.
- It's a good idea to wear an antistatic wrist strap when working with electronic equipment and to use a foam pad of some sort to conduct any electricity away from you.
- Beware of sharp metal edges when removing the cover to your computer.

Now you're ready to begin. Whether replacing a disk drive, optical drive, or battery, the initial steps are the same. You have to open up the computer and remove the fan duct.

✔ **Follow these steps to open up the computer:**

1. Turn off the computer and disconnect it from any power source, phone or network lines, and peripherals.

2. On the right side of the back of your CPU, loosen the screw(s) (see Figure 18.1) with a flathead screwdriver. Note that the screw(s) do not come out of their slots. They should just be loosened.

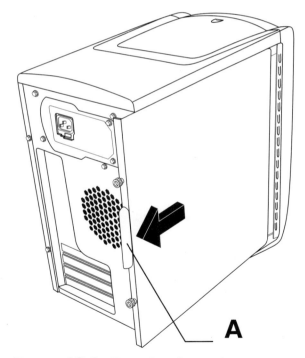

FIGURE 18.1 The right side panel gives you access to your computer workings (A).

3. Standing behind the back of the computer, put one hand on the top to hold it steady.

4. Grab the handle on the right side panel and pull it toward you.

5. Finally, lift the panel up and remove it from the CPU.

In some cases, you also have to remove the fan duct to get at your drives and battery. To do so, with the computer on its side, press the two tabs shown in Figure 18.2 down and push the fan down and out.

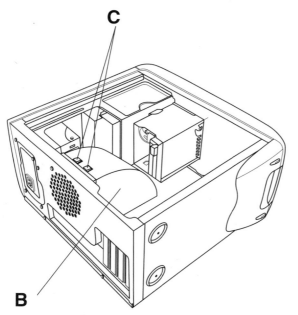

FIGURE 18.2 Push the tabs marked C in this illustration to remove the fan duct (B).

Replacing a Disk Drive

At some point, all drives wear out. If your disk drive isn't functioning properly anymore, or if you want to upgrade to a different model of drive, you can replace it. It's recommended that you purchase your replacement drive from HP. That way, you're ensured of equipment that will fit correctly into your CPU.

 tip Click the Hot Deals icon on your desktop to go to the online store where you can buy your equipment.

✔ **After you have purchased your replacement drive and have opened your computer, follow these steps to install the new drive:**

1. With the computer on its side, remove the power and Integrated Drive Electronics (IDE), or disk drive, cables that are on the back of the disk and hard drives (see Figure 18.3).

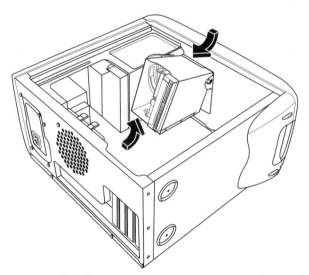

FIGURE 18.3 The drive cage houses the disk and optical drives.

2. Press the drive cage release tab as shown in Figure 18.3.

3. With the release tab still pressed down, move the cage upward and pull it gently out.

4. Take out the screws on each side of the disk drive and remove the drive.

5. Place the new drive into the drive cage so that the screw holes match.

6. Replace the screws in each side of the drive cage.

   When you're done, you can proceed to the "Closing Your Computer" section later in this chapter to close up your computer.

Changing an Optical Drive

Your computer has two optical drives, in some combination of CD, DVD, or CD-Writer, depending on your specific model. You might decide that you'd like to upgrade to a drive with more capacity or that you'd like two CD-Writer drives, for example.

✔ **To replace an optical drive, follow these steps:**

1. With the computer panel and fan duct removed, and the computer on its side, unscrew the two screws on the bottom drive (marked C in Figure 18.4). If you want to remove the top drive, undo both screws B and C.

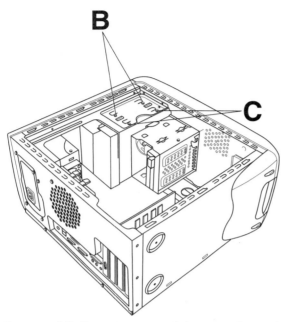

FIGURE 18.4   Either optical drive can be replaced.

2. Push one or both drives out through the front panel of the computer. There will be cables coming off the back of the drives.

3. Remove the cables that are attached to whichever drive you want
to replace and pull the drive entirely free of the computer casing
through the front panel.

4. Being sure that the jumper setting on the new drive you're going to
install is set for Cable Select (CS), slide it through the front of the
computer.

5. Reattach the cables to the drive and replace the drive in the casing.

6. Replace the screws.

7. You're ready to close up the computer with the steps in the last section of this chapter.

tip Whenever you're detaching cables, make a little diagram for yourself or place colored tape on each cable and attachment point to identify where each reattaches.

Replacing the Battery

Your computer contains a battery that provides a backup specifically for your timekeeping feature (your date and clock). If you turn your computer off or your computer should crash, the battery ensures that these settings don't become inaccurate.

If this battery starts to go, you'll notice that your computer clock is no longer accurate. That's when it's time to replace it. Most HP computers use a CR2032 lithium battery with a 3-volt, 220mAH rating, but just to be safe, verify this with the manual for your Pavilion or Presario model.

caution   **If you don't use the right kind of battery, it could actually explode. Therefore, please, be sure you check your documentation and buy only the recommended battery type.**

✔ **Here's how you replace a battery:**

1. With the computer panel removed (note with some models the fan duct and drive cage might have to be removed as well), push gently on the metal latch that holds the battery in with a screwdriver until it pops out of its socket.

2. Place the new battery in the socket. Be sure the positive side faces up.

3. That's it. Now just reassemble your computer.

Closing Your Computer

To close your computer, depending on what you might have removed to do your upgrading task, you may have to replace the drive cage, replace the fan duct, and put the side panel back on.

Replacing the Drive Cage

The first thing to put back into place is the drive cage.

✔ **Follow these steps to put your computer back the way it was:**

1. With the drive cage held at a 45-degree angle, slide the two protrusions on the drive case into the slots in the chassis (see Figure 18.5).

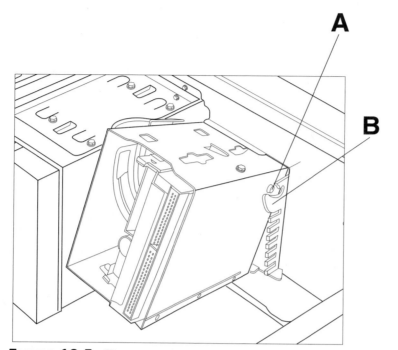

FIGURE 18.5   The protrusions, marked A, fit along the slots marked B.

2.   Match the track on the side of the drive cage with the guide on the fixed drive cage (see Figure 18.6) and push them together as you move the drive into place.

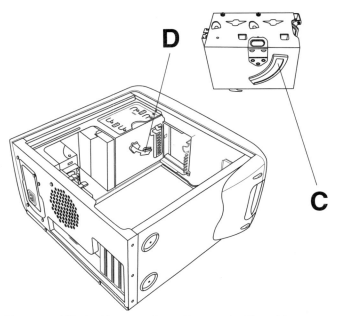

FIGURE 18.6 You need to align tracks C and D.

note To test that you've got the drive cage in properly, try gently pulling it up. If it comes free without pushing on the release tab, it's not properly aligned, and you'll have to try again.

Replacing the Fan Duct and Side Panel

Here are the last two steps in reassembling your computer. The fan duct has to slot over the fan that keeps your computer from overheating, and the side panel has to go back in place.

✔ **Follow these steps to reassemble your computer:**

1. Hold the fan duct at a 45-degree angle.

2. Line up the bottom of the duct with the hole on the fan base (see Figure 18.7).

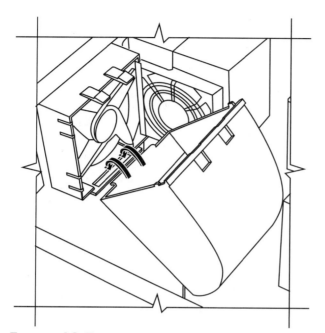

FIGURE 18.7 The fan duct cover should lock into place.

3. Turn the fan duct until it is in position and check that it's on there tightly.

4. Place the side panel on the CPU chassis, making sure the nodes on the panel match up with the holes in the chassis.

5. Slide the panel forward until it clicks into the proper closed position (see Figure 18.8).

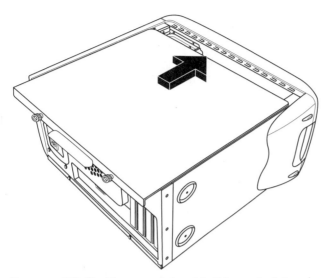

FIGURE 18.8 The panel should slide easily into place.

6. Tighten the screws on the panel.

That's it!

Chapter Summary

In this chapter, you learned about some of the simple upgrading and repair techniques you can use to replace your disk or optical drives. You also learned how to replace your backup battery when it runs dry.

chapter

19

Supercharging Your Computer

In this Chapter

✔ Installing add-in cards

✔ Replacing your hard drive

✔ Networking your computers

Pavilions and Presarios have plenty of power and features, but, if you've pushed your computer to the limit, you might find you'd like more hard drive space; more functionality, such as higher-end video graphics; or the ability to network two or more computers to orchestrate your computing power. This chapter looks at ways you can take your computer to the next level.

Opening Your Computer

The steps involved in opening your computer and removing the fan duct and drive cage are covered in Chapter 18. Please refer to them to get ready to install an add-in card or hard drive. Also review the safety tips in that chapter. After the computer is open and the fan duct removed, you can proceed with the steps in this chapter.

Installing Add-In Cards

Add-in cards, also called expansion boards, are circuit boards that you connect to a computer to add functionality. Some commonly used add-in cards are video adapters to add video memory and graphics processing, sound cards to enable your computer to play and record sounds, and accelerator boards that enhance the computer processing speed.

caution   Avoid installing too many add-in cards because each pulls on the electrical current coming into your computer. Check your manual to see what your specific system can handle.

✔ **If you want to replace a damaged expansion board or install a more sophisticated one, it's easy to do by following these steps:**

1. With the computer panel off and the computer on its side, locate the card slots shown in Figure 19.1.

E

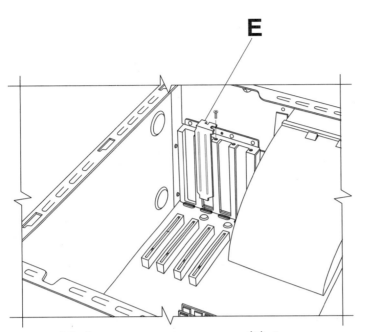

FIGURE 19.1 Empty slots have a cover (E) that you must remove.

2. Loosen the screw on the slot cover (E) and remove the cover.

3. Push the new card into the slot, with a downward motion (see Figure 19.2)

4. Reattach the screw to the card itself.

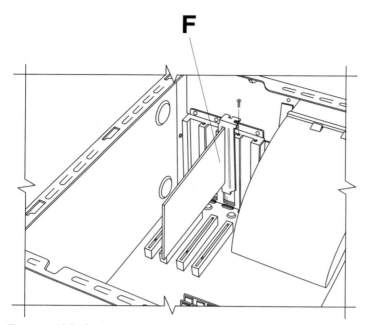

FIGURE 19.2 You can add several cards (F), but don't overextend your power.

5. Reassemble the computer.

 note **If you're replacing a card that's already installed, after Step 1, you must remove the existing card by disconnecting any cables attached to it, unscrewing the bracket of the card, and removing it.**

Replacing the Hard Drive

The hard drive is the large storage medium on your computer. Hard drives shipped with Pavilions and Presario today have a very large capacity, but what's sufficient today might not be tomorrow. You might decide to replace your hard drive to put one with more capacity in its place or to replace a damaged hard drive.

✔ **The hard drive comes out of your computer quite easily with these few simple steps:**

1. With the computer open and the drive cage removed, unscrew the two screws on the top of the hard drive, as well as a single screw on the bottom.

2. Disconnect any cables from the back of the hard drive.

3. Slide the old hard drive out.

4. Slide the new hard drive into place and reattach the screws.

5. Replace the drive cage and side panel.

Networking Your Computers

Do you want to create a home network of computers, including your HP Pavilion or Compaq Presario? Millions of households now have more than one computer and the benefits of networking them are many.

First, you can access the Internet from all your computers through a single connection. You can also send files to a printer or other hardware, no matter which computer it's connected to in your house. In addition, you can access files on your network from any computer, removing any need to email or hand-carry files from one computer to the other.

Typically, computers are attached in one of three ways: with network cables attached to the Network Interface Card (NIC) installed in each computer, through standard phone lines, or through a wireless connection device using infrared technology.

Choosing Your Network

There are several types of networks, such as Ethernet, Home PNA (using your home phone line), or Wireless HomRF. In choosing the type of network you want to install, you should consider how easy it is to connect the computers by cable, how fast you want your network to be, and cost.

PCs Made Easy

Understanding Home Networks

In setting up a network, you have to be sure you have a network card and modem in each computer and make a choice of network method, either cables, infrared wireless, or through your phone lines. Visit *HPShopping.com* to view home networking products (see Figure 19.3). After you've purchased the option you prefer and followed manufacturer instructions to install network cards or cables, you're ready to set up your network using Windows XP's Network Setup Wizard.

tip **You can follow the instructions earlier in this chapter for installing add-in cards to install your network card.**

FIGURE 19.3 HP offers solutions for networking that work perfectly with your Pavilion.

- Ethernet is the fastest type and is not all that expensive. However, if you choose Ethernet you must run cables from a central hub to each computer.
- If the computers are remote so that cabling is difficult, but each is near a phone line, you could use those lines to connect them. Note that you can then use your single phone line for voice calls and Internet access at the same time. However, this sharing can make for a slower connection.
- If your computers are not all near a phone line, wireless might be your only option. Here cost is a factor. Where an Ethernet connection might cost you $75 or so to connect two computers, a wireless connection might run almost $200. Also, wireless connections can be hampered by anything metal in your home, such as water pipes or door knobs.

caution **Wireless networks pose a standards challenge. Different vendors use different variations on the technology. If wireless is the way to go, find a wireless standard that several vendors support, such as Bluetooth, when purchasing your wireless network. Otherwise, if you want to expand your network someday, you may find yourself with a compatibility problem.**

Setting Up the Host and Guest Computers

✔ **The first step in setting up your network is to set up a host computer that gives access to the Internet and then to set up each computer in the network:**

1. Select Start, Control Panel.
2. Click Network and Internet Connections.
3. Click Set up or change your home or small office network. The Network Setup Wizard appears.

4. Click Next. The first window confirms that you have network cards, modems, and cables on all computers, and that all computers, printers, and external modems are on and connected to the Internet.

5. Click Next. The Select a Connection Method dialog box appears (see Figure 19.4).

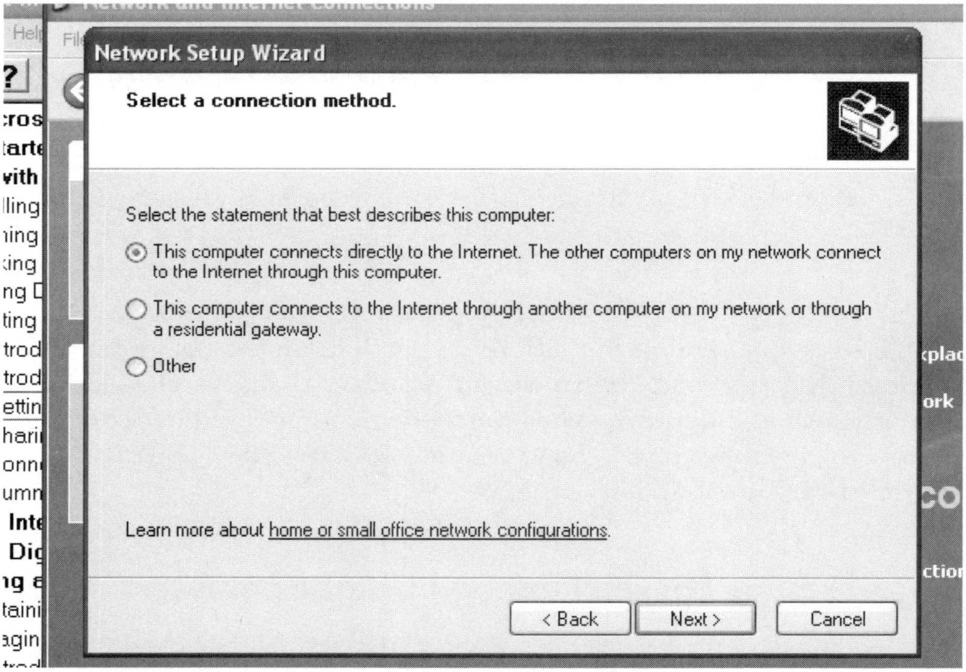

FIGURE 19.4 The host will always be the computer on your network that has a direct Internet connection.

6. Click to select the first option, This computer connects directly to the Internet, and then click Next.

7. You are now asked to select your connection from a list of connections that Windows offers. Click your Internet provider, such as MSN Internet Access, and then click Next.

8. Type the word "host" in the computer description text box. If you want, you can also change the computer name.

9. Click Next. If you want, you can change the name of your network or accept the one that's listed.

10. Click Next. The next dialog box, shown in Figure 19.5, lists all the settings you've made.

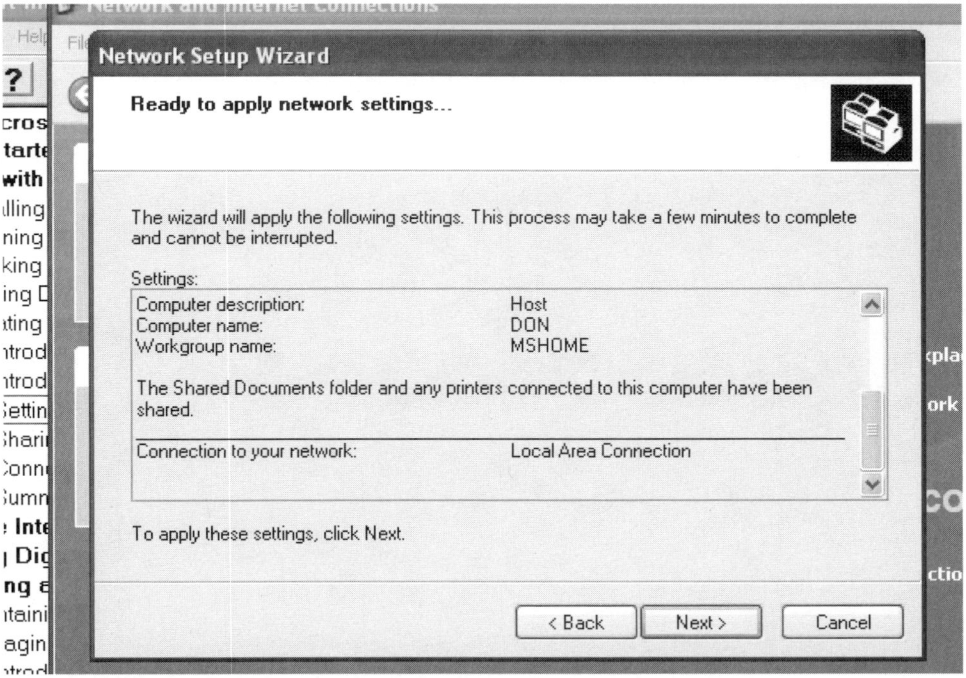

FIGURE 19.5 Note that the Shared Documents folder has been set up to share with any printers.

11. Click Next, and all the settings will be configured. The final wizard page offers you the opportunity to configure your network to include computers that don't use Windows XP.

12. Assuming you have no non-Windows XP computers, click the Just finish the wizard option and then click Next.

13. Click Finish.

Now you have to set up each computer on the network to connect to the host using the Network Setup Wizard, which guides you through the process.

✔ **After all computers are set up, to view shared resources, follow these steps:**

1. Select Start, Control Panel.

2. Click Network and Internet Connections.

3. Click My Network Places.

4. Click View Workgroup Computers.

5. Double-click the Host computer. All shared resources are listed (see Figure 19.6).

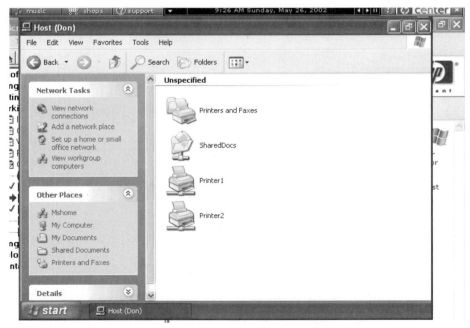

FIGURE 19.6 Now you can share files and hardware among all computers on the network.

Chapter Summary

In this chapter, you learned about installing add-in cards to add functionality to your computer. You also walked through the steps involved in replacing your hard drive, which you might do to increase your computer's storage capacity. Finally, you got a basic tutorial on home networking and the benefits it offers from shared Internet access and hardware.

20

Troubleshooting

In this Chapter

✔ Top tips from HP Technical Support

✔ Solving a problem with HP Help and Support

Your computer is the sum total of pieces of hardware, such as mouse, monitor, CPU, and keyboard; dozens of computer programs; and an operating system called Windows XP. All of that is connected to the Internet, where additional files are sent and received and downloaded all the time. The interaction of all of these components may occasionally cause you problems. For that reason, I've compiled some of the top tips of HP technical support folks to help you stay out of trouble or to solve problems when they arrive.

This chapter also walks you through solving a typical computing problem using the online HP Help and Support system so that you can see the many ways HP helps you to solve problems on your own.

Top Tips from HP Support

Here are some pieces of advice from the folks who help Pavilion and Presario users day in and day out. Following this advice might save you problems down the road, or get you out of trouble. Although HP Support people are some of the best in the business and love to help Pavilion and Presario owners have a positive experience, they like it even more when you can avoid problems altogether!

- *Tip 1*—HP consumer products work better together. Whenever possible, use HP hardware and drivers for peripherals you connect to your HP Pavilion or Compaq Presario. If you do use non-HP peripherals, always make sure you have the most current drivers for those products from their manufacturers. Most of these companies allow you to download the most recent drivers from their Web sites.
- *Tip 2*—You can get the most recent software for HP Pavilions from the HP Pavilion section of HP's Customer Care Web site (*www.hp.com/cposupport/eschome.html*) seen in Figure 20.1 and for your Presario at http://www29.compaq.com/falco/sp.list.asp. Here you can get product-specific information and software. Enter your model information as specifically as possible, including product name and model number including any letters, such as Pavilion 520N, to get the most targeted results.

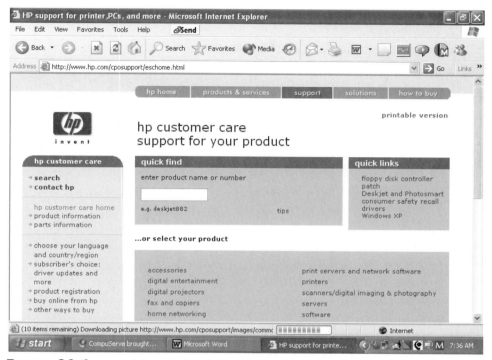

FIGURE 20.1 Search by product name to find recent software updates.

- *Tip 3*—You can use the HP Subscriber's Choice program to be notified automatically of new software versions for your Pavilion or Presario, get tech support alerts that relate to your product, or sign up for email newsletters that include product tips or project ideas. Go to http://www.hp.com/cposupport/ eschome.html to sign up.

- *Tip 4*—If you have problems with non-HP software that was included with your Pavilion or Presario when you bought it, try visiting the software manufacturer's Web site. Most provide online support. A few addresses to help you out are the following: Microsoft for help with MS Works, Encarta Online Deluxe, Outlook Express, Internet Explorer, and Windows XP (*www.microsoft.com*); MusicMatch for assistance with Music-

PCs Made Easy

Match Jukebox (*www.musicmatch.com*); and Adobe for support of Adobe Acrobat Reader (*www.adobe.com*).

- *Tip 5*—Turn on the Windows Update feature by selecting Start, Control Panel and clicking the Windows Update link (see Figure 20.2). With this feature, you can scan for any updates to Windows that should be downloaded to keep your system current, resolve glitches in the operating system software, or set yourself up for automatic updating.

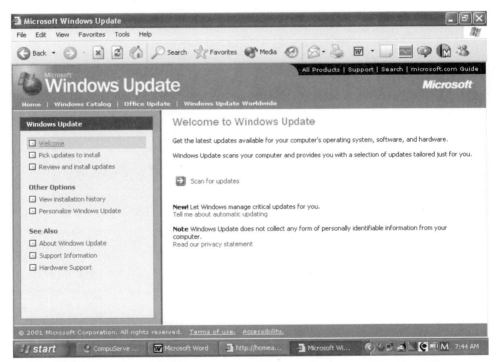

FIGURE 20.2 Microsoft provides an update service to keep Windows XP current.

- *Tip 6*—When trying to resolve system problems, use the Three Strike Rule. First, use Microsoft System Restore to go back one day. If you still have a problem, use Microsoft System Recovery to go back one week. If that still doesn't work, try again, going back one month. If none of these works, then and only then should you use the nondestructive System Restore to restore your computer's factory settings.

- *Tip 7*—If you're having trouble with video or sound devices, it's possible your hardware or its drivers aren't compatible with Windows XP. Microsoft maintains a list of products and drivers that have been updated for Windows XP and tested by Microsoft. If you are having a problem and can find a driver or product that has been determined to be XP compatible, it could solve your problem. Go to *www.microsoft.com/hcl/* to see listings such as the one shown in Figure 20.3.

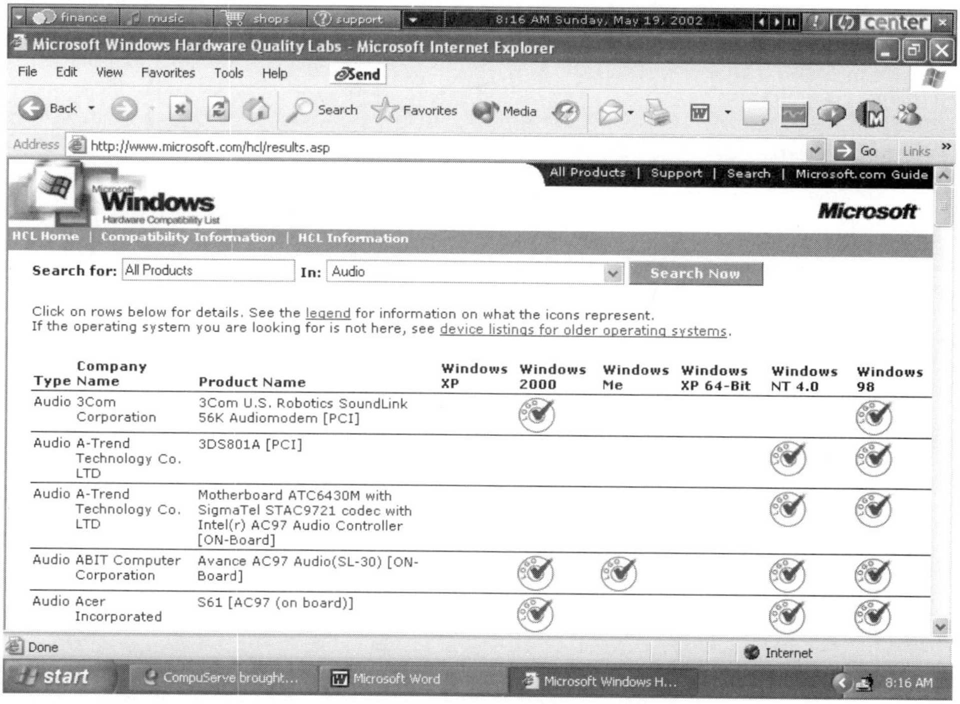

FIGURE 20.3 Look for an XP-tested driver from this list and download it.

Troubleshooting with Help and Support

It's one thing to show you how to navigate around a help system and another to show you how you can use the help system to run down a problem you're having. That's what this section is about. I've taken a typical problem—my modem isn't working—and written about the steps you can try to solve it. You'll find along the way that there is a wonderful combination of tools—from help text to automated diagnostic tests, Troubleshooter procedures, and instant live support to help you through. The exact steps you might use to solve this problem could differ, but here's one way to use the Help system to find a solution.

caution   **If you were actually having trouble with your modem and couldn't connect to the Internet, some of the live support features wouldn't be accessible to you.**

✔ **To solve a problem with a modem, follow these steps:**

1. Select Start, Help and Support. The Help and Support Center appears.

2. Click the link for Fixing a Problem in the Pick a Help Topic section. The Fixing a Problem window shown in Figure 20.4 appears.

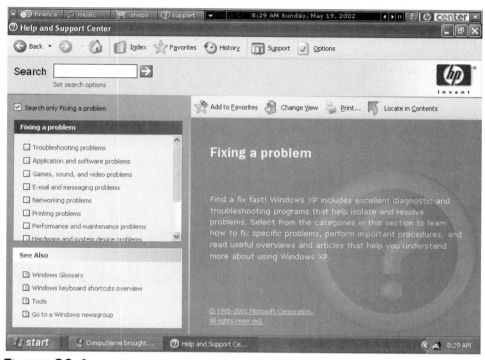

FIGURE 20.4 At this point, you could click the Troubleshooting problems link for general troubleshooting information.

3. Click the Hardware and System Device Problems link on the left side. (I chose Hardware and System Device Problems as being most specific to my problem.) The information in the right pane of this window changes to Hardware and System Device Problems.

4. Click the Modem Troubleshooter (see Figure 20.5). (Note that I could also have clicked the task, Test a Modem, at this point. Also, I could have reached this troubleshooter by choosing Troubleshooting problems, List of Troubleshooters, in Step 3 instead of clicking Hardware and System Device Problems. There are often several routes to the same solution.)

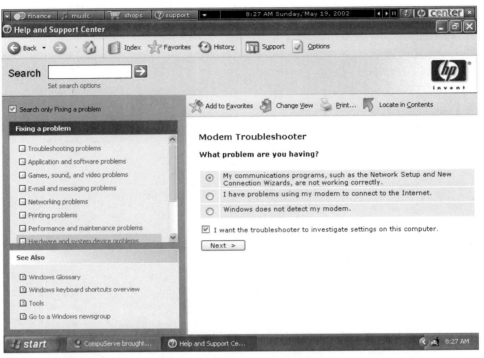

FIGURE 20.5 Troubleshooters are like wizards in that they walk you through a process step by step.

5. Because I was getting a message that no modem was detected when I tried to connect to the Internet, click the choice Windows does not detect my modem, and then click Next. The next step deals with the possibility that your connection to your modem or phone line is causing the problem.

6. Click No, my modem is connected correctly, but I still have a problem and then click Next. The window in Figure 20.6 appears.

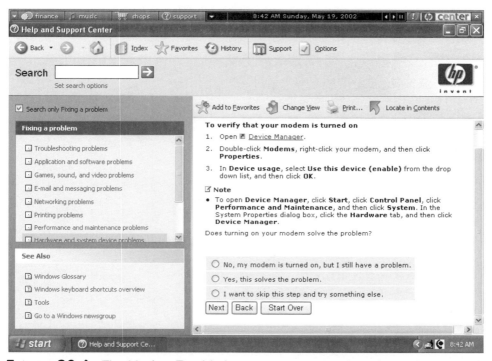

FIGURE 20.6 The Modem Troubleshooter is trying to isolate the problem based on your input.

At this point, you should note a few things. The Troubleshooter is suggesting there could be a setting you need to make in Windows XP, and it has provided a link to that setting (Device Manager) and directions on how to modify the setting. At any point during the Troubleshooter, you may solve the problem and indicate that by selecting the Yes, this solves the problem option.

On the other hand, if you continue to tell the Troubleshooter that you haven't solved the problem, you are presented with a final window, shown in Figure 20.7, that suggests you either check the Windows Hardware Compatibility List by following a link to it, or that you contact your modem manufacturer.

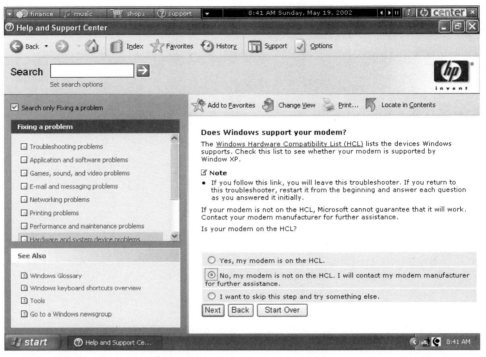

FIGURE 20.7 First the Troubleshooter identifies problems that can be fixed locally and then it directs you to online and manufacturer resources.

caution **Sometimes when you go to a link in the Troubleshooter that is on the Internet, you can't get back to the Troubleshooter without starting to run it again from the beginning.**

✔ **Take a look at a different way of solving this problem and a different tool:**

1. From the Help and Support Center main window, click Hardware.

2. On the window that appears, click Modems. The options in Figure 20.8 appear.

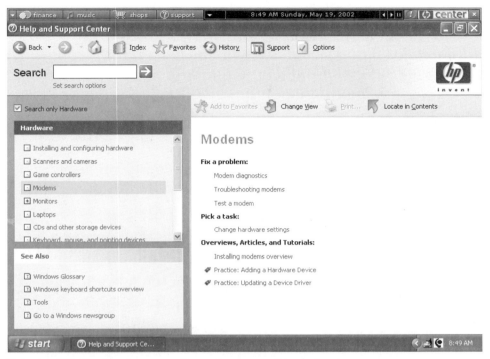

FIGURE 20.8 Modem-specific options are all together here.

3. Click Practice: Adding a Hardware Device. An interactive training module opens up (see Figure 20.9). You follow the steps in the printed and spoken instructions to see exactly how to complete a specific process.

FIGURE 20.9 You'll be asked to make specific choices to walk through a procedure in these tutorials.

tip **Many of the windows in the Help and Support Center include a Related Topics link. If you didn't get exactly the answer you needed or it didn't give you all the information you need about a topic, clicking this link can be an easy way to find the exact information you want.**

Troubleshooting Tips

The choices you make in the Help and Support Center will depend to some extent on the way you organize things in your own mind. For example, some windows will offer solutions organized by tasks or by the tools you'd use to fix a problem. If you think of problems in terms of tasks, such as the task of testing a modem, rather than in terms of a tool, such as Modem Troubleshooter, that's the option you're likely to pick. These may lead you to similar or identical solutions, but in a slightly different way.

There's no wrong choice to make in the Help and Support Center, but some paths are more direct or fruitful than others. Here are some tips to using the feature most efficiently:

- Try to make the most specific choice you can for your problem. For example, if you're having trouble installing an external modem, rather than clicking the Modems option on the Hardware list, you'd click the Installing and Configuring Hardware option.
- Use the Add to Favorites button to quickly return to information you encounter during a help search that you think you might like to come back to.
- If you are dealing with a topic that you have no knowledge about, look for Overview tutorials first to give you the context to understand more specific help information.
- If you encounter a term you don't understand, click the Index button to see a searchable list of terms to get more information about that item.

Ask a Friend

One feature that's definitely worth looking into is the Remote Assistance feature. This allows you to connect with somebody you trust who knows more about computers or the specific problem than you so that he or she can view what's on your screen. Your friend can even use his or her computer to take over yours (with your permission) and make changes for you.

To use this feature, you and the friend have to be using the Windows XP operating system. You must be using Windows Messenger, or an email program such as Outlook Express that is Messaging Application Programming Interface (MAPI) compliant. Finally, you both have to have an Internet connection.

✔ **Follow these steps to obtain help remotely using email:**

1. Select Remote Assistance from the Help and Support Resources area of the Help and Support Center.

2. Click Ask a Friend to Help.

3. Click Invite someone to help you. The form appears asking you to enter an email or Windows Messaging choice (see Figure 20.10).

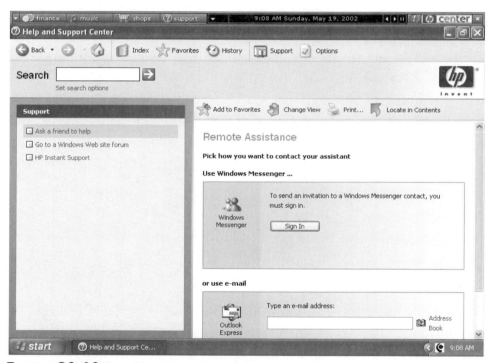

FIGURE 20.10 Your friend must be online to receive your invitation, which you can send using Windows Messaging or email.

4. Enter an email address and then press the arrow titled Invite this Person. The Invitation form in Figure 20.11 appears.

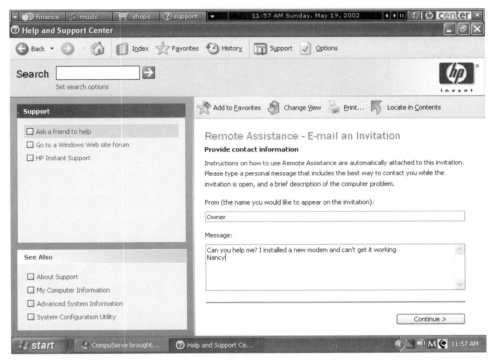

FIGURE 20.11 You and your friend both have to have Windows Messaging activated to use that feature. With email, you can invite anybody with an email address to help.

5. Change the name in the From box, if you like, and enter a message asking for help.

6. Click Continue. The window in Figure 20.12 appears, asking you to make settings for how long the invitation should be available and to enter a password the person must use to log onto your computer. Note that you'll have to contact the person to provide the password, but, because you're turning over access of your computer to someone else, using a password is a very good idea.

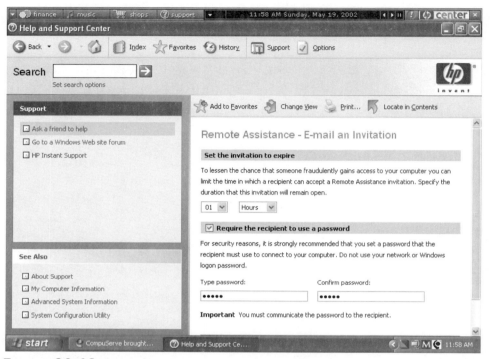

FIGURE 20.12 If your friend might not get online for another hour or two, set the availability of the invitation accordingly.

7. Click Send Invitation. An email is sent to the person, and a confirmation that your invitation was sent appears on your computer.

The other person will receive an email that looks like the one shown in Figure 20.13. This email contains your message and a link the recipient can follow to get instructions on how to proceed.

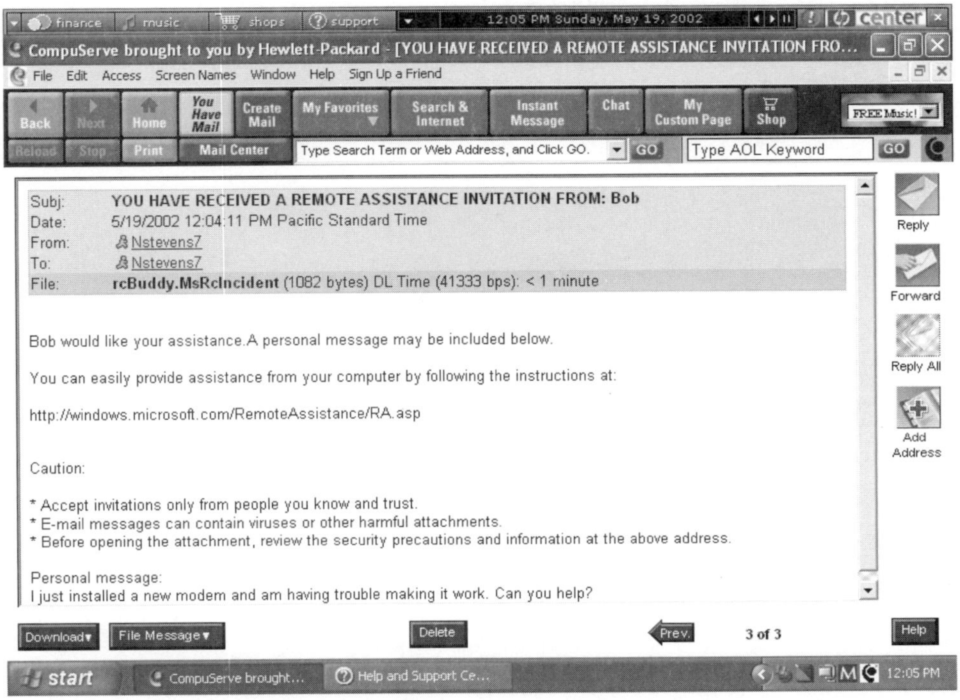

FIGURE 20.13 This email provides instructions for connecting to your computer.

✔ Here's what your friend must now do to help you out:

1. Download the file that is attached to the invitation email and open it (rather than save it) when prompted.

2. Click Yes to accept the invitation. A prompt appears to connect to the sender's computer using a password, if that option was selected by you.

3. Enter the Password and click Yes. A dialog box appears confirming that you want to be connected to the person's computer. Click Yes.

The dialog box shown in Figure 20.14 appears, with controls for talking, sending files, or controlling the settings on the requestor's computer.

FIGURE 20.14 Use these controls to initiate chats or to look at computer settings.

 tip **You can also use the Remote Assistance feature to allow an HP Technical Support person to take over your computer and make adjustments.**

HP Instant Support

HP Instant Support is a real-time exchange with an HP Technical Support person available to Pavilion users. You submit your question in writing and then wait a brief time for a response to appear. In essence, you can carry on a text-based conversation using this feature. The HP Support person will keep a log of your problem so that, if you must sign off to try a solution, you can come back. Whoever is available will have information about your problem.

✔ **To use HP Instant Support from a Pavilion, follow these steps:**

1. From the HP Help and Support Center window, click HP Instant Support. The window shown in Figure 20.15 appears.

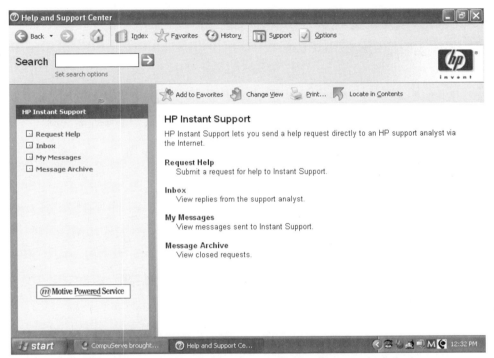

FIGURE 20.15 You can keep track of all your messages and responses from one of these four areas.

2. Click Request Help to initiate a session.

3. On the six-step Request Help procedure, Step 1, select a topic for your inquiry and click Next.

4. In Step 2, click Next (or, if you want to run a communications test first to ensure that you can connect with Support, click Run twice and then Next).

5. In Step 3, enter a description of the problem (Figure 20.16) and click Next.

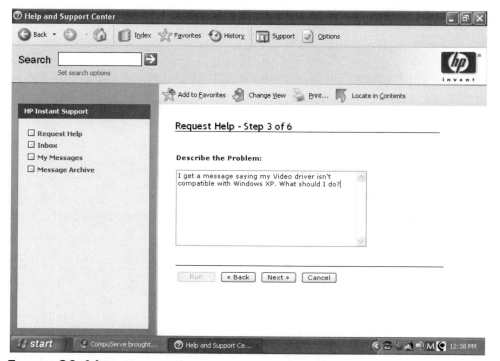

FIGURE 20.16 Try to make the description you enter here as concise, yet complete as possible.

Information is gathered about your system, and your message is sent to Support. In a few moments, you'll receive a response. Now you can follow directions provided, answer questions, ask more questions, and so on to solve your problem.

Chapter Summary

In this chapter, you got some insider tips from HP Technical Support about how to keep your computer troublefree or to solve problems. Then, you walked through the process of using the wealth of help tools available for solving a typical computing problem.

Using Organize from HP and Compaq

In this Chapter

✔ Customizing HP/Compaq Organize

✔ Accessing Files

✔ Working with Software

✔ Linking to Web Sites

Organize from HP is available on both HP and Compaq computers, with each sporting a slightly different look and feel. This appendix provides an overview so you can begin to appreciate the centralized functionality Organize offers (the HP version is featured in figures in this appendix).

B y using Organize you can coordinate access to files and software, and links for Web favorite sites in one easy-to-use interface. You can also play multimedia files without opening a multimedia player, select customizable view options, and search your hard drive with ease.

Customizing HP/Compaq Organize

Organize is organized by categories, as you can see in Figure A.1. One of the great things about HP/Compaq Organize is that you can customize it to look and feel the way you like. You do that by adding elements to categories, adding new categories, and changing the skin and view applied to Organize.

FIGURE A.1   Organize puts everything you use everyday one click away.

Dragging and Dropping Elements

One of the simplest ways to customize Organize is to add elements to it. For example you can easily drag and drop a desktop shortcut, such as one to Internet Explorer, to an Organize category. Consider dragging Internet Explorer to the Web Services category, for instance, or Works to the Productivity category. Your desktop shortcut remains intact, but a new copy of the shortcut appears in the command central that Organize offers.

Creating New Categories

Creating a new category is simple: Just right-click on the tab of any category and a shortcut menu appears. Click on Add Category, and the Add New Category dialog box appears (Figure A.2). Enter a Category Name, then click OK. The new category becomes available.

You can now drag desktop shortcuts to the category, drag items from other Organize categories to the new category, and use Delete and Move Up/Move Down commands from the category shortcut menu (right-click on any item in the category to display this) to reorganize the category listing.

FIGURE A.2   Simply enter a new category name here to add your favorite types of programs and links to Organize

Customizing Organize's Look

To change the appearance of Organize, you can use the Organize Preferences (Figure A.3). Here you can choose a different skin (1 column or 2 column view), select an icon size, specify the type of Internet connection you have (Cable/DSL/T1 or Dialup), set Organize to launch when you startup your comptuer, and adjust the speed with which images are displayed in the Picture Viewer media playback panel.

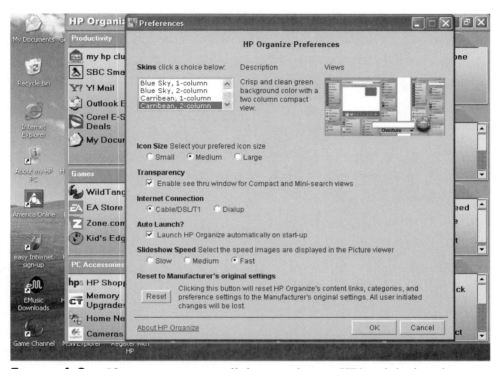

FIGURE A.3 If you want to reset all these settings to HP's original settings, click the Reset button in this dialog box

To open the Organize Preferences dialog box, click on the icon showing a hammer and wrench icon in the right side of the Organize title bar.

Accessing Files

When you start up Organize (Start, All Programs, PC Help & Tools, HP or Compaq Organize) there are a few file folders already available to you. The My Pictures folder is included in the Pictures category, and the My Music folder is in the Music category. Clicking on these makes the files stored there immediately accessible to you.

You might consider adding the My Documents folder to the Productivity category by creating a shortcut (click Start, then right-click on My Documents, then click Add to Desktop) and click and drag the My Documents shortcut to the Productivity category. Use this method for any file folder on your computer.

Using Software

Just as you can open folders to access your files in Organize, you can open software applications to get your work done.

Launching Programs with a Single Click

Some programs, such as Outlook Express in the Productivity category and MusicMatch in the Music category, are already included. Others you can drag and drop to easily copy shortcuts from your Windows desktop to any Organize category.

 tip **To remove a program from an Organize category right-click on it, and select Delete.**

Full Screen Multimedia with Media Player

The largest panel of HP/Compaq Organize Player is the HP Organize Player, which can play pictures, video, and audio files (see Figure 4). With this player you can control the following functions:

- Play
- Stop
- Back (to the first item)
- Forward (to the last item)
- Back one item
- Forward one item
- Volume
- Open (a media file)

FIGURE A.4 This central panel of Organize offers a powerful multimedia player

Getting Online with Organize

Organize offers several links to online sites in its categories, but you can add more any time you like. You can also use a built-in search feature to search the Web with a variety of popular search engines.

Connecting with Web Sites

Several of the content items included with HP/Compaq Organize are actually links to popular Web sites. For example, the Games, PC Accessories, and Web Services categories offer links to online games, online shopping, and Yahoo's Best of the Web. You can add other Web links by right-clicking any content item and selecting Add link. The Add

New Content dialog box appears. Enter a name for the link which will appear on the category list, then locate the Web address or location of a document on your computer using the Browse PC button. That's it!

Searching the Web

The Search feature in Organize helps you search the Web using several popular search engines such as Yahoo, AltaVista, and Ask Jeeves. Just select the appropriate search engine by clicking the button to the left of the Search area (which may be named Yahoo or Lycos, for example, depending on which search engine is currently selected). Then enter a keyword and click Search to find what you need. If you want to find a document on your computer choose My Computer in the drop down list, then enter a term you would find in the document title, and click Search.

Index